Overcoming Violence against Women and Girls

Overcoming Violence against Women and Girls

The International Campaign to Eradicate a Worldwide Problem

MICHAEL L. PENN AND RAHEL NARDOS

in collaboration with
William S. Hatcher and Mary K. Radpour
of the Authenticity Project

ROWMAN & LITTLEFIELD PUBLISHERS, INC.
Lanham • Boulder • New York • Oxford

ROWMAN & LITTLEFIELD PUBLISHERS, INC.

Published in the United States of America
by Rowman & Littlefield Publishers, Inc.
A Member of the Rowman & Littlefield Publishing Group
4720 Boston Way, Lanham, Maryland 20706
www.rowmanlittlefield.com

PO Box 317
Oxford
OX2 9RU, UK

British Library Cataloguing in Publication Information Available

Library of Congress Cataloging-in-Publication Data

Penn, Michael L., 1958-
  Overcoming violence against women and girls : the international
campaign to eradicate a worldwide problem / Michael L. Penn and Rahel
Nardos.
      p. cm.
Includes bibliographical references and index.
  ISBN 0-7425-2499-X (cloth : alk. paper) — ISBN 0-7425-2500-7 (pbk. :
alk. paper)
  1. Women—Violence against. 2. Sex discrimination against women. 3.
Women—Violence against—Prevention. 4. Sex discrimination against
women—Prevention. I. Nardos, Rahel. II. Title.
  HQ1237 .P45 2003
  362.88'082--dc21
                            2002010307

Printed in the United States of America

For my wife, Katharine;
our parents, Rachael and William, and Rosemary and Charles;
our children, Charles and Corina;
and our friends, Tahereh and Hussein

Contents

Preface

This book is inspired by an approach to scholarship that seeks to place knowledge at the service of development. It assumes that knowledge of complex phenomena is best derived from a diversity of methods and that there are often technical as well as ethical dimensions to most human endeavors. This approach thus assumes a position of epistemological and methodological openness—ever mindful of the fact that "nature gives most of her evidence in answer to the questions we ask."[1]

The approach that inspires and animates this book recognizes an essential complementarity between the empirical and rational demands of science and the ethical conduct required of human beings if our relationships to one another and to nature are to secure life and promote development. This approach is, therefore, not simply a new paradigm from which to view the problems of the world, but an approach to living in the world that unites the philosopher, the researcher, and the practitioner and makes of these three, one. From this perspective, the qualities of character that distinguish the student, scholar, or practitioner are as critical to securing human happiness and progress as are his or her knowledge, skills, and insights.

At the heart of this approach is an ethical commitment to the oneness of the human race and the conviction that life and development are sustained by the creation and maintenance of unity within the context of diversity. In contrast to a wholly pragmatic and materialistic perspective, this approach affords consideration of ethical and spiritual principles vital in all of its undertakings. These principles are derived from empirical research, reasoned discourse, and the writings of the world's religious and philosophical systems, as they constitute the primary reservoirs of humanity's ethicospiritual heritage.

This book has been written in the hope of providing university students, policymakers, activists, public health workers, clinicians, and lay citizens alike with a clear overview of the problem of gender-based violence worldwide, as well as a sense of the important work now under way to eradicate it. The book is thus an integration of a vast range of data and insights from all the major disciplines that have contributed to our understanding of this problem over the course of the twentieth century. I have been guided throughout this work by the desire to contribute a document that would move the current international discourse along by providing a historical, interdisciplinary overview that is at once critical, constructive, and visionary.

The inspiration for a book of this nature began to emerge during my undergraduate years at the University of Pennsylvania, where I studied psychology, history, and religion. In these early days of interdisciplinary study, I became mindful of the value of an integrative approach for making sense out of some of the more complex problems confronting human beings at this unique juncture of human history. Furthermore, during my graduate training in clinical psychology and afterward, in my career as a psychopathologist, clinician, and consultant to nongovernmental organizations, I became acutely aware of the role of violence in the subjugation of women and the prevention of humanity's advancement worldwide. As the women of the world assembled in Vienna, Austria, for the UN/ECE High Level Regional Preparatory Conference for the Fourth World Conference on Women, I was one of a handful of men who had been invited to join them. In preparation for that meeting, I authored a paper entitled "The Role of Men in Eradicating Gender-Based Violence." That paper, enriched by the new insights imparted to me through my association with the Authenticity Project, and especially with my colleagues on the project, William S. Hatcher and Mary K. Radpour, provided the seeds that have grown into the present book. My able and hardworking student Rahel Nardos, who went on to undertake studies in medicine at Yale, consented to assist in gathering research for this work.

I wish to extend my heartfelt and sincere thanks to the Hackman Scholars Program at Franklin and Marshall College for its generous financial support during the development of this book and to David Gould, Dr. Hossain Danesh, Christine Zerbini, and Dr. Beth Bowen for their helpful feedback on an earlier draft. I wish also to thank the members of the Authenticity Project in the United States, Canada, and Russia for their generous intellectual and spiritual support in bringing this project to completion. Last, but most important, I would like to thank Dr. Constance Chen, who urged me to push forward when I so desperately needed from someone a word of encouragement.

—MICHAEL L. PENN
Lancaster, Pennsylvania
September 2002

Introduction

Across the planet, and over the centuries, various forms of violence against women and girls have been an everyday part of humanity's social life. In the middle of the nineteenth century, however, a movement bent on eradicating gender-related abuses and uplifting the station of women burst upon the world. Among the progenitors of this movement were two women, one from the East, the other from the West.

At a time and in a country in which women were denied the most basic rights, the Persian poet and scholar Qurratu'l-'Ayn (also known as Táhirih) openly proclaimed the equality of the sexes. In the 1840s Táhirih became the first Middle Eastern woman ever reported to have removed her veil in public. A social history of the period captures the reactions she provoked as she presented herself "adorned and unveiled" before a company of men at a gathering known as the Conference of Badasht:

> Suddenly the figure of Táhirih, adorned and unveiled, appeared before the eyes of the assembled companions. Consternation immediately seized the entire gathering. All stood aghast before this sudden and most unexpected apparition. To behold her face unveiled was to them inconceivable. Even to gaze at her shadow was a thing which they deemed improper. . . . Quietly, silently, and with utmost dignity, Táhirih stepped forward and, advancing towards Quddús, seated herself on his right-hand side. Her unruffled serenity sharply contrasted with the affrighted countenances of those who were gazing upon her face. Fear, anger, and bewilderment stirred the depths of their souls. That sudden revelation seemed to have stunned their faculties. 'Abdu'l KháliqiIsfáhání was so gravely shaken that he cut his throat with his own hands. Covered with blood and shrieking with excitement, he fled away from the face of Táhirih. A few, following his example, abandoned their companions and forsook their Faith. A number were seen standing speechless before her, confounded with wonder.[1]

In 1848, when the authorities could no longer abide either the new spiritual teachings that she championed or the remarkable social audacity she displayed, they arranged for Táhirih's execution. As the hour of her death approached, she calmly noted, "'You can kill me as soon as you like, but you cannot stop the emancipation of women.'"[2] In that same year in Seneca Falls, New York, Elizabeth Cady Stanton, joined by one man, Frederick Douglass, and a company of inspired women, initiated the women's movement in the West.

Stanton's oration at the opening of the Seneca Falls convention was no less memorable than Táhirih's bold unveiling at the Conference of Badasht. On Wednesday, 19 July 1848, Stanton arose and addressed the assembled delegates:

> Verily, the world waits the coming of some new element, some purifying power, some spirit of mercy and love. The voice of woman has been silenced in the state, the church, and the home, but man cannot fulfill his destiny alone, he cannot redeem his race unaided. . . . The world has never seen a truly great and virtuous nation, because in the degradation of woman the very fountains of life are poisoned at their source. It is vain to look for silver and gold from mines of copper and lead. It is the wise mother that has the wise son. So long as your women are slaves you may throw your colleges and churches to the winds. . . . Truly are the sins of the fathers visited upon the children to the third and fourth generation. God, in his wisdom, has so linked the whole human family together that any violence done at one end of the chain is felt throughout its length, and here, too, is the law of restoration, as in woman all have fallen, so in her elevation shall the race be recreated.[3]

Although the women's movement would enjoy several impressive victories in the decades following the momentous events in Persia and Seneca Falls, it would take a full century before efforts to eradicate gender-based violence would begin to capture the attention of the world. The processes contributing to the globalization of this campaign can be traced to the founding of the United Nations and the subsequent creation of the Commission on Human Rights and the Commission on the Status of Women and to the adoption of the Universal Declaration of Human Rights in December 1948.

The Globalization of the Effort to Eradicate Gender-Based Violence

The establishment of the United Nations Commission on the Status of Women was among the most significant early developments in the globalization of the women's movement. At its inaugural meeting, held in February 1947, the commission resolved to work "to raise the status of women, irrespective of nationality, race, language or religion," to establish "equality with men in all fields of human enterprise, and to eliminate all discrimination against women in the provision of statutory law, in legal maxims or rules, or in interpretations of customary law."[4] As significant and far reaching as these goals were, no mention was made of the need to eliminate sexual and/or physical violence against women and girls. It would take several more decades before this problem would receive sustained international public attention and be adopted as a significant concern of the world body.

Nevertheless, one of the earliest and most important accomplishments of the Commission on the Status of Women—an accomplishment that would ultimately prove vital to the campaign to eradicate gender-based violence—was the commission's influence on shaping the language of the Universal Declaration of Human Rights. Upon the commission's insistence, the declaration, which was adopted in Paris on 10 December 1948 by unanimous vote, was divested of its gender-insensitive language and tailored to affirm, explicitly, the equality of women and men.[5]

Another significant step in advancing women's human rights was taken in 1952 when the UN General Assembly adopted the Convention on the Political Rights of Women. Entered into force in 1954, this convention was the first instrument of international law framed specifically for the protection of the political rights of women everywhere. It provides that the women of the world, whatever their homeland, are entitled to vote in any election, run for any political office, exercise any public function, and hold any public position that a man may hold.

In the areas of work and education, the Commission on the Status of Women also began to gain an appreciation for the impact of inequality on women's quality of life. Near the end of the 1940s it collaborated with the International Labour Organization on women's economic rights. The fruit of that collaboration was the inclusion in the 1948 Universal Declaration of Human Rights of an article (article 23) specifying that everyone, without discrimination, has the right to equal pay for equal work. The commission also collaborated with UNESCO (United Nations Educational, Scientific, and Cultural Organization) in developing basic educational programs that would afford women and girls the same access to education that is provided to men and boys. Although great disparities in access to education continue in many countries, this early work brought to the United Nations a consciousness of the importance of education to women's advancement.

Since the right to nationality is the political basis for many other rights and since many national laws require that married women automatically take their husband's nationality, international human rights observers noted that this tradition left many women vulnerable to losing their own nationality without their consent. Divorced women or women who chose to leave their husbands were particularly vulnerable to becoming stateless. Recognizing this vulnerability, the Commission on the Status of Women completed a draft treaty on the nationality rights of married women and in 1955 submitted it to the UN General Assembly. The Convention on the Nationality of Married Women provided for the right of a woman to retain her nationality if she so desired, even if her nationality would be different from that of her husband. Although the convention was approved in 1957 and the treaty came into force in 1958, the resistance of some governments to many of the treaty provisions signaled the difficulties that would attend any effort to secure nationality rights for women independent of the nationality of their husbands.[6]

A second measure adopted by the United Nations relating to marriage was the Convention and Recommendation on Consent to Marriage, Minimum Age for Marriage, and Registration of Marriages. Adopted by the General Assembly in November 1962 and entered into force in December 1964, the convention was necessary because of the widespread practice of forced child marriage. It requires that no marriage take place without the full and free consent of both parties but leaves it to individual governments to determine the minimum age at which one may enter into a marriage. With the exception of provisions in the Declaration on the Elimination of Discrimination against Women (1967), and the Convention on the Elimination of All Forms of Discrimination against Women (1979), the agreements framed between 1955 and 1962 constitute all the international agreements entered into by the United Nations related to women's rights in marriage.[7]

In the 1950s the Commission on the Status of Women began to express reservations about what amounted to violence perpetrated against women in the name of customary law, religious practices, and traditional ceremonies. Such traditional practices—which include female genital circumcision, virginity tests, dowry and widow burnings, and early-childhood marriages—were brought to the attention of member states who were encouraged to "take immediately all necessary measures with a view to abolishing . . . all customs which violate the physical integrity of women, and which thereby violate the dignity and worth of the human person as proclaimed in the Charter and in the Universal Declaration of Human Rights."[8] In the UN General Assembly the response of member states was mixed. Some maintained that only a gradual process of education could lead to the eradication of such practices; some suggested that the effort to abolish traditional practices was in violation of the UN Charter, which proscribes interference in the domestic affairs of member states; and others felt that traditional practices that compromise the health and well-being of women and girls should be abolished.

When the World Health Organization refused to undertake a study on the effects of genital circumcision for the Commission on the Status of Women, the question of the adverse effects of traditional practices on the well-being of women and girls was abandoned for approximately twenty years and did not become a focus of international attention again until the UN's International Women's Year in 1975.[9] In 1979 the World Health Organization sponsored a seminar on traditional practices affecting the health of women and children, but strong efforts to eradicate such practices did not begin to gain momentum until the mid-1980s when a growing number of individuals and organizations, both within and outside of the human rights community, began to consider female genital circumcision a form of gender-based violence. Such practices, a growing number of voices began to insist, could no longer be justified in the name of the sanctity of culture, religion, or tradition.

During the 1960s and 1970s, as former African colonies began to seize their independence, the number and diversity of member states at the United Nations grew dramatically. In addition, the economic and social consequences of centuries of oppression and injustice had crippled the human and material resources of many colonized nations and had begun to present acute threats to the lives of millions of people—particularly of women and girls—throughout the developing world. For this reason the survival-related concerns of women in developing countries began to eclipse the UN's earlier focus on securing women's legal rights.

Concurrently, the economic and health-related problems associated with the emergence of fledgling nations from colonial rule served to awaken the Commission on the Status of Women to the disproportionate impact of poverty and inequality on the lives of women and girls:

> The work of the Commission on the Status of Women in the 1960s and 1970s thus began to take it beyond the negotiating tables in New York and Geneva and into the fields and rice paddies of the developing world. Such issues as women's needs in community and rural development, agricultural work, family planning and the impact of scientific and technological advances on women became increasingly prominent in the Commission's work. This was the first step in a growing perception among United Nations bodies concerned with development, that the Charter's promise to 'promote social progress and better the standards of life in larger freedom' could not be met without the full participation of women in society.[10]

Realizing the grassroots needs of so many of the world's women, the Economic and Social Council, along with the General Assembly, called upon governments to turn to the United Nations for technical assistance in their development efforts. In addition, organizations within the UN system—such as the United Nations Children's Fund and the United Nations Development Programme—were asked to give special attention to the social and economic advancement of women in the developing countries.

In an effort to highlight women's vital role in national and international development, and with a view to promoting the equality of men and women in the international arena, the Commission on the Status of Women recommended that 1975 be designated International Women's Year. The General Assembly not only endorsed this recommendation but also suggested that, in addition to the themes of development and equality, International Women's Year be used to heighten awareness of the importance of women in promoting world peace.

Perhaps the most significant event of International Women's Year was the first global conference on women's issues ever to be held. The conference took place in June 1975 in Mexico City. Delegations, 113 of them headed by women, from more than 133 member states were present. According to a history of the advancement of women, the UN's Secretary-General, in his opening remarks to the assembled delegates, observed that the conference in Mexico City was "the first major step in a worldwide attempt to achieve equality between men and women and to end separation of the sexes in matters of education, opportunities and economic priorities."[11] At the close of the conference the delegates adopted the Declaration of Mexico on the Equality of Women and Their Contribution to Development and Peace. The declaration specified a set of principles that stress the role of women in promoting and maintaining peace in all spheres of life, including the family, the community, the nation, and the international arena.

The World Plan of Action for the Implementation of the Objectives of the International Women's Year was also drafted at the Mexico City conference. This document specified three main objectives: to promote gender equality; to facilitate the integration of women in all development efforts; and to strengthen the contribution of women to the global movement for world peace. Although the plan left it to each country to specify the means whereby these objectives were to be met, it also outlined minimum goals to be achieved by 1980, the midpoint of the Decade for Women, which would begin in 1976. These goals included efforts combating problems affecting female migrant workers, female prisoners, and women and girls forced into prostitution; achieving equality of access to education for women at all levels of schooling; increasing employment opportunities for women throughout the world; passing laws to ensure greater participation by women in politics and governance; and making significant improvements in women's access to adequate nutrition, housing, health care, and family planning.

The United Nations declared the period between 1976 and 1985 the UN Decade for Women. During this period the women's international human rights movement reemerged as a major concern and began to gather renewed support and unprecedented momentum. The adoption in 1979 of the Convention on the Elimination of All Forms of Discrimination against Women, together with international women's conferences in Copenhagen, Denmark, in 1980 and in Nairobi, Kenya, in 1985, not only brought women's issues to the fore but also began to strengthen the effectiveness of nongovernmental organizations (NGOs) that were moving to the forefront in the effort to promote the advancement of women. Such organizations began to link violence and discrimination against women to a variety of national and international crises, including war, homelessness, illiteracy, poverty, malnutrition, overpopulation, poor health, and high rates of infant mortality. As a result of their growing strength and effectiveness, NGOs began to transform the United Nations into a world body that is not only responsive to the needs and wishes of governments but also receptive to policy recommendations and guidance from the grass roots.

The Convention on the Elimination of All Forms of Discrimination against Women, an important action taken during the UN Decade for Women, was adopted by the United Nations General Assembly on 18 December 1979 and entered into force as an international treaty on 3 September 1981. Since its adoption, more than 150 nations have agreed to be bound by its provisions.

The spirit and objectives of the convention are animated by the same vision and goals that gave birth to the United Nations: "to reaffirm faith in fundamental human rights, in the dignity and worth of the human person, in the equal rights of men and women."[12] As an international treaty, the convention accomplishes two major objectives. First, it establishes an international bill of rights for women and specifies a set of actions to be taken by the nations of the world to ensure that these rights are enjoyed. Second, it mandates the establishment of the Committee on the Elimination of Discrimination against Women (CEDAW), which is charged with ensuring that the provisions of the convention are observed.

The adoption of the Convention on the Elimination of All Forms of Discrimination against Women was a major action during the UN Decade for Women. But at the Copenhagen conference which took place in 1980 at the midpoint of the UN Decade for Women, it became clear to the delegates that the goals articulated in Mexico City could never be achieved by laws alone. Many recognized that, without a sustained measure of grassroots social action and a high level of political commitment, the goals were just that—goals. Following Copenhagen, at least some of the focus of the movement for the advancement of women began to be concentrated on mobilizing more effectively at the grass roots. In addition to concentrating on grassroots efforts, one of the most important developments of the Copenhagen conference would be little noticed: Some of the delegates began to discuss the lack of involvement of men in improving the status and role of women in society.

The third global conference on women was held in 1985 in Nairobi at the end of the UN Decade for Women. At that conference, and at the preparatory conference that took place in Vienna the preceding year, delegates agreed that the goals for the second half of the Decade for Women had not been achieved. However, the experience gained in international consultation at the two previous conferences generated a spirit of confidence and optimism that united the hearts of the delegates in ways that the previous conferences had failed to do. When they left Nairobi, many did so with a profound sense of sisterhood and solidarity that cut across traditional lines of race, class, and culture.

The second major accomplishment of the Nairobi conference was the clear emergence of a consensus among the delegates that gender-based violence would have to be addressed as a human rights issue in the international legal and political arenas. The major document coming out of that conference, the

Nairobi Forward Looking Strategies for the Advancement of Women, noted that

> Violence against women exists in various forms in everyday life in all societies. Women are beaten, mutilated, burned, sexually abused and raped. Such violence is a major obstacle to the achievement of peace and the other objectives of the Decade and should be given special attention. Women victims of violence should be given particular attention and comprehensive assistance. To this end, legal measures should be formulated to prevent violence and to assist women victims. National machineries should be established in order to deal with the question of violence against women within the family and society. Preventive policies should be elaborated, and institutionalized forms of assistance to women provided.[13]

The call raised at the Nairobi conference for addressing gender-based violence began to bear fruit. In May 1990, the UN's Economic and Social Council recognized that gender-based violence in the family and society "is pervasive and cuts across lines of income, class and culture." "Efforts to eradicate it," the council noted, "must be matched by urgent and effective steps." The council called upon governments to take immediate and decisive steps to establish appropriate penalties for violence against women, as well as to reduce its impact in the family, the workplace, and society.[14]

In 1992 the Committee on the Elimination of Discrimination against Women moved to rectify the omission in 1979 of gender-based violence from the Convention on the Elimination of All Forms of Discrimination against Women. At its eleventh session, CEDAW resolved to include gender-based violence under the rubric of gender-based discrimination. Gender-based discrimination, according to CEDAW, is "violence which is directed against a woman because she is a woman or which affects women disproportionately. It includes acts which inflict physical, mental or sexual harm or suffering, threats of such acts, coercion, and other deprivation of liberty." CEDAW went further to request that states parties undertake appropriate and effective measures to end all forms of gender-based violence, whether such violence be by public or private act.[15]

Joining the voices raised against gender-based violence is the Vienna Declaration and Programme of Action, adopted by the World Conference on Human Rights, held in Vienna, Austria, in June 1993. Part I, paragraph 18, of that document addresses violence against women:

> The human rights of women and of the girlchild are an inalienable, integral and indivisible part of universal human rights. The full and equal participation of women in political, civil, economic, social and cultural life, at the national, regional and international levels, and the eradication of all forms of discrimination on grounds of sex are priority objectives of the international community. Gender based violence and all forms of sexual harassment and exploitation, including those resulting from

cultural prejudice and international trafficking, are incompatible with the dignity and worth of the human person, and must be eliminated.[16]

Part I, paragraph 38, continues:

> The World Conference on Human Rights stresses the importance of working towards the elimination of violence against women in public and private life, the elimination of all forms of sexual harassment, exploitation and trafficking in women, the elimination of gender bias in the administration of justice and the eradication of any conflicts which may arise between the rights of women and the harmful effects of certain traditional or customary practices, cultural prejudices and religious extremism.[17]

In 1993 the UN Declaration on the Elimination of Violence against Women—adopted by the General Assembly at its forty-eighth session on 20 December 1993—became the first international human rights instrument designed exclusively to deal with violence against women.

Although not legally binding, the Declaration on the Elimination of Violence against Women (hereafter referred to as the Declaration) provides the first set of international standards to address the problem of violence against women and girls. The preamble to the Declaration affirms that the root cause of gender-based violence is the "historically unequal power relations between men and women, which have led to domination over and discrimination against women by men and to the prevention of the full advancement of women." In affirming that "violence against women is one of the crucial social mechanisms by which women are forced into a subordinate position compared with men," the preamble recognizes that violence is both a result and a cause of gender-related inequities.[18]

As it is with the Convention on the Elimination of All Forms of Discrimination against Women, the notion of equality embodied in the Declaration is free of theoretical speculation. It seeks to ensure that women are allowed and enabled to enjoy the most fundamental of all human rights, namely, the right to physical and psychological integrity and safety. Specifically, the Declaration defines violence against women as physical and sexual violence that takes place within the family (and that consists of battering, sexual abuse of female children, dowry-related violence, marital rape, female genital circumcision, and other traditional practices that have proven to be harmful to women; nonspousal violence; and violence that attends various forms of female exploitation); violence against women in the community (which consists of rape, sexual abuse, harassment, and intimidation in the workplace and educational institutions, trafficking in women, and forced prostitution); and violence against women that is either perpetrated or condoned by the state.

Among the most significant contributions to gender equality embodied in the Declaration are the obligations imposed upon the state both to "condemn" gender-based violence and to pursue all "appropriate means" and "without delay" to ensure the elimination of violence directed against women within their national borders. Commenting on state responsibility in this regard, the UN's Special Rapporteur on Violence against Women observed:

> The problem of violence against women brings into sharp focus an issue that has been troubling the international community—State responsibility for the actions of private citizens. In the past, a strict judicial interpretation had made the State responsible only for actions for which it or its agents are directly accountable. In this case it would relate to issues such as women in custody and women in detention and perhaps the problem of women during armed conflict. The question of domestic violence, rape and sexual harassment, etc., were seen as the actions of individuals and thus beyond the "human rights" responsibility of the State.[19]

By specifying a proactive role for the state in all situations in which women are more likely than men to be victims of violence, the Declaration on the Elimination of Violence against Women makes it possible to conceptualize even private acts of violence against women (for example, domestic violence) as violations of women's human rights. Inasmuch as the equal protection of all citizens from violence on account of race, class, religion, or sex is fundamental to any functional and operational definition of equality, the Declaration is a major advance in establishing the equality of women and men worldwide.

The four actions taken between May 1990 and December 1993—the actions of the UN's Economic and Social Council in 1990 and CEDAW in 1991, the Vienna Declaration in June 1993, and the UN Declaration on the Elimination of Violence against Women in December 1993—were the first concrete signs of the international community's moral and legal commitment to eradicating this global, age-old problem. They are among the most significant developments in human rights law in the twentieth century and are the first to challenge the legal and moral foundations on which misplaced justifications for allowing gender-based violence to continue are based.

In its resolution 44/82, the UN's General Assembly designated 1994 the International Year of the Family. This act catalyzed a number of processes that clarified the steps necessary to protect and promote the advancement of women and girls. At its thirteenth session, for example, the Committee on the Elimination of Discrimination against Women chose to mark the International Year of the Family by analyzing three articles in the Convention on the Elimination of All Forms of Discrimination against Women that have special significance for the status of women in the family: articles 9, 15, and 16.

Article 9(1) of CEDAW disallows nationality laws that discriminate against women by limiting their nationality rights in situations in which men's rights are not so limited. In some countries, for example, women are unable to confer on foreign husbands such rights as may be conferred by men on their foreign wives (such as the right of residency or the right to become a citizen after a brief residency period). Furthermore, inasmuch as article 9(2) provides women and men with equal rights with respect to the nationality of children, women who are now prevented from doing so may soon be able to pass citizenship on to their offspring. (At present the constitutions of several nations provide that children born outside of the country may become citizens only if their father is a citizen.) Commenting on the significance of article 9, Marsha Freeman, the director of International Women's Rights Watch, observes:

> Nationality is fundamentally related to women's exercise of personal liberty and freedom of movement. If a woman's nationality or that of her children is dependent upon her husband's nationality, her ability to make adult decisions as to residence, travel, her children's welfare, or even marriage is severely limited.[20]

Article 15 of CEDAW provides for the equality of women before the law. The right of women to attain the age of majority (or legal age) at the same age as is applied to men; the right of women to undertake contractual obligations and to sell, buy, and administer property; the right of women to inherit and administer estates; the right of women to appear before the court on their own behalf and to have their testimony given weight equal to that of men; and the right of women to choose freely where they will live or travel without male consent are all provided for under article 15.

Article 16 covers marriage and family law and is designed to promote equality within the family and to protect women from the discriminatory effects of customary laws, traditions, and religious practices that usurp the rights of women and/or girls to choose their own spouse and to give their consent to marriage. Article 16 also provides that during marriage men and women should be equally responsible for household and family duties, should have equal rights to family decision making, should be equally responsible for children, and have equal power in discharging familial authority.

In September 1995, during the fiftieth-anniversary year of the United Nations, the Fourth World Conference on Women was held in Beijing, China, with delegations from 189 countries. This gathering represented the largest UN conference ever held. The platform for action and the Beijing Declaration emerging out of the conference were adopted unanimously by 189 countries and are among the most comprehensive human rights documents ever articulated on behalf of the world's women. The platform for action seeks to uphold the Convention on the Elimination of All Forms of Discrimination against Women (1979) and to build on the Nairobi Forward-Looking Strategies for the Advancement of Women (1985). While the platform for action's overall objective—empowering all women—conforms to the purposes and principles of the Charter of the United Nations, its immediate aim was to establish a basic group of priority actions to be carried out during the five-year period between 1995 and the turn of the century. The platform for action contained twelve areas of critical concern that were to receive special attention:

1. The persistent and increasing burden of poverty on women

2. Inequalities and inadequacies in, and unequal access to, education and training

3. Inequalities and inadequacies in, and unequal access to, health care and related services

4. Violence against women

5. The effects of armed and other kinds of conflict on women, including those living under foreign occupation

6. Inequality in economic structures and policies, in all forms of productive activities, and in access to resources

7. Inequality between men and women in the sharing of power and decision making at all levels

8. Insufficient mechanisms at all levels to promote the advancement of women

9. Lack of respect for, and inadequate promotion and protection of, the human rights of women

10. Stereotyping of women and inequality in women's access to, and participation in, all communication systems, especially in the media

11. Gender inequalities in the management of natural resources and in the safeguarding of the environment

12. Persistent discrimination against, and violation of the rights of, the girl child[21]

In its effort to contribute in new ways to the eradication of all forms of inequality and abuse, the platform for action outlines specific actions to be taken by governments to address each of the problem areas adumbrated above. In its comprehensiveness it has left almost no institution of civil society untouched. Included in the platform are actions prescribed for national and local governments, community organizations, nongovernmental organizations, educational institutions, the public and private sectors, and the mass media as directed by the state. Thus the platform for action is one of the most comprehensive documents ever articulated in the interest of promoting and protecting women's human rights.

Since articulation of the platform for action, measures have been undertaken to improve the status of women within the United Nations itself. For example, the numbers of women in professional and decision-making positions at the UN have increased and are expected to continue to increase. These changes not only facilitate the realization of the important goals outlined in the platform for action but also serve as greater evidence of the UN's commitment to the advancement of women in all fields of human endeavor. Beyond these steps, the United Nations has, since the Beijing conference, sought to forge even stronger bonds with nongovernmental organizations at the grassroots levels and has begun to work to encourage a wider spectrum of civil society to contribute to the advancement of women and their protection from human rights abuses.

Where Do We Go from Here?

Despite the progress made during the last half century, and notwithstanding the detailed and much-needed prescriptions for change addressed to governments and institutions of civil society, violence against women and girls continues to be a public-health scourge of global proportions. According to the UN's Special Rapporteur on Violence against Women, appointed just before the Beijing conference in 1994, violence against human beings, and particularly against women and girls, continues to be a major factor hindering the realization of human rights goals:

> War, repression, and the brutalization of public and private life have destroyed the possibility of human rights being enjoyed as a universal phenomenon. Violence against women, in particular, has inhibited women as a group from enjoying the full benefits of human rights. Women have been vulnerable to acts of violence in the family, in the community and by States. The recorded incidents of such violence have reached such unprecedented proportions that they have shocked the conscience of the world.[22]

As is clear from the foregoing review, over the course of the last half century organized efforts to eradicate gender-based violence and discrimination have tended to be centered on international law and human rights. The underlying assumption appears to be that when the national and international legal instruments necessary for securing gender equality and for protecting women's rights have been fashioned and applied, gender-based discrimination and abuse will find an inhospitable environment and will gradually disappear.

As vital as legal and human rights measures are, they are, as an increasing number of individuals and organizations are beginning to recognize, insufficient to effect the magnitude of change necessary if gender-based violence and discrimination are to be eradicated. Inasmuch as violence against women and girls is sustained by long-standing, maladaptive patterns of thinking and relating, legal strategies, unaccompanied by efforts to address the intrapersonal dimensions of the problem, are likely to prove ineffective. Indeed, as Shoghi Effendi observed, inasmuch as the inner and outer dimensions of human life are inseparable, it is futile to attempt the reformation of the one without the other. Humanity is organic with the world, he noted; the inner life of each individual molds the environment and is itself also deeply affected by it. The one acts upon the other, and every abiding change in the life of humanity is the result of these mutual reactions. Conscious awareness of the reciprocal relationship between personal development and institutional and societal transformation is thus an essential component of any viable scheme to advance the realization of human rights goals.

In this regard, the distinction that Cornel West has made between the pitfalls of "structural liberalism" and the limitations of "conservative behaviorism" is of heuristic value here. Structural liberalists, noted West, tend to identify social, historical, and institutional impediments when seeking to remedy widespread social problems. Conservative behaviorists, by contrast, tend to limit their analyses to person-centered variables, such as people's values, attitudes, beliefs, and so forth. Liberal structuralists resist talking about values too much because it takes the focus away from structures, especially the positive role of government, while conservative behaviorists "talk about values and attitudes as if political and economic structures hardly exist."[23] In contradistinction to this dichotomous debate, we suggest that the global campaign to elevate the status of women, to promote gender equality, and to eradicate gender-based violence is most likely to be effective if it is fueled and upheld both by enforceable local and international laws and by processes that address the inner terrain of human consciousness, human values, and human spiritual and moral development.

Moreover, as legal theorist and researcher Amede Obiora has suggested, the impact of the broad legal culture on the persistence of gender-based discrimination and violence cannot be overlooked. "Legal culture" has been described as "the network of values and attitudes which determine why, when, where and how people employ legal structures and why legal rules work or do not work." It is, according to Obiora, "the legal culture that provides the impetus for the use, abuse, or avoidance of the law."[24] The legal culture and social fabric depend upon covenantal arrangements that, in the words of Jonathan Sacks, Great Britain's chief rabbi, "prevent us—from a sense of honor, or fidelity, or decency—from doing certain things." Such arrangements extend well beyond a mere code of laws and embrace a people's internalized, fundamental values. If the legal culture of a nation or community is not oriented toward the advancement and protection of women, a proliferation of laws, however much needed, will not remedy gender-related abuses.

There are at least three dimensions to a legal culture: the outer form, or *legal structure* of a community; the inner form, or *philosophical principles* that animate that structure; and the *actors* or citizens within a community who embody in their deeds the degree of commitment they have to the values and principles that animate their legal and/or social system. The outer aspect of a legal culture is utilitarian and has to do with mechanisms designed to facilitate application of a community's constitution and/or body of laws. The inner aspect is abstract and has to do with metaphysical principles that the laws of a community are designed to embody, protect, and advance. In addition to the facilitation of order and social processes, the desire to protect such values as justice, equity, human nobility, and a sense of collective trust are the implicit or explicit goals that buttress most nontotalitarian legal systems. Indeed, even in contemporary Western cultures where law is presumed to be merely utilitarian or functional, the strength of the law rests, to no insignificant degree, on its ability to evoke a sense of respect, and sometimes even reverence, for the legitimacy of the social order that the law is designed to serve.

A people's awareness of, and appreciation for, the underlying values that serve as the foundation of law give a legal culture its enduring strength and render a legal system more than "a mere code of laws."[25] In the absence of a concern for underlying values, laws lose their power to protect against many forms of exploitation and abuse. Harold Berman, one of the world's foremost legal historians and philosophers, notes that, in the final analysis, what empowers law is the "deeply or passionately held conviction that law is not only an instrument of secular policy but also part of the ultimate purpose of life."[26] The legal scholar Roshan Danesh further observes that law is best understood "not only as positive rules but also as a relationship between rules and standards and the architecture of beliefs, traditions, and texts that support and give meaning to those rules. A crisis of internal fidelity exists," he notes, "when legal rules and the institutions that create and interpret them have become unmoored from any generative aspirative frame."[27] Traditionally, the aspirative frame for law was provided by religion. Religious systems, which are the primary fount of law, embody the notion that laws exist in order to facilitate the realization of human aspiration for that which is, in some sense, transcendently good for both the individual and the community. But more than this, laws rooted in religion were intended to prevent crimes not only by threat of punishment but also by inspiring in adherents the acquisition of a sound character. And while the trend toward secularization of law is both understandable and necessary in a context of cultural and religious pluralism, the larger project of connecting laws designed to protect and advance human rights with a tenable framework of values that citizens are both familiar with and embrace would seem vital to ensuring success. For underlying the failure of nations, communities, and families to protect and advance the rights of women and girls are not only legal and human rights standards that leave women vulnerable but also maladaptive values and attitudes that run counter to the spirit of equality and humanity that many legal systems have been explicitly designed to advance. These patterns of thought require as much attention by the international community as do the laws that have been, and will be, framed in defense of women's human rights. It is for this reason that the global campaign to eradicate gender-based violence would do well to add to the worldwide concern for articulating human rights law a similar concern for promoting psychological maturation, spiritual growth, and self-mastery.

There are three places that we can turn for insights into the psychological, spiritual, and ethical dimensions of this challenge: the emerging body of behavioral research on the development of emotional competence; the work of contemporary moral philosophers who are creating systems of ethics and programs of moral development that are based on universal human values; and the world's ethicospiritual traditions, which have provided some of the most enlightened discourse to date on the processes of self-mastery. It is, therefore, toward these relatively neglected dimensions of the global campaign to eradicate gender-based violence that we turn in the present volume.

Following an epidemiological overview of the problem of gender-based violence and discrimination, we draw special attention to the Authenticity Project, an international moral education project that seeks to develop materials that might frame a global approach to moral and spiritual development. The Authenticity Project (whose members include the first author of this volume, as well as William S. Hatcher, Mary K. Radpour, Leslie Asplund, Sheri Dressler, and Lonya Osokin) grounds its approach to moral development in the assumption that the highest values that a civilization can promote are the cultivation of human consciousness and the development of authentic human relationships. All other values, the project suggests, should be evaluated in light of the extent to which they are in harmony with these overarching goals.

Moral education, according to the Authenticity Project, is concerned, first, with understanding the nature of value and, second, with applying this understanding in one's relationships with others. There are two types of value: *intrinsic* value, which arises from the inherent properties and capacities of an entity; and *extrinsic* value, which is ascribed to an entity through subjective preferences and social conventions. An example of the latter is the value generally ascribed to money. Although little more than ink on paper, and although highly ephemeral, money derives a great deal of value by social agreement. Its value is thus extrinsic to its inherent qualities and nature. That which is of intrinsic value, by contrast, derives its value, not by social agreement, but from the inherent qualities and potentialities of the entity in question. The sun, for example, is of value irrespective of any individual's opinion about it. Its value is inherent in its being the primary source of light and warmth in our biosphere and the sine qua non for life and development in the natural world.

Similarly, the human person is of inherent value. The value of the human person is inherent in the facts that persons represent the fruit and arrowhead of evolution on Earth and that the maintenance and advancement of civilization—in all of its forms—depends upon the cultivation of persons. The protection and development of this value is the supreme objective of any legitimate social order. Any system of government, any set of laws, any ideology or cultural practice that unduly jeopardizes the realization of the inherent potential of a human being is in violation of that person's inalienable right to become. Such a society has betrayed its legitimate raison d'être. According to the Authenticity Project, true morality consists in apprehending the inherent value of the self and others and in living in relationship in such a way as to afford the development and expression of humanity's full potential. The creation of the capacities necessary for authentic relationships is the objective that fuels the work of the Authenticity Project.

The Nature of Authentic Human Relationships

The signs of authenticity in relationships are said to be the practice of justice and the presence of altruistic love. Nonauthentic relationships, by contrast, are characterized by conflict, disharmony, manipulation, cruelty, jealousy, and so forth. "Altruistic love," the project writes, "is not just a feeling of emotional warmth towards others, but is an objective, attractive force that operates according to certain objective laws and principles. Moral education means learning these laws and principles so that we become ever more subject to the force of love in our lives. Morality, then, *is the pursuit of authentic relationships* or, stated more fully, *the process of developing our innate capacity to sustain authentic relationships.*" The Authenticity Project illustrates this unique perspective with an analogy from physics:

> Current physical theory has discovered four fundamental forces. The force of gravity and the strong nuclear force are purely attractive forces. The weak nuclear force, however, is a purely repulsive force: it has no (currently known) attractive form. Finally, electromagnetic force has both an attractive and a repulsive form. Now [we] affirm that altruistic love, like gravity, is a purely attractive force. True love *cannot* be the cause of conflict or estrangement between two people any more than the force of gravitational attraction between two physical bodies can push them apart.
>
> Of course, physical bodies can be pulled apart by forces that overcome their mutual gravitational attraction. But, whenever we observe two physical bodies moving away from each other, we know that such a configuration is occurring in spite of their mutual gravitational attraction, not because of it. In the same way, whenever we see conflict and disharmony in human relationships, we know that it is due to some factor other than love. . . . Thus, moral education is the pursuit of relational authenticity by learning the laws that govern the action of love and then implementing that knowledge in our relationship with others. The moral person is one who has acquired the capacity for genuine love and self-sacrifice. He demonstrates this by his integrity and trustworthiness in his relations with others, by consistently treating others with genuine kindness and encouragement. . . . In other words, the basics of morality are stark in their simplicity: either a

person has acquired the capacity for self-sacrifice, which he demonstrates through active, humble, reliable service towards others, or he has not, in which case his behavior will reflect various pathologies of inauthenticity . . . (such as greed, untrustworthiness, jealousy, self-centeredness, coldness, indifference, anger, cruelty).[28]

Because the acquisition of the capacity for authentic morality requires continual, often painful self-evaluation, a number of strategies have been developed throughout history to transform basic morality into something that can be more easily achieved. For example, although one of the overarching goals of religion is to facilitate the achievement of authentic moral relationships, this goal is frequently transmuted in such a way that religion becomes primarily an ideology. Once religion becomes an ideology, its doctrines become the supreme value, and morality is conceived as their protection and propagation by all possible means. Although all religions present a philosophy of life and teach the belief in certain doctrines and ideas, authentic religion conceives of belief in such doctrines, not as an end in itself, but as a means for developing the capacity for authentic relationships (both with God and with other human beings). Thus, the error of ideologized religion lies, not in seeking to propagate and advance certain doctrines, but rather in exalting these doctrines above authentic relationships, thereby interchanging means and ends.

> We will use the term *ideology* to designate any philosophy which holds that certain doctrines, ideas, or propositions are more important than human beings. Thus defined, any ideology (irrespective of what its specific doctrinal content may be) contradicts the basic assumption of authentic religion, which holds that (while God may be the Supreme Value in Existence) the human being is the supreme value in creation. Moreover, any moral system holds that lesser values may be sacrificed to obtain greater values. An ideology thus sanctions (at least implicitly) the deliberate sacrifice of human beings, or of authentic human relationships, if it is deemed necessary for the propagation of the doctrines of that ideology. In regarding its doctrines as more important than human beings, an ideology considers these doctrines as God—as the supreme value in existence. Ideology is thus idolatry. It is the worship of certain ideas.[29]

As it is with ideology, culture-specific values and traditions are also frequently invoked in support of the continuation of practices that may be harmful to the equal participation, development, and/or well-being of subgroups such as women and girls within a culture. The continuation of such practices is inspired by the belief that cultural values are the only ultimate values and that these values are necessarily local and accidental, rather than intrinsic and universal. Inasmuch as this perspective renders all cultural values fundamentally equivalent, the argument is that each cultural group must be left free from outside interference in deciding the values that should animate community life.

Legitimate as is the concern for preserving a people's right to determine the nature and course of their own lives, the work of the Authenticity Project assumes that there are also intrinsic, universal values that derive from the universal nature and needs of all human beings—irrespective of race, culture, or historical time period. The global community is said to have a moral responsibility to safeguard these values, even when the parties concerned would prefer to operate free from external influence. To do otherwise would be to render the preservation of culture the supreme value, irrespective of the impact of culture-specific practices on the lives of human beings. The articulation of an international body of laws designed to preserve human rights is an explicit rejection of the assumption of absolute cultural relativity by the community of nations. At the same time, inasmuch as the adoption of a universal set of moral values on the local level is not likely to be realized unless large segments of the population are persuaded of their logic and need, the promotion of such values depends upon processes of education and persuasion.

The Nature of Moral Education

The Authenticity Project recognizes that an approach to moral education that nurtures in children and youth a hunger for moral and spiritual growth while also developing morally relevant *capacities* is likely to be more effective in eliminating the root cause of abuses of power in the family, the community, and the state than are approaches that focus on the transmittal of moral lessons or rules. What is needed is the development of an inner agent of self-control that encourages right action because of its own inherent beauty. Iraj Ayman, a scholar specializing in moral philosophy, refers to this capacity as the capacity for "spiritual discernment."[30] According to educator Irene Taafaki, developing spiritual discernment requires that institutions around the world promote moral growth. The role of educators is to use a variety of processes to nurture children and youth to go beyond knowing what constitutes moral ideas to developing moral insight and practicing moral behavior, the goal being to develop moral wisdom rather than a rote following of rules. Moral wisdom then becomes the "inner lens" through which children are able both to discern what is right and to do those things that enhance both their own well-being and that of others.[31]

A pedagogy of moral education, notes Taafaki, would include active learning rather than the passive inculcation of moral lessons; a loving and encouraging environment wherein educators demonstrate in their own lives the qualities they wish to teach; use of the arts, literature, and folklore from cultural and religious communities around the world; and cooperative learning exercises that enable children and young people of diverse backgrounds to work together in exploring and resolving a range of socially and morally relevant problems. The promotion of a spirit of service to humanity is an integral part of the pedagogy of moral education. Such service enables children and youth to enhance their understanding of the relevance of moral behavior for the development and solidarity of family and community and for the cultivation of a sense of "at-oneness" with others.[32]

In addition to a concern for moral development, the concept of "emotional intelligence," first articulated by researchers John Meyer and Peter Salovey and later popularized in a book by Daniel Goleman, embodies the idea that human beings can be assisted to develop emotional skills that empower them to relate to themselves and to others in more adaptive and harmonious ways.[33] We feel that inasmuch as emotional immaturity and poor impulse control are at the root of many forms of gender-based violence, efforts that are designed to enhance the capacity of children and youth to better understand and manage their own emotions are likely to contribute to reducing high rates of many forms of violence and abuse that occur in the home. Thus, in addition to examining processes of moral development that might be applied to the problem of gender-based violence, in this volume we also explore the promise embodied in this emerging paradigm of applied research.

Last, as has already been noted, we feel that the world's sacred and philosophical traditions contain many useful insights into the challenge of self-mastery and intrapersonal growth. We have thus taken the liberty to quote these traditions throughout the work when the insights contained in them appeared to us to be relevant and useful. We have taken care to emphasize the fundamental spiritual truths that appear to be common to all the world's faiths, as we believe that it is these spiritual truths, embodied perhaps most simply in the Golden Rule, that provide peoples of all faiths, as well as those of no faith, with penetrating insights into the conditions necessary to make anew the social world.

This book is divided into three parts and nine chapters. Parts I and II explore the epidemiology of gender-based violence and discrimination. Chapter 1 provides a general overview of structural violence and of discriminatory practices that continue to jeopardize the health and development of women and girls across the planet. Chapter 2 examines the many forms of sexual violence directed against women and girls; and chapter 3 adumbrates the continuing problem of physical abuse. Chapter 4 of part II provides an introduction to culturally sanctioned forms of gender-based violence. Chapter 5, which opens part III's exploration of efforts to eradicate gender-based violence, explores the potential impact that equal access to education would have on the life chances of women and girls. Chapters 6 and 7 examine the psychological and spiritual dimensions of the global campaign to eradicate gender-based violence. It is in these chapters that we discuss in detail the work of the Authenticity Project. Chapter 8 lays out a role for men; and chapter 9 closes the volume by exploring some of the reasons we should have hope that the global campaign to eradicate gender-based violence can and will meet with success.

Part I

GLOBAL PREVALENCE OF GENDER-BASED INEQUALITY AND VIOLENCE

1

Confronting Structural Violence against Women and Girls: The Principle and Practice of Gender Equality

Notwithstanding the international struggle to achieve it, there is considerable variation throughout the world as to what is meant by "gender equality" or "gender equity" and how such equality might be achieved. Amede Obiora, for example, recently conducted a study that examined the attitudes of a select population of Nigerian men and women to the effort to legislate equality in gender relations. In the course of her study, a majority of her subjects, both male and female, were confounded by the notion of equality that is commonly articulated in mainstream Western legal discourse. "Insisting instead that 'all fingers are not equal,' some of these respondents suggested that 'respect,' not 'equality,' was a more appropriate and realistic paradigm for ordering (male/female relationships)."[1] Obiora's work, and that of many other feminist scholars, illustrates the difficulty of articulating a notion of gender equality that facilitates social transformation while also respecting the diversity of views that must be brought to bear on this issue. And although an exploration of the full range of views articulated by scholars of diverse backgrounds is well beyond the scope of this work, it is clear that, at minimum, equality must mean the right to live free of gender-based violence and exploitation. Furthermore, providing the same rights and opportunities for women as are presently available for men in civil and political life, in education and employment, would seem indispensable to any viable definition.

For example, notwithstanding the extraordinary achievements in the advancement of women recorded during the twentieth century, a survey of the current status of women reveals that there is still much structural work to be done if women and girls are to enjoy the same opportunities for development and participation that are available to men and boys. This is particularly true for women and girls who live in those parts of the world where access to legal support in defense of women's civil and human rights is either unaffordable or unavailable.

The need for progress in advancing equality is apparent in two interconnected areas: one has to do with our understanding and embrace of the *principle* of gender equality, and the other involves redressing disparities in access to those material conditions necessary to translate the idea of equality into *concrete form*. We begin this work on the global campaign to eradicate gender-based violence by examining these two dimensions of equality. We attempt to show how structural violence against women and girls is supported and sustained by the cultural and philosophical assumption of ontological inequality between women and men. We go further to articulate an organic model of gender equality that emphasizes the complementary nature of human relationships within a broader commitment to the essential oneness and interdependence of humankind.

Gender Inequality and Structural Violence

In a widely read document on the status of women and girls, UNICEF reports that women the world over are routinely subjected to discriminatory restrictions of such fundamental freedoms as travel, marriage, testifying in court, inheriting and owning property, securing credit, and obtaining custody of their children. UNICEF goes further to note that in many countries girls enjoy less nutritious food, fewer visits to health care facilities, lower rates of vaccination, and less nurture than boys.[2] With respect to the distribution and allocation of workload and income, a number of studies report that although women and girls continue to work many more hours daily than men, they own almost none of the world's wealth. As one group of researchers affirms, "Women constitute half the world's population, perform nearly two-thirds of the work hours, receive one-tenth of the world's income and own less than one one-hundredth of the world's property."[3] In Nepal, for example, boys work approximately one-half of the hours worked by girls.[4] Studies out of Africa and Asia reveal that while boys are engaged in play, girls aged ten to fourteen put in seven or more hours of domestic labor per day. In Java, young girls tend to spend 33 percent more hours per day working either at home or in the market than do boys of the same age. In the Ivory Coast, girls aged ten to fourteen work three to five hours per day carrying out household chores; their male counterparts, by contrast, work on average two hours per day.

Even among industrialized nations disparities in the unpaid workloads of males and females have become evident. For example, studies of Italy and Australia reveal greater unpaid workloads for girls than for boys.[5] The difficulties imposed by this reality are rendered all the more salient when we consider that the number of households headed by poor women is sharply increasing.[6] In the United States, for example, the proportion of female-headed households among poor African Americans may be as high as 71 percent.[7]

Among the growing number of economically disadvantaged women who work outside the home, historical and unequal power relations between men and women continue to result in exploitation of female labor. The UN's Special Rapporteur on Violence against Women recently reported that economically disadvantaged women are more vulnerable to sexual harassment, trafficking, and sexual slavery; that they are employed as bonded and low-paid labor in many economic enterprises throughout the world; and that as migrant workers, they often face innumerable hardships in foreign countries.[8]

In addition, while adoption of modern technology contributes significantly to the destruction of the livelihoods of a growing number of rural women, so-called sweatshops and similar sites for the economic exploitation of female labor have begun to proliferate. More than a decade ago, a widely cited special report in *Ms.* magazine noted, "All other things being equal, if the proportion of the poor in female-householder families were to continue to increase at the same rate as it did from 1967 to 1978, the poverty population would be comprised solely of women and their children before the year 2000."[9] That women with children now constitute the fastest-growing group of homeless people and refugees would suggest this prediction was not as gross an exaggeration as it first seemed. The feminization of poverty is now a feature of many societies worldwide.

Despite the inability of millions of women to gain access to adequate income, current data indicate clearly that women in developing countries tend to manage money better than men do. A recent study involving Malaysia, Cameroon, and Bolivia revealed that among three priority problems related to women's status, women themselves cited mismanagement of household finances by their husbands.[10] Numerous other studies, including data from the World Bank, have shown that as compared to men, when women have access to economic resources, they tend to expend a larger percentage of available funds on their families.[11] Thus, when women prosper, families prosper. Conversely, when women fall prey to poverty, so do the world's children.

Although women are the first, and often the only, educators of children, women and girls receive the least exposure to formal education. The World Bank reports that two-thirds of the 960 million illiterate people in the world are women. Furthermore, of the 130 million children who received no primary education in 1990, 81 million were girls.[12] As compared to boys, even in developed nations, fewer girls enroll in and complete school. According to Neera Sohoni, "Parental reluctance to enroll and maintain girls in schools even when primary and secondary education may be free and compulsory is associated with their limited view of girls as liabilities rather than assets. As an Indian proverb puts it crudely, 'Investing in a girl is like watering a plant in a neighbor's garden.'"[13] Girls may also be demotivated and are less likely to complete school owing to a number of factors such as sexual harassment and violence, in-class gender discrimination, gender stereotyping in the curriculum and textbooks, teachers' lower expectations for their success, early pregnancies, and childhood marriages.

The United Nations reports that the average age at marriage for girls in Bangladesh is 11.6 years; in two villages in India, the average age of marriage proved to be 14.4 years. Among Nigerians, 25 percent of all marriages of girls occur before age 13, 50 percent by age 15, and 80 percent by age 20. Boys, by contrast, tend to marry when they are much older. Data from the United States, Bangladesh, Brazil, Ethiopia, Indonesia, Sudan, Turkey, and the United Arab Emirates reveal that the percentage of married girls aged 15 to 19 is three to ten times higher than the percentage of married males aged 15 to 19.[14] One consequence of early marriage for girls is that they are afforded less opportunity to complete their education. Another consequence is that their reproductive role renders them more vulnerable to illness and early death. For example, in some countries, such as Bangladesh, the maternal mortality rate (MMR) for mothers aged 10 to 14 is five times greater than among mothers aged 20 to 24; in the United States, pregnant girls under age 15 evidence a maternal mortality rate that is three times as high as that of women aged 20 to 24.[15]

For centuries traditional arrangements have instilled in many people and cultures a tendency not only to prefer sons but also to neglect female children. Professor Hoda Mahmoudi points out that female life expectancy has actually declined in Ghana, Kenya, Liberia, Niger, and the Philippines over the past few decades. "When the difficult decision needs to be made in terms of which child to feed," noted Mahmoudi, "a boy is preferred over a girl."[16] Son preference is practiced most widely in Southeast Asian countries including Bangladesh, India, Nepal, and Pakistan; Middle Eastern and North African countries like Algeria, Egypt, Jordan, the Libyan Arab Jamahiriya, Morocco, the Syrian Arab Republic, Tunisia, and Turkey; and in some sub-Saharan African countries such as Cameroon and Madagascar. There is also some evidence of abnormal sex ratios in mortality figures of some Latin American countries such as Ecuador, Mexico, Peru, and Uruguay, indicating the possibility of son preference in these nations as well.

In countries practicing son preference, there is a tendency to abort girls following sex-determination tests like amniocentesis and sonography. A study of amniocentesis in a large Bombay hospital found that 95.5 per cent of fetuses identified as female were aborted.[17] Similarly, another study, conducted in Maharashtra (West India), indicated that of 8,000 fetuses aborted, 7,999 were female.[18]

In cases where technological prebirth sex determination is beyond the reach of the poor, female infanticide sometimes substitutes for abortion. If the delivery is at home, the child is often born, killed, and buried the same day. If delivery occurs at the hospital, a mock illness is frequently declared within a week to ten days, after which the child is killed. Different ways of killing female infants have been documented, including force-feeding the infant excessive cow's milk and hanging the bottle upside down from the cradle so that the child chokes; feeding the infant a mixture of soapy water and dissolved salt until she chokes; using a cloth with dripping water to cover the face of the infant to suffocate her; giving the poisonous milk of the Calatropis plant to the infant; feeding the child with husks of paddy grains until she chokes; administering pesticides; and so on.[19]

The one-child rule in China appears to be intensifying the problem of abortion, infanticide, and orphanage as parents struggle to fill their one-child quota with a son. The UN's Special Rapporteur cites a 1995 Amnesty International report on China indicating that in 1994, 117 boys were born for every 100 girls, a figure significantly higher than the world average of 106 males for every 100 girls.[20] Those who are unable or unwilling to kill their own infants sometimes abandon them, subjecting them to a life as orphans. Tom Hilditch recounts the work of a British documentary team that captured the condition of children at some of the government-run orphanages in China as follows:

Mei-ming has lain this way for 10 days now: tied up in urine-soaked blankets, scabs of dried mucus growing across her eyes, her face shrinking to a skull, malnutrition slowly shrivelling her two-year old body. The orphanage staff call her room the "dying room", and they have abandoned her for the very same reasons her parents abandoned her shortly after she was born. She is a girl. When Mei-ming dies four days later, it will be of sheer neglect. Afterward, the orphanage will deny she ever existed. She will be just another invisible victim of the collision between China's one-child policy and its traditional preference for male heirs. She is one of perhaps 15 million female babies who have disappeared from China's demographics since the one-child-per-family policy was introduced in 1979. Yet Mei-ming's brief and miserable life may not have been in vain. Before she died, she was discovered by a British documentary team that entered her orphanage posing as American charity fund-raisers. The footage the team shot, through a concealed camera, would provide the first video evidence of the existence of dying rooms. And when the documentary, *The Dying Rooms*, was shown in Britain in June, over the protest of China's embassy in London, little Mei- ming's dying cries for help were heard around the world.[21]

Recently, UNICEF estimated that as many as 77 million females are missing and feared dead as a result of female infanticide, deliberate malnutrition, selective abortions, and outright violence against girls. In his explication of this fact before the U.S. House of Representatives, Congressman Tom Lantos noted: "The combined total of females missing in Bangladesh, Afghanistan, India, Pakistan and China exceeds 77 million human beings. The way this figure is arrived at is obvious. On the basis of actuarial figures, there should be so many adult women and so many adult men. There are 77 million adult women who are not there. They are not there because they were killed as infants or were the victims of gender violence in later years."[22] Lantos points out that this figure is more than the combined populations of California, New York, Texas, and Florida.

Evidence from China, Korea, and Singapore reveals a strong desire to prevent female births.[23] An article by Sohoni on the status of female children notes:

> Anecdotes and proverbs in many countries refer to the pride with which the male child is welcomed, and the gloom that casts a shadow on the coming of a baby girl. In the Arab language, for instance, any unexpected silence or conversational gap in an assembly invites the comment 'Khilqat bint' or 'Why the silence? Has a girl been born?' A phrase from the Korean language translates to: 'A girl lets you down twice, once at birth and the second time when she marries.'[24]

Such comments reveal the disdain and disappointment that accompany the birth of many female children.

Some parents who decide to keep their baby girls often neglect them. In her book *Women and Literacy*, Jennifer Horsman gives an insight into the childhood experience of one of her case-study subjects, a woman in Nova Scotia, Canada:

> Pat left her abusive home and said she was unable to continue at school because the psychiatric drugs she was being given prevented her thinking. She was abused and rejected as a child; her mother had wanted a boy and so refused to acknowledge her. Her childhood was one of neglect and violence. "The doctor that delivered me told me the whole story. He said: 'Right from birth . . . she wouldn't hold you; the staff had to take over. She just said, I don't want nothing to do with her'. And when I was taken home . . . she would just leave me in a room with the door closed and ignore me." When she accused her brother of sexually abusing her, her mother refused to believe her. She suffered from a serious illness which was misdiagnosed as psychological and left untreated.[25]

A communication from UNICEF received by the UN's Special Rapporteur on Violence against Women indicated that in 1990, 71 percent of all babies under the age of two admitted to one hospital were boys. Where, many were compelled to ask, were the sick girl children? Girls between the ages of two and five years have higher death rates than boys in many developing countries—despite the well-documented biological fact that female newborns are less susceptible to infections than are male babies, and despite the fact that mortality rates in other parts of the world are lower among female babies than among male babies.[26]

Perceptions, attitudes, and convictions have both motivating and steering effects on human action, such that the social conditions that are created and accepted are a function of the assumptions made about the world. In this way is the social reality an inevitable outcome of the psychological reality. The legal, social, and economic status of women worldwide would suggest that women and girls continue to be perceived as neither as important nor as valuable as men and boys; and although in some minds this assumption is gradually losing its hold, many institutions continue to be structured in ways that automatically replicate the unequal treatment and disparate outcomes already described.

In an illuminating paper entitled "Women in the Informal Sector in Malaysia," Lee Lee Lou Ludher tells the story of a Malaysian woman named Govindamah who opened a roadside stall to sell *nasi lemak* (rice cooked with coconut milk). Despite her husband's protestations, Govindamah felt compelled to open the stall to support her family of five after her husband had lost his job as a van driver and had refused to take other odd jobs open to him. Although their eldest daughter, Vani, had already left school to work in a local factory, this additional income proved insufficient to feed their other two daughters and one adopted son:

> It took Govindamah a few days to gather enough courage to tell her husband that she had decided to make some packets of 'nasi lemak' to sell at the road junction. He was furious. He abused her, ridiculed her and assured her that she would fail. But the more she countered his criticisms, the more convinced she became that her venture could succeed. The next morning she got up bright and early, cooked 5 cups of rice, made the 'sambal' (a hot chili mixture) with whatever 'ikan bilis' (anchovies) remained in the house, added pieces of cucumber and laced the 'nasi lemak' with tiny pieces of omelet. She wrapped them into small packets to sell for 50 sen each, placed them in a basket, and crept out of the house, bound for the spot at the T-junction. She looked searchingly into the faces of passers-by. Three ladies stopped and bought packets. Govindamah was encouraged. Soon more stopped and eventually she had a pocketful of notes and coins and an empty basket. Unable to contain her happiness, she ran home to share her joy with her daughters, who agreed to help her. But the minute her husband walked in, all the excitement stopped. He grumbled about his cold tea and left. Nevertheless, Govindamah prepared her baskets for the next day, barely able to wait for her second round of success. As her 'nasi lemak' business grew, Govindamah added more products: tea, snacks and cakes. Vani assisted during her off-shift hours. Customers requested a stall with tables and chairs, which Govindamah secured from her cousin in exchange for a 50% share in the business. The business prospered, but there were problems. When gangsters demanded protection money, Govindamah and her cousin were too afraid to resist. Because they had no license, municipal council enforcement officers often came by threatening to confiscate all their items. They were reluctant to go to the authorities, having heard how difficult it could be to get a license. So there they were: their promising business in jeopardy and nowhere to turn.[27]

Govindamah's situation, notes Ludher, is not unusual. As have millions of other women throughout the world, Govindamah became an entrepreneur because economic necessity demanded it. Also like millions of other women,

Govindamah contributes significantly to her community's economy while also spending her earnings on food and education for her children. Nevertheless, because she is an entrepreneur in the informal sector, operating outside the formal and legal economy, Govindamah's business is not eligible for the support or legal protection that is offered to legitimate businesses that are owned and operated primarily by men.

Ludher reports that between 1985 and 1992, approximately 47 percent of women in the Malaysian female labor force were employed in the informal sector. These data are in line with statistics from other developing regions of the world. Despite their contributions to the country's overall economy, however, women employed in the informal sector face three significant challenges: they tend to receive relatively low pay; they lack access to resources such as capital, credit, education, and training; and they are typically excluded from policymaking processes.

With respect to low pay, Ludher notes that women in the informal sector are not paid according to salaries commensurate with market rates; rather, they tend to be compensated on the basis of rates assigned to domestic labor. Since domestic laborers earn very little, even professional women in the informal sector make far less than their counterparts in the formal sector. Business women in the informal sector also have great difficulty securing loans from banks and other financial institutions. This is because the procedures and policies of most financial institutions have been articulated without regard to women's unique employment circumstances. Ludher explains:

> Few women in the informal sector know how to keep accounts in forms financial institutions would recognize. Salmah, Foziah and 4 other ladies, for example, measure their profits by the number of gold bangles and chains they are able to buy for themselves and their loved ones and the savings they have for their Muslim pilgrimage (a goal they set for themselves). These women don't speak the same language as financial institutions. They would, however, be trustworthy clients, repaying every cent borrowed. But which bank would believe them—no collateral, no bank account, no income statement or balance sheet to prove their success and their honesty![28]

In this respect, experiences with the Grameen Bank in Bangladesh and with microcredit schemes in Kenya and Ghana are worth noting, as they demonstrate some of the most positive outcomes of the economic and financial empowerment of poor rural women.[29]

In both developing and industrialized regions, large numbers of women are driven into the informal sector because they lack skills and education. Since workers in the informal sector are generally not organized, their views are rarely taken into account and they almost never participate in policymaking. Marginalization of women in this way perpetuates their lower social and economic status and contributes to the notion that they are neither as important nor as valuable as men. This erroneous and discriminatory notion, in turn, keeps open the door to women's abuse.

Jean Zorn, professor of law at the City University of New York, tells the story of Wagi Non, a woman living in the Western Highlands of Papua New Guinea who was ordered to be imprisoned for thirty-two weeks for having committed adultery. Learning that Ms. Non's husband had left her and their four children in the care of his relatives for five or six years and had neither sent money nor visited, a judge of the National Court ordered her released. In his commentary on the case, the judge took exception to Papua New Guinea's customary law that was invoked by the village court to justify the sentence:

> I cannot help feeling that going off and leaving the wife and children without sup-
> port and protection, yet expecting her to remain bound by custom, is a custom
> that must be denigrating to her status as a woman. It is denying her the equality
> provided in the Constitution. . . . The Village Courts must recognize the nature of
> the change in Papua New Guinea and that the enforcement of custom must not
> conflict with the principles and rights given in the Constitution. . . . Customs that
> denigrate women should be denied a place in the underlying law in Papua New
> Guinea because they conflict with the National Goals of equality and participation
> which have been laid down clearly in the Constitution.[30]

This case is exceptional in that it affirms the priority of the principle of gender equality over the preservation of custom, no matter how deeply entrenched or long established; indeed, reflecting on the inequities perpetrated both by tradition and by force of customary law, Papua New Guinea's Supreme Court tendered the following observations:

> It is clear there are serious problems existing in the Highlands with respect to
> family law. . . . Women are still in a subservient situation, they are not safe unless
> they have a man to protect them. Men can have several wives and new girlfriends,
> however, women cannot have several husbands nor mix with other men. . . . There
> is no consideration in any breakdown of marriage for the men's neglect or their
> desertion or their mistreatment. . . . Men treat women clearly as property and
> when women wish to exercise their equal rights guaranteed under the Constitu-
> tion, men create trouble.[31]

Rarely are the structural arrangements that impede the just treatment of women addressed in such direct and practical ways. If for nothing other than enlightened self-interest, similar efforts must be made the special concern of men at all levels of the social order; for in the absence of sustained confrontation with traditions that sabotage the equal protection and development of women and girls, men and boys will be unable to achieve "the greatness which might be theirs."[32]

Chief among traditional barriers frequently invoked to preclude the active and equal participation of women is religion. A recent petition circulated among academics throughout the Western world in support of the women of Afghanistan captures the abuses that were routinely carried out there in the name of religion:

> Madhu, the government of Afghanistan, is waging a war upon women. Since the Taliban took power in 1996, women have had to wear burqua and have been beaten and stoned in public for not having the proper attire, even if this means simply not having the mesh covering in front of their eyes. One woman was beaten to death by an angry mob of fundamentalists for accidentally exposing her arm while she was driving. Another was stoned to death for trying to leave the country with a man that was not a relative. Women are not allowed to work or even go out in public without a male relative; professional women such as professors, translators, doctors, lawyers, artists, and writers have been forced from their jobs and stuffed into their homes. Homes where a woman is present must have their windows painted, so that she can never be seen by outsiders. They must wear silent shoes so that they are never heard. Women live in fear of their lives for the slightest misbehavior. Because they cannot work, those without male relatives or husbands are either starving to death or begging on the street, even if they hold Ph.D.s.
>
> Depression is becoming so widespread that it has reached emergency levels. There is no way, in such an extreme Islamic society, to know the suicide rate with certainty, but relief workers are estimating that the suicide rate among women, who cannot find proper medication and treatment for severe depression and would rather take their lives than live in such conditions, has increased significantly. There are almost no medical facilities available for women. At one of the rare hospitals for women, a reporter found still, nearly lifeless bodies lying motionless on top of beds, wrapped in their burqua, unwilling to speak, eat, or do anything, but slowly wasting away. Others have gone mad and were seen crouched in corners, perpetually rocking or crying, most of them in fear. One doctor is considering, when what little medication that is left finally runs out, leaving these women in front of the president's residence as a form of protest.
>
> It is at the point where the term "human rights violations" has become an understatement. Husbands have the power of life and death over their women relatives, especially their wives, but an angry mob has just as much right to stone or beat a woman, often to death, for exposing an inch of flesh or offending them in the slightest way. Women enjoyed relative freedom, to work, dress generally as they wanted, and drive, and appear in public alone until only 1996. The rapidity of this transition is the main reason for the depression and suicide; women who were once educators or doctors or simply used to basic human freedoms are now severely restricted and treated as subhuman in the name of right-wing fundamentalist Islam. It is not tradition or 'culture', but it is alien to them, and it is extreme even for those cultures where fundamentalism is the rule.
>
> Everyone has a right to a tolerable human existence, even if they are women in a Muslim country. If we can threaten military force in Kosovo in the name of human rights for the sake of ethnic Albanians, citizens of the world can certainly

express peaceful outrage at the oppression, murder and injustice committed against women by the Taliban.[33]

Confronting Islamic justifications for the mistreatment of women in her address to the delegates assembled at the Fourth World Conference on Women, Mohtarma Benazir Bhutto, then prime minister of the Islamic Republic of Pakistan, affirmed that "in distinguishing between Islamic teachings and social taboos, we must remember that Islam forbids injustice—injustice against people, against nations, against women." She continued:

> Islam shuns race, color, and gender as bases of distinction among fellowmen. It enshrines piety as the sole criterion for judging humankind. It treats women as human beings in their own right, not as chattel. A woman can inherit, divorce, receive alimony and child custody. Women were intellectuals, poets, jurists, and even took part in war. The Holy Book of the Muslims refers to the rule of a woman, the Queen of Sabah. The Holy Book alludes to her wisdom and to her country being a land of plenty. The Holy Prophet (peace be upon him) himself married a working woman. And the first convert to Islam was a woman, Bibi Khadija. Prophet Mohammed (peace be upon him) emphatically condemned and put an end to the practice of female infanticide in pre-Islamic Arabia.[34]

As has been affirmed by the UN's Special Rapporteur, whatever the source—whether it is time-honored traditions, well-established customary laws, or deeply entrenched religious prescriptions—those social or institutional practices that constitute definite forms of violence against women can be neither overlooked nor justified.[35]

The Idea of Gender Equality: Implications for the Organization of Society

While the liberation of women from the forms of structural violence, exclusion, and discrimination chronicled above would go far in advancing efforts to achieve structural equality, as has been pointed out by Martha Schweitz, advancements in these areas alone are not sufficient to bring about a condition in society that many would regard as "equal":

> Gender equality has long been regarded in the West as freedom to be treated without regard to sex. Women have essentially demanded the right to be treated as men. This struggle so defined has produced enormous progress in a great many societies worldwide. Nevertheless, it has become increasingly apparent that this approach is not complete, as it leaves untouched and unchallenged the social structures of hierarchy and power as well as the societal assumption of the male as the norm. Moreover, it debases women (and ultimately impoverishes society) by depriving them of the opportunity to discover what is different about their in-

dividual and/or collective contribution to work, family, and community from that of the men around them. It would appear that the increasingly active participation in the global dialog on women's rights of women from non-Western backgrounds, and from a wider range of social strata in the West itself, has accelerated the shift in search of new paradigms of equality. Not only do these voices bring a focus on issues far different from those of personal independence, career and sexual freedom that animated the early days of the contemporary Western women's movement, such newer voices have also been willing to express their distaste for what they often perceive in the West to be the masculinization of women.[36]

Carol Gilligan and Jean Baker Miller have been especially persuasive in their efforts to articulate approaches to gender equality that respect and promote women's unique qualities and capacities. In her widely read book, *In a Different Voice,* Gilligan notes that while the feminist movement has thus far concerned itself with securing for women those public rights and opportunities that have been exclusively the right of men, the focus has begun to shift to exploring those characteristics that distinguish men from women and to ensuring that these qualities be given an equal voice in determining the course and tone of human affairs.[37]

Similarly, in *Toward a New Psychology of Women,* Jean Baker Miller argues that if gender equality is to result in transformation of the psychosocial order, these distinguishing characteristics, as much as women as individuals, must be given an adequate arena for expression and development. "Humanity has been held to a limited and distorted view of itself," notes Miller, "from its interpretation of the most intimate of personal emotions to its grandest vision of human possibilities—precisely by virtue of its subordination of women. Until recently, 'mankind's' understandings have been the only understandings generally available to us. As other perceptions arise—precisely those perceptions that men, because of their dominant position, could not perceive—the total vision of human possibilities enlarges and is transformed."[38]

Indeed, when the question of gender equality is taken seriously, what we are really dealing with is the complete transformation of the world, brought about by a transformation in human consciousness and values. This transformation is not simply a matter of equalizing the gender of those who are in positions of power and authority but requires an abdication of that patriarchal spirit that renders power the supreme value.

As Moojan Momen has noted, within a patriarchal framework those who have power are important. To say that they are important is to affirm that they are noticed—that their deeds are recorded in newspapers and in history books; it is to say that they find it easier to have their needs met and their wants satisfied. Those who do not have power, whether men or women, are largely ignored and do not count. They may not even appear in the social structure, in the sense that no account is taken of them when decisions affecting their lives and futures are made. "A good example of this was Greece in the fifth and fourth millennium B.C.E.," writes Momen.

> [T]his was a time when Greek civilization peaked, when Socrates, Plato and Aristotle lived in Athens, and Alexander the Great conquered most of the civilized world. It is recorded in history books as the "great and glorious age" of Greece. But it looked that way only to those who were in power. What about the women of Athens who were considered intellectually and physically defective, who were married at an early age and confined to their husbands' houses thereafter with no rights or freedoms? What about the numerous slaves in Athens? Was it a "great and glorious" age for them? One suspects not—but we will never know because they were unseen. No historian bothered to record their thoughts and feelings.[39]

In many respects, the collective childhood and adolescence of humanity has been characterized by the unbridled pursuit of power. This pursuit, one might legitimately argue, is at the root of conflict and injustice in our history. Each of us has inherited a history of injustice in which the strong have consistently dominated the weak: men have dominated women, more powerful tribes and nations have conquered and enslaved weaker ones, and war has predominated over intellectual prowess and social harmony. To pursue gender equality is to renounce the pursuit of power and to pursue the cultivation and institutionalization of those qualities of heart that have been largely associated with the feminine spirit.

Such a society would need to acquire the maturity and confidence necessary to renounce the pursuit of power as the greatest value and would replace power seeking with cooperation, compassion, and service to the entire human race as the supreme objectives. "The world in the past has been ruled by force," wrote 'Abdu'l-Bahá at the beginning of the twentieth century, "and man has dominated woman by reason of his more forceful and aggressive qualities both of body and mind. But the balance is already shifting—force is losing its weight and mental alertness, intuition and the spiritual qualities of love and service, in which woman is strong, are gaining ascendancy. Hence the new age will be an age less masculine, and more permeated with the feminine ideals—or, to speak more exactly, will be an age in which the masculine and feminine elements in civilization will be more evenly balanced."[40]

As we will discuss at greater length in a future chapter, what is deemed the cause of injustice and oppression is the *seeking* of power and not power itself. Without power we can do nothing, neither good nor evil. The error lies, therefore, not in possessing power but in pursuing power for its own sake; that is, in making power the *end* rather than the *means* of pursuing morally and socially productive objectives. Indeed, each of us possesses a certain degree of power, but to use that power to establish and/or maintain our dominance over others constitutes a moral and spiritual error. From such a perspective, to pursue power is to misuse power.

Thus we hold that notwithstanding the obvious importance of greater gender equality in redressing structural violence, the problem of gender inequality is not solved when women hold half the seats in schools around the world and half the positions of power in government, industry, education, and the healthcare professions. It is solved only when the pursuit of power is far less of a value in the conduct of human affairs. The cultivation of a social order that is animated by a more feminine spirit would both require and bring about a spiritual, psychological, and moral revolution in the way that life is conducted on the planet.

Organic Equality and Human Interdependence

An emerging model of gender equality, referred to as "organic equality," seeks to advance the full development and participation of women while honoring those qualities and characteristics that may, in the aggregate, distinguish men from women.[41] The notion of organic equality draws upon the biological sciences for its root metaphor and is based upon four fundamental assumptions: first, that humanity may be likened to an organic system composed of multiple and diverse "parts"; second, that each part is dependent upon the whole for its viability and that no part is unimportant; third, that the parts necessarily differ from one another; and fourth, that only when all parts are working together harmoniously can it be said that the organism (humanity) is in good health.

An embrace of organic equality requires abandonment of the competitive, individualistic, power-seeking model of human beings that underlies much contemporary legal and social discourse and affords a view of male-female relations within a paradigm of complementarity. 'Abdu'l-Bahá drew upon an organic/complementarity metaphor as he described the degree of interdependence that obtains between women and men:

> There is a right hand and a left hand in the human body, functionally equal in service and administration. If either proves defective, the defect will naturally extend to the other by involving the completeness of the whole; for accomplishment is not normal unless both are perfect. If we say one hand is deficient, we prove the inability and incapacity of the other; for single-handed there is no full accomplishment. Just as physical accomplishment is complete with two hands, so man and woman, the two parts of the social body, must be perfect.[42]

The vision of gender relations embodied in organic equality assumes that the right of each and all to participate fully and unencumbered is a logical extension and minimum requirement of interdependence and complementarity; it further assumes that a variety of forces have rendered men and women distinct from one another, not in essence, but in some basic needs and capabilities that have been acquired over the course of history. Nevertheless, it is anticipated that these differences, liberated from the distorting influences of injustice, oppression, and neglect, will reveal the full range of strengths and capabilities available to humanity. When a state of organic equality is more fully realized, the masculine and feminine elements of civilization will be more evenly balanced. All of us, men and women alike, are apt to benefit from such a change. Thus, viewed from an organic perspective, sexual equality is not solely a "woman's issue"; it is an issue intimately connected with the destiny of all humankind.

Organic equality seeks a conception of justice that is rooted in awareness that the well-being of any part of the world system is best achieved by protection and cultivation of the whole. At the same time, a biological metaphor of complementarity and interdependence recognizes that since all parts of the human system are not the same (that is, are not identical), local, national, and international laws, policies, and procedures must be articulated in such a way as to ensure that the particular rights, responsibilities, and needs of all member groups are honored and advanced.

Inasmuch as it recognizes the uniqueness of women's contributions, seeks to release the transformative forces associated with the feminine spirit, and proscribes yet another round of struggle for power and dominance, organic equality comports well with the postmodern perspective of Mary Daly. "What is at stake is a real leap in human evolution, initiated by women," observes Daly. "[R]adical feminism . . . opens up human consciousness adequately to the desire for nonhierarchical, non-oppressive society, revealing sexism as the basic model and source of oppression. Without the power of this vision to attract women and men so that we can and will transcend the whole array of false dualisms, there will be no real change. The liberation 'movements' that leave sexism unchallenged can, of themselves, only spin delusions of progress, bringing about endless, arbitrary variation within the same senescent system."[43]

The Ontological Basis of Gender Equality

It may be argued that although the effects of gender inequality are visible in the social, political, and interpersonal arenas, the fundamental basis for the equality of the sexes is neither political nor sociological. It is metaphysical; it is that both men and women share the same spiritual capacities. Let us examine these human capacities more fully before going further.

Notwithstanding the thoughtful critiques of *essentialism* that have emerged over the past twenty-five years,[44] and despite wide variation in morphological or cultural form, the characteristics that distinguish humans from all other forms of life are evidenced in the unique capacities associated with human consciousness. Whether male or female, and of whatever race or culture, humans are unique in possessing the power of *metacognition*. Metacognitive capabilities distinguish human beings from other types of knowers (such as apes and chimpanzees) because they enable us, not only to acquire knowledge about ourselves and the world, but also to reflect critically upon the object(s) of our knowledge. In this sense we have the ability, not only to think, but also to think about our thinking. We may ask ourselves whether our thinking is internally consistent or logical; whether it is in conformity with what we observe through our senses; whether our inner convictions conform to our outward behavior, and so on. These powers, whether realized or in potentiality, are the powers that distinguish humans from all other species and provide the ontological bases of the equality of women and men.

Humanity's unique capacity for use of language and complex symbol systems enables the acquisition of two distinct types of knowledge: knowledge of those things that can be perceived by the senses, and knowledge of intellectual or abstract realities (gravity, justice, God, etc.). All other animals are limited in their perceptions and manipulations to the concrete world of matter. Consider, for example, humanity's capacity to engage in scientific investigation. By careful observation of that which may be perceived by the senses, humans are able to discover the operation of forces (as well as the laws and principles that govern such forces) that are not themselves directly observable. Thus the human intellect brings forth from nature its hidden secrets and enables us to harness natural forces for benefit or harm.

The power to predict the future states or conditions of many natural systems would be entirely useless if we did not also have the power to influence such systems on the basis of our goals and current understandings. This fact alone is sufficient proof that human beings must, to a significant degree, also have the power to exercise will. Concerning this point, William Hatcher writes:

> By deliberately establishing, in the short run, certain particular conditions of a system, we can bring about, in the long run, certain desired future states of the system, i.e., configurations that are favorable to our goals and our [perceived] interests. This is the power that scientific knowledge gives us, the power to control our future—to participate in the processes of the natural world and not just endure them. In other words, scientific knowledge has the effect of *increasing our autonomy with regard to the natural world*.[45]

C. J. Herrick wrote in a similar way seven decades ago: "Man's capacity for intelligently directed self-development confers upon him the ability to determine the pattern of his culture and so to shape the course of human evolution in directions of his own choice. This ability, which no other animals have, is man's most distinctive characteristic, and is perhaps the most significant fact known to science."[46] Furthermore, despite the proliferation of twentieth-century theories that attempted to divest humans of will, the ethical basis of human rights law is that human beings have an inherent degree of freedom to shape the direction and quality of their own lives and that this freedom ought not to be abridged arbitrarily.

The human capacity to know, however, is clearly not limited to knowledge of natural forces. We may also acquire intuitive and creative knowledge, which enables us to develop the arts and to refine human relationships; we may acquire spiritual and divine forms of knowledge through prayer and meditation; and by combining many ways of knowing and many types of knowledge, we may find patterns of purpose and meaning that give life depth and that may evoke in us uniquely human attitudes and emotions such as awe, humility, and wonder.

Humans are likewise united in the capacity to engage important cosmological and philosophical concerns, such as the purpose of human life, the goal(s) of human development, the meaning and implications of death and suffering, and so forth. If the prosperity of humankind is to be achieved, these fundamental human capacities need to be recognized as equally inherent in women of all cultures and races and must be allowed and encouraged to unfold and flourish. Furthermore, those qualities in which the women of the world are particularly strong must be brought to the fore of collective consciousness so that the new age will be one in which the masculine and feminine qualities will be more evenly balanced.

2

Sexual Violence against Women and Girls

Incest and Child Sexual Abuse

Of the abuses suffered by female children, few are as harmful and widespread as sexual exploitation. A recent study found that 29 percent of all rapes are committed against children who are less than eleven years old and that another 32 percent of all rape victims are between the ages of eleven and seventeen. The overwhelming majority of these children are victimized not by strangers but by fathers, stepfathers, brothers, uncles or other close relatives, and friends.[1] The problem of incest and child sexual exploitation cuts across all racial, cultural, and economic groups.

A study conducted in the Maternity Hospital of Lima, Peru, revealed that 90 percent of mothers aged twelve to sixteen had been raped and that most had been raped by close relatives.[2] In an islandwide sampling of women in Barbados, 33 percent reported having been sexually abused in childhood or adolescence.[3] In a Jamaican study, 4 percent of the 450 thirteen- and fourteen-year-old girls had been raped by persons they knew.[4]

The psychological and social consequences of child sexual exploitation and abuse are impossible to calculate. Some well-known consequences include severe disruption in healthy patterns of trust and attachment, low self-esteem, eating disorders, preoccupation with suicide, multiple personality disorder, increased vulnerability to rape and future abuse, anxiety attacks, post–traumatic stress disorder (PTSD), insomnia, dissociation, borderline personality disorder, drug addiction, sexual promiscuity, school failure, and depression.[5] Although throughout the world awareness of the problem of sexual abuse is increasing, prevalence rates of abuse appear to be increasing as well.[6]

The exploitation of children through pornography and prostitution has been described as "a global growth industry," fueled by galling poverty, greed, and a callous demand for cheap sex:

It is destroying the lives of millions of girls and boys in rich and poor nations alike, and much too little is being done nationally and internationally to check it. In some countries, children as young as seven years of age are bought and sold by adults who might be their parents, their guardians, their teachers or even agents for institutions masquerading as charitable organizations. Physically and emotionally enslaved, the children are then rented out and abused by men, and sometimes women, from all walks of life.[7]

Traditionally, both experts and laypersons have accounted for the sexual abuse of minors by invoking the image of "the dirty old man" or by reference to various types of mental illness. However, as has been noted more recently by feminists, given the widespread nature of childhood sexual abuse, it is unreasonable to assume that most child abusers are particularly unusual human beings suffering from one or another diseased state.[8] An alternative explanation is that *deeply entrenched psychological, social, and cultural practices must contribute significantly to the likelihood that many males, from a wide range of cultural backgrounds, will be prone to abuse children sexually.* As Linda Gordon, author of *Heroes of Their Own Lives: The Politics and History of Family Violence*, notes, in focusing almost exclusively on the "perversion" of the culprits, child-protection and development agencies have avoided confronting social patterns that promote men's sexual exploitation of children.

If progress is to be made toward the eradication of this worldwide problem, insights must be acquired into those social and cultural factors that contribute to childhood sexual victimization. While several cultural factors contribute to the sexual abuse of children, three rarely discussed factors are sexual inequality in child-rearing practices, the failure of a significant proportion of men to appreciate adequately the harmful effects of child sexual abuse, and men's neglect of the psychospiritual challenge of self-mastery.

Sexual Inequality in Child-Rearing Practices

Several studies have shown that sexual abuse of children is most likely to be perpetrated by males who feel little responsibility for the welfare of the abused child. Gordon refers to such males as "social fathers" and has found that they are often in transient relationships with mothers and have only casual contact with their children. As a result, such men are less likely to have internalized a consciousness of the child's welfare.

Gordon's research revealed that while fathers living with their children might be expected to have more opportunity for an illicit sexual relationship, in fact, incestuous fathers were less likely to live with their children than were other types of abusive fathers. The best explanation for her findings, she suggests, "is that fathers living with their children had more responsibilities for and intimacy with the children than absent fathers." If there is an "incest taboo," she continues, "that taboo grows from nurturant attitudes toward children, constructed through internalizing a conception of the child's interest as distinct from the adult's interest."[9] Gordon's perspective is supported by other studies that show that fathers in reconstituted families are more likely to abuse their stepchildren sexually and that such abuse is more likely to be severe.[10] Indeed, as Richard Jolly, former director-general of UNICEF, observed in his December 1993 address to nongovernmental organizations accredited to the UN: "A growing body of evidence suggests that close and early father–child links—what anthropologists call a high 'paternal investment'—greatly reduces the likelihood of violence in men."[11]

It would thus appear that the the greater the involvement men have in nurturing children, the less likely they are to abuse those children. In most cultures women bear a disproportionate share of the responsibility for the care of children. For example, Philippine data, which are consistent with data from around the world, suggest that fathers, in general, spend less than a quarter of the time that mothers do in providing care for children.[12] Furthermore, in a wide range of cultures, as the number of children increases, so does the time spent by the mother, but not the father. Thus, according to one report, "the experience of a 'growing family' is solely or disproportionately borne by women."[13]

Increasingly, both men and women have been expressing concern about men's alienation from some of the more intimate aspects of family life. For many men, the time available for family and work has not been sufficient to build true bonds of affection and intimacy. Furthermore, within a growing number of cultures that associate male expressions of intimacy primarily with eroticism, many males may have relatively few skills in relating to any females in nonsexual ways. Since the capacities for relational intimacy are cultivated principally through sustained, nurturing relationships, some men's failure to develop such relationships within the matrix of the family may well contribute to a proclivity to seek closeness through sexual contact.

Potent barriers to many fathers' greater participation in child care that cannot be ignored include poverty, lack of nurturing experience, and lack of social support for male involvement in the lives of children. Recent studies also show that a growing number of men are becoming sexually involved with young teenage girls who are often impregnated and then abandoned. Perhaps such men are less likely to be engaged in the lives of their children because the sexual activity that brought these children into the world was largely in pursuit of pleasure, rather than the development of family.[14]

With respect to the impact of poverty on fathering, Andrew Hacker points out that in the United States, nearly two-thirds of all black babies are now born outside of wedlock and that over half of all African American families are headed by women. These figures, Hacker notes, are from three to five times greater than for white households.[15] Andrew Cherlin of Johns Hopkins University points out that the real problem is not "the lack of a male presence but the lack of male income."[16] This perspective is corroborated by Elijah Anderson's ethnographic research, which has shown a clear link between black males' participation in the lives of their children and the economic opportunities that are or are not available in their communities.[17]

Similarly, Fernando Barros has presented data from a longitudinal study involving three hundred father–child pairs that illustrate the deleterious impact of poverty on fathering. Employing five indicators of father involvement (presence of the father in the home at twelve months; father's reaction to the pregnancy; father's support for the woman during pregnancy; presence of the father in the hospital during labor and delivery; and father's involvement in child care at twelve months), Barros demonstrated that the poorer the family, the less likely the father was to be involved with his child.[18] According to Joseph Mahase, UNICEF representative in Barbados, in areas such as the Caribbean that have relatively high rates of female-headed households, the historical patterns of slavery and economic marginalization have resulted in a peripheral role for men in families. If men are not able to fulfill their role as economic provider, they can often find no other place in the family for themselves. Some marginalized men drift from the family; others remain and become sources of social, psychological, and/or spiritual pathologies.

While many studies show that men who are unable to support their families financially tend to neglect their children, it is also true that men with considerable economic means tend to evidence a similar pattern of family disengagement. Such a realization led Louise Silverstein to write: "Limiting the definition of fathering to the provider role in the family has been central to the problem of male privilege, and thus the subordination of women within society at large. . . . Our cultural definition of the fathering role as employment in the *public* world, rather than caretaking in the *personal* world of the family," she continues, "has been responsible for the inability of most men to be aware of and to articulate their needs for intimacy and emotional connectedness."[19]

Underestimating the Damage
Caused by Childhood Sexual Abuse

In addition to emotional disengagement, in many societies men are socialized to regard sex as the ultimate source of pleasure, power, and control. Also, throughout the world, little has been done either to publicize the widespread nature of childhood sexual abuse or to publicize its devastating psychological and social consequences. Even in settings where opportunities to discuss the harmful effects of child sexual abuse are available (e.g., marriage licensing centers; churches, synagogues, and mosques; psychology courses; and medical schools), in proportion to its impact, this subject often receives little attention. Numerous studies conducted over the past three decades have shown that sexual violence—and particularly sexual violence committed by trusted ones against children—inflicts emotional injuries that can have profound implications for victims' total psychological and social development. These facts need to be more widely appreciated.

The concept of "spirit injury," introduced by Patricia Williams of Columbia Law School, captures the profundity of the damage often done by childhood sexual assault. Spirit injury, Williams affirms, leads to the slow death of the psyche, of the soul, and of the identity of the individual.[20] To few violations is the notion of spirit injury so apt as it is to the sexual abuse of children. Throughout much of their lives, sexually abused children may have great difficulty establishing trusting, loving relationships with themselves or others. They often have difficulty feeling safe or valued. They commonly mutilate themselves or allow others to abuse them. When abused children cannot flee from the abuser, they learn to escape abuse by using the powers of imagination. In this way, they become vulnerable to the development of somatoform and dissociative disorders. These disorders are characterized by a loss of identity, self-consciousness, and memory. In brief, the sexual exploitation of children commonly results in the death or gross distortion of the child's psyche. In this sense, sexual violence against children is among the most toxic forms of violence to which children are exposed.

Within a cultural paradigm that emphasizes an increasingly materialistic conception of human beings, it is easy for many to limit the perception of harm to that which can be registered by the senses. If we do not "see" that we are hurting others—if they do not show bruises, wounds, or broken bones—concern may be minimized by holding to the belief that no real harm has been done. This is particularly true of sexual abuse for three reasons. First, sexually abused children are generally far too confused about their experiences either to complain about them or to manifest outward signs of distress. Distress is thus often "masked." Second, for a variety of reasons, sexually abused children often show unusual allegiance to, and identification with, the abuser.[21] Third, as noted earlier, through a variety of media—including films, books, and music—men are generally conditioned to equate all kinds of sexual activity (including sexual violence) with pleasure, rather than pain.[22] Thus, even when actual violence is used, that violence may be easily integrated into an abuser's schema for pleasure. In light of these realities, much more needs to be done by national and international agencies, health-care officials, community organizations, and religious institutions to provide education on the untoward effects of sexual abuse on the lives and development of children.[23]

Trafficking in Women

The sale of women and children, especially girls, into prostitution and enforced marriage is escalating in many countries. In Asia, Africa, and the Middle East such practices are common. In the Philippines, Thailand, and Sri Lanka, "sex tourism" industries have fueled a crisis in the exploitation of female children that is unmatched in history. The Bangkok-based international organization ECPAT (End Child Prostitution in Asian Tourism) reports a half million prostitutes sixteen years or younger in Thailand, the Philippines, and Sri Lanka. They report another fifty thousand who are under thirteen.

The child-sex industry is fueled by tens of thousands of pedophile tourists from the so-called pedophile ring of wealthier nations that includes the United States, Belgium, Canada, Britain, Germany, Sweden, Japan, Australia, and New Zealand. "They fly to southern Asia for child sex knowing they face little risk of being caught and small penalty if they are. The lure of tourist dollars leads government and law enforcement officials in these countries to look the other way."[24] Anti-Slavery International (ASI), a London-based human rights organization, also reports sexual slavery among poor Turkish women, Mozambican refugees in South Africa, and women from Bangladesh who are shipped as "mail-order brides" to the United States and Europe.[25]

Although child prostitution has existed for centuries, escalating levels of child sexual exploitation, growing interest in human rights, and significant advancements in global communication have combined to bring the severity and ubiquity of this problem into clearer focus. In August 1996 child-welfare activists from around the world gathered in Stockholm to consult about ways to fight the growing problem of child prostitution. A second meeting was held more recently. Judicial systems around the world have also begun to show greater commitment to cracking down on sex tourists. For example, in March 1999, a Thai court sentenced Bernd Karl-Heinz, a thirty-six-year-old German citizen, to forty-three years in prison for sexually abusing children; in the Philippines, Victor Keith Fitzgerald, a sixty-six-year-old Australian, was sentenced to seventeen years' imprisonment for purchasing sex from a twelve-year-old girl; and in Sri Lanka, Benjamin Dennis, a Canadian citizen, received a one-year suspended sentence for sexual assault of two boys, aged twelve and fourteen. In addition, owing largely to the work of ECPAT, thus far eleven countries have criminalized the sexual abuse of children committed by their citizens overseas.

While growing awareness of the sexual exploitation of children has resulted in these noteworthy developments, the sex tourism industry continues to grow, in part because of the AIDS pandemic. Pedophiles and sex tourists believe that they are unlikely to catch AIDS from very young children. Furthermore, many Asian clients pursue children, not only because they believe that sex with virgins will enable them to avoid AIDS, but also because they believe that such practices promote longevity.

One of the most comprehensive analyses of the global problem of trafficking in women was completed recently by Lois Chiang for the three-volume work *Women and International Human Rights Law*. According to Chiang, women and girls are typically brought into the trafficking industry through forced prostitution, forced marriage, or forced labor. They may be lured by a ploy or brought in forcibly by abduction. The women who are targeted for trafficking are typically from the poorest regions of the world, from rural areas, and from families and communities where levels of education and sophistication about such practices are relatively low. Despite this general pattern, Chiang notes that university students in China and women in urban centers in both Montreal and Paris have also been abducted.

Those engaged in the trade and sale of women and girls include members of gangs who establish trafficking rings on behalf of organized crime; locals who recruit known girls and women from the neighborhood; former abductees and/or prostitutes who win their freedom by promising to find replacements; and fathers and mothers who knowingly sell their children into sexual slavery, forced marriages, or debt bondage for personal gain or in order to provide for the remaining family members in harsh economic circumstances. Some women and girls volunteer their services with the expectation that they will be able to escape poverty, relieve the economic pressures on their family, and/or flee from an abusive relationship in a context in which other avenues of escape may not exist.

Common ploys used to entice women and girls into the trafficking industry include offers to work in factories as laborers, offers to work in homes as nannies and housekeepers, and opportunities for employment in hotels and bars as hospitality service workers. Others are lured into fraudulent marriages as mail-order brides. Trafficking, as Chiang notes, is frequently carried out at particular points in the year when women and girls are most vulnerable:

> Thus in Nepal, recruiters return to participate in local festivals in June, late August, or early September. These months, known as the "hungry months," precede the harvest so poverty is most acute. In China, traffickers look for women who have spent all their money and are stranded in an unfamiliar urban center far from home. In the Philippines, fierce typhoons may ruin farmers who then send a wage-earner to the big city, most commonly, a daughter. Traffickers are well aware of the vulnerable situations girls and women face. As one Hungarian pimp in Romania revealed, he "took the kind of girl no one would miss if she disappeared. Girls who were having trouble with their parents or who lived alone, so when they were resold, no one would look for them."[26]

Once forced or tricked into the trafficking business, many women are then subject to various forms of physical and psychological abuse so as to render them less likely to attempt escape or to bring their case before authorities. This period is referred to as a "breaking-in" period and may include repeated rapes, various forms of torture such as electric shocks, and beatings by brothel owners or guards. In cases in which girls are sold as virgins, psychological and physical abuse substitutes for rape as a means of forcing victims to comply.

Having been sold or traded to a brothel, family, or criminal organization, a captive is required to comply with whatever orders she is given. She typically has no control over the clients she will service, when, how many, or in what ways. She is rendered a slave and is subject to all of the limitations imposed upon slaves with respect to rights to her body, labor, and income. In some cases, women and girls are "employed" inasmuch as they are told that they have been purchased from a recruiter or her family and can repay her purchase price by working until the debt is clear. Once she pays off the debt, she is told, she will be free to go. As Chiang explains, the debt typically includes the expenses incurred for her housing and food, her purchase price, the money required for her "transportation" from her home to the brothel, cost of travel papers and passports, medical care, clothing, and protection money paid to the police. In addition to these, taxes and interest are not infrequently added. Inasmuch as women who are paid are typically paid a small fraction of the money that their services bring in, it is virtually impossible for most of them to purchase back their freedom.

Beyond these informal means of control, the enslavement of women in various parts of the world is supported by local and national authorities that profit, sometimes enormously, from trafficking in women. They are thus willing to do all they can to ensure that brothel owners are able to keep enslaved women under their control. Should women escape, they are often returned by the local police, fined or imprisoned by the judicial system for entering the country illegally, or subject to punitive action for engaging in illicit prostitution. Realizing that they cannot turn to local authorities for help, many women give up all hope of escape.

Women who are able to escape frequently learn that they are not welcome back in their families or communities. Often, writes Chiang, women who manage to escape and return to their families are rudely confronted with the fact that they are now ostracized, stigmatized, and considered "spoiled" or "damaged" goods. Not only is the woman typically shunned, but also any children she has as a result of her experience are similarly stigmatized:

> When asked about leaving a brothel, [one] girl replied, "Where would I go? If I tried to go home, my family would cut my throat." Other women find out that they have been rejected when their families do not come to take them home, or when they are publicly scorned and ridiculed upon their return to their villages. The stigmatization, coupled with the lack of opportunities for these women, results in many of those trafficked (particularly in prostitution) returning to the brothels.[27]

Contributing to the maintenance and growth of child prostitution are religious and cultural practices that condone or encourage the sexual exploitation of the girl child. In India, for example, a significant percentage of child prostitutes are females who have been initiated as *devadasi,* or Hindu temple servants. Traditionally, devadasi were dedicated for life to the goddess Yallamma before reaching puberty. This "divine marriage" had once served to elevate a low-caste girl into a devotional career of temple singing and dancing. Today, however, this practice is a widely accepted means of selling young girls into enslavement to temple priests for their sexual pleasure or for prostitution. Although the practice of devadasi has been outlawed, its continued growth renders it one of the primary sources of child prostitution in India.

In Brazil, child prostitution may be the worst in the world. As in other places, most child prostitutes are victims of extreme poverty, poor education, and/or domestic violence. Thus the intersection of economic conditions, insufficient education, and escalating levels of domestic violence provides a milieu in which child sexual exploitation can flourish. Another factor contributing to the growth of the industry is the lack of a coordinated international approach. When one nation in a region begins to crack down on sex tourism, other areas absorb the new business. As a result, sex tourism has spread rapidly to Africa, the former Soviet bloc, Cambodia, and other regions of the world.

A related problem of considerable and growing concern in the United States is the abduction and sexual abuse of adolescents and children. Recent U.S. Senate subcommittee hearings suggest that there were nearly one million persons reported missing in the United States in 1994 alone. Ninety percent of those missing were children or youth; and while a significant number of abducted children are abducted by parents or relatives, the National Incidence Studies of Missing, Abducted, Runaway, and Thrown-away Children (NISMART) estimates that teenagers (50 percent) and girls (75 percent) were the most common victims of nonfamily (or "stranger") abduction. Furthermore, the overwhelming majority of nonfamily abductions involved the rape or sexual exploitation of the victim. In fact, so prevalent has the sexual molestation of children in America become that President Clinton signed into law measures that mandate notification of a community when a convicted sex offender has been released from prison.[28]

The Role of Human Rights Law in Eradicating Trafficking

The Convention for the Suppression of the Traffic in Persons and Exploitation of the Prostitution of Others (hereafter referred to as the Trafficking Convention), the Convention on the Elimination of All Forms of Discrimination against Women (Women's Convention), and the Convention on the Rights of the Child (Children's Convention) all contain provisions designed to combat trafficking in women and girls. The Trafficking Convention, which came into force in 1951, is the first international human rights instrument that affirms prostitution and human trafficking are both incompatible with human dignity and damaging to the welfare of the individual, the family, and the community. The Trafficking Convention lays down the principles required for the punishment of those who procure women for trafficking, requires punishment of those who exploit prostitutes (irrespective of the prostitute's age or consent), and requires parties to the convention to: (1) abolish any form of registration or supervision of prostitutes; (2) take measures to prevent prostitution and rehabilitate victims of prostitution; (3) take appropriate steps to deal with trafficking in persons on the level of immigration and emigration procedures; (4) repatriate victims of international trafficking; (5) ensure that employment agencies protect those seeking employment from the prostitution industry. As is evidenced by the growing trafficking industry, the Trafficking Convention has been relatively ineffective in combating this problem. There are three reasons for this: first, the lack of sustained international commitment to the eradication of trafficking; second, a relative paucity of information relevant to states parties' compliance with the convention; and, third, the lack of an international enforcement strategy effective enough to hold traffickers responsible before the law.

The Convention on the Elimination of All Forms of Discrimination against Women contains an article that requires all states parties to take appropriate measures (both legislative and otherwise) to eliminate all forms of trafficking in women and the exploitative practices that attend the prostitution of women. Article 6 of the Women's Convention goes beyond the provisions contained in the Trafficking Convention by requiring all states parties to confront the root causes of trafficking, rather than limit their focus to punishing perpetrators after trafficking crimes are committed.

The Women's Convention also goes further than the Trafficking Convention in that simultaneous with its adoption was the articulation of a formal committee, known as CEDAW, that is designed to monitor the compliance of states parties with the convention's provisions. While CEDAW's enforcement powers are limited, the committee does receive regular country reports from all 154 signatories to the convention and is empowered to use such data to monitor the progress of states and to request action on the part of the UN General Assembly should efforts to uphold the provisions of the convention not be manifested in state actions.

The Convention on the Rights of the Child, which covers persons under the age of eighteen (unless domestic laws specify that majority occurs at an earlier age), deals specifically with the trafficking and exploitation of children. This convention requires states parties to: (1) take appropriate measures to prevent the illicit transfer and nonreturn of children abroad; (2) to take steps required to protect children from all forms of neglect and physical, mental, or sexual violence and abuse when they are in the care of parent(s), legal guardian(s), or any other persons; (3) to protect children from economic exploitation; (4) to protect children from abduction and/or sale for any purpose and in any form; (5) to take steps to promote the full psychological and physical recovery and social reintegration of children who have been victimized by any form of exploitation, abuse, torture, or any form of inhuman, degrading, or cruel treatment; and (6) to ensure that a child not be separated from his or her parent against their will, save when such separation is deemed in the best interest of the child.

In 1991 a working group convened by the Coalition against Trafficking in Women assumed responsibility for identifying international human rights approaches to the exploitation of women in prostitution. The product of this effort was a draft of the Convention against Sexual Exploitation (CASE), which was subsequently introduced at the 1993 World Conference on Human Rights and the 1993 preparatory meetings for the Beijing Women's Conference. CASE defines sexual exploitation as "a practice by which person(s) achieve sexual gratification or financial gain by advancement through the abuse of a person's sexuality by abrogating that person's human right to dignity, equality, autonomy, and physical and mental well-being" (CASE appears in appendix C of this book). Sexual exploitation, according to CASE, is dehumanizing inasmuch as it treats human beings as objects, divests human beings of their dignity, and denigrates victims' sense of self-worth. Furthermore, as has been noted by Elizabeth Defeis in her analysis, CASE also addresses the "private sexual subordination of individual women and violence against women that escapes direct condemnation in both the Women's Convention and the Declaration on Violence Against Women."[29] The forms of sexual exploitation recognized by CASE include female infanticide, wife and widow murder, battering, prostitution, genital mutilation, female seclusion, dowry and bride price, sexual harassment, rape, incest, sexual abuse, and torture. CASE also provides for the provision of services to those exposed to sexual exploitation.

As Defeis notes, CASE's approach to the eradication of prostitution is both unique and comprehensive. Unlike earlier conventions, CASE condemns all forms of prostitution, regardless of the victim's age, consent, race, or geography, and affirms that all sexual exploitation, including prostitution, is a violation of a person's fundamental human rights. CASE also criminalizes the promoters and customers of prostitution, while decriminalizing the women whose circumstances have brought them into the practice. Commenting on this unique aspect of CASE, Defeis writes:

> While this approach has been criticized as unrealistic and incorporating a double standard, it is necessary to draw a distinction between the victim and the perpetrator. While much prostitution is maintained through force and physical coercion, very often prostitution is the result of earlier sexual and emotional abuse, economic disadvantage, manipulation, and deception inflicted on the victim. Prostitution is thus a continuing form of rape, sexual abuse, and battery.

The distinction commonly made between voluntary and forced prostitution is also rejected in CASE. The argument that prostitution is often the result of personal choice that some women willingly make is not persuasive. The data suggest that few women appear to make a considered decision to become or remain prostitutes. Rather, in most cases the choice to enter into prostitution is the result of conditions that the prostitute neither originally chose nor would probably choose again, should the conditions that led to prostitution be different.

CASE advocates a comprehensive approach to remedying the conditions that lead to the flourishing of prostitution and the intergenerational transmission of the practice. Such conditions include economic development policies and practices that channel women into conditions of sexual exploitation, sex tourism industries that often have implicit or explicit government support, mail-order-bride businesses, the sexual exploitation of women and children in refugee camps, and the sexual exploitation of women and children using new media ad technologies.

Rape and Sexual Abuse by Armed Forces

On 21 January 1993, Amnesty International (AI) issued a report on abuses against women, including rape, in the conflict in Bosnia-Herzegovina. In this document AI presented testimony suggestive of widespread, systematic, and prolonged sexual violence against women that appeared to have the implicit or explicit approval of political and military leaders. In addition to its use in Bosnia-Herzegovina, sexual violence against women and girls has been a part of official military strategy in a number of wars and conflicts over the course of history. For instance, rapes on a mass scale have been recorded in antiquity during the wars of ancient Greece and in the Crusades. Rapes were also committed during the U.S. Civil War and the war in Vietnam. The Yugoslavians reported rapes committed by Stalin's Red Army during World War II; the Nuremberg trials revealed that the Nazis would routinely use rape to inflict dread and terror; and in 1971, the rape of two hundred thousand to four hundred thousand Bengali women occurred during Bangladesh's struggle for independence from West Pakistan. More recently, on 15 August 1993, Prime Minister Hosokawa of Japan formally recognized that the Japanese government kidnapped and forcibly confined seventy thousand to two hundred thousand Korean, Chinese, Filipina, and Indonesian women during the Second World War to serve as sexual slaves, or "comfort women." Indeed, in her statement to the U.S. House of Representatives Committee on Foreign Affairs subcommittee hearings on human rights, Dorothy Thomas, director of the Women's Rights Project, noted that in the last few years alone the use of rape as a military tactic has been well documented in countries as diverse as Peru, Somalia, Liberia, India, and Burma.[31]

In March 1994 the United Nations/Organization of American States International Civilian Mission in Haiti condemned the use of rape against Haitian women and implicated armed civilian auxiliaries, attachés, members of the Front for the Advancement and Progress of Haiti, and Haiti's armed forces in a political campaign of violence and terror that targeted women. Similarly, in Rwanda, militiamen raided homes, hospitals, and camps in pursuit of women and girls who were subject to rape, sometimes in public, as part of the official strategy designed to terrorize and evacuate the locals.[32]

The use of rape as an official military strategy continues because it has proven to be effective from both economic and strategic perspectives. With respect to the short-term military advantage it confers, relatively poor and technologically unsophisticated tribes, ethnic groups, or nations—which may be ill equipped to engage in ongoing combat with neighboring enemies—can, nevertheless, inflict considerable terror and loss by adopting military tactics and campaigns that target a community's women and children. In addition, as was witnessed in the conflict in Bosnia-Herzegovina, sexual assault so devastates and demoralizes the integrity of the family and the community that victims are often compelled to flee contested areas in humiliation and shame. For despotic leaders bent on the cultural, ethnic, and/or racial genocide of another people, rape has thus become an invaluable military tool.

Although the 1949 Geneva Conventions as well as the 1977 protocols view rape, enforced prostitution, and all other forms of indecent assault as crimes under national and international rules of war, Rhonda Copelon noted recently that where rape and other forms of sexual assault are mentioned in these documents, they are categorized either as an outrage upon personal dignity or as crimes against honor. Crimes of violence, including murder, female circumcision, cruel treatment, and torture, are treated separately.[33] In Copelon's view, conceptualizing rape as a crime against dignity and honor, as opposed to a crime of violence, is a serious problem:

> Where rape is treated as a crime against honor, the honor of women is called into question and virginity and chastity is often a precondition. Honor implies the loss of station or respect; it reinforces the social view, internalized by women, that the raped woman is dishonorable. And while the concept of dignity potentially embraces more profound concerns, standing alone it obfuscates the fact that rape is fundamentally violence against women—violence against a woman's body, autonomy, integrity, selfhood, security and self-esteem as well as her standing in the community. This failure, to recognize rape as violence, is critical to the traditional lesser or ambiguous status of rape in humanitarian law.[34]

The fundamental question, in Copelon's view, is no longer whether human rights provisions regard rape as a war crime; rather, it is whether rape represents a "grave breach" of the provisions of the Geneva Conventions. For only those war crimes that are judged to be grave breaches of the conventions give rise to "universal jurisdiction." The implication of universal jurisdiction is that all nations have an obligation to do everything within their power to bring the perpetrators of such crimes to justice. Since rape is not specifically mentioned in the list of crimes considered grave breaches in the Geneva Conventions, it is possible for some international jurists to argue that rape can be redressed only by the state to which the wrongdoer belonged or in which the wrong occurred, and not by an international tribunal. To obviate this danger, Copelon maintains that it is important that rape be recognized and classified as a form of torture in international human rights documents and their provisions.

Rape as a Widely Used Weapon and Instrument of Domination and Control

The use of rape as an official strategy of war is not the only context in which rape and sexual abuse appear to be socially sanctioned. In an illuminating work on rape in cross-cultural perspective, Patricia Rozée distinguishes between "normative" and "non-normative" rape. According to Rozée, nonnormative rape is "illicit, un-condoned genital contact that is both against the will of the woman and in violation of social norms for expected behavior."[35] Normative rape, by contrast, is defined as "genital contacts that the female does not choose, but that are supported by social norms."[36]

Normative rape may also take the form of "punitive rape." In this widely used form of rape, rape is used to punish, and thereby silence and control, women leaders. Koss, Heise, and Russo, for example, report that in India, a highly successful leader of a women's development program was gang raped by male community members because they disapproved of her organizing effort against child marriage. "The woman was raped in front of her husband," report Koss et al., "who was warned, 'Keep your wife in line or we'll rape her again.'"[37] In another widely publicized case, Cecilia Rodriguez, Texas-born human rights activist and the Zapatistas' U.S. representative, was abducted, raped, and sodomized by "unknown assailants" during a visit to Mexico for peace talks between the Mexican government and the Zapatista Army for National Liberation (EZLN).[38] Alternatively, punitive rape often takes the form of sexual torture, inflicted by state security forces against women held in detention.[39]

Although rarely investigated, punitive rape is also common among street children who have little or no social and legal protection. Among the street children of Brazil, for example, *ronda,* a form of ritualized gang rape, is a common way of controlling a group's behavior and punishing rule breakers. Girls are particularly vulnerable to such rapes because of their relatively low number on the streets, as well as their dependence on males for protection.

Other forms of normative rape identified by Rozée include ceremonial rape, exchange rape, theft rape, and status rape. "Status rape" is said to occur when "unchosen genital contact . . . occurs primarily as a result of acknowledged differences in rank between the individuals involved" (such as master and slave, nobleman and commoner, chief and clanswoman, priest and parishioner).[40] In "ceremonial rape" females are expected to submit to genital contact as part of socially sanctioned ceremonies, procedures, or rituals. Virginity tests and "ritual defloration," according to Rozée, are common examples of this type of rape. Ritual defloration "is intended to bring a young girl to womanhood [and is] . . . also known in the literature as opening the vulva or introcision. This may be accomplished with fingers, objects such as a stick or stone knife, or by penile penetration."[41] "Theft rape," Rozée notes, includes the involuntary abduction of women as slaves, prostitutes, concubines, or spoils of war. Last, "exchange rape" occurs when males use "female genital contact as a bargaining tool, gesture of solidarity, or conciliation."[42] Wyatt has suggested that a particularly common form of exchange rape is what she calls "survival rape." Survival rape occurs when young, poor women are sexually involved with older men in order to obtain the goods or services they may need in order to survive.[43]

Survival rape is particularly prevalent among refugee women and street girls who lack economic resources and social support. Economic desperation renders them susceptible to sexual exploitation in exchange for essential needs such as food, shelter, security, and documentation. Among refugee women, rape can take place prior to flight when they are targeted by the police, the military, or even male community leaders who barter women and children for arms and ammunition. Rape also occurs when refugees are attacked by pirates, smugglers, border guards, or other refugees. Finally, refugees may be sexually violated in the country of asylum by persons in authority, other refugees, and members of the local population. Refugees who are most at risk for sexual violence include unaccompanied women, lone female heads of household, unaccompanied children, children in foster-care arrangements, and those women and children in detention or detention-like situations.[44]

Beyond the aforementioned forms of normative and nonnormative rape, forced prostitution by parents or male partners is a growing problem in a number of countries throughout the world. This problem has been recognized as a significant source of distress among women of Pakistan. In her report on violence against women, Coomeraswamy recounts the story of Ayesha, a Pakistani woman who was beaten and forced into prostitution by her husband, who was addicted to heroin:

> On 19 May 1995, Ayesha was finally compelled to abandon her home for fear of her life. According to Ayesha, her young children and the neighbor's children were involved in a quarrel to which she responded by reprimanding all the children. Her husband, after hearing about this, became angry with Ayesha and subjected her to beating. Since this was not the first incident of beating, Ayesha threatened to go to Mandi Hira Singh police station to report the beating. Ayesha then went to report the matter to the police. At the police station, Ayesha met

some of her husband's relatives who advised her not to go and threatened her with an ax and a butcher's meat chopper. Later that day, Ayesha escaped to the police, claiming that the matter could not be settled within the family. She also met her uncle who advised the same. In the meantime, Ayesha's husband had learned of her intentions to report the incident. He, along with some other relatives, followed her to the police station. Once he arrived and had assured Ayesha's uncle that he would neither beat nor hurt her, Ayesha's uncle convinced her to return to the village. They returned the same day. That night, Ayesha's husband suddenly took the children out of the house and returned with six of his relatives. According to Ayesha, her husband and his six relatives all beat her. After the beating, her in-laws held her down while her husband retrieved a kitchen knife and cut off her nose. After this, Ayesha ran away to her relatives in Karachi where she remains.[45]

The Health Consequences of Rape

The physical and psychological consequences of rape may endure a lifetime. Some of the physical complications resulting from rape include chronic pelvic pain, arthritis, gastrointestinal disorders, headaches, chronic pain disorders, psychogenic seizures, and premenstrual symptoms.[46] A study of rape in Bangladesh reports that 84 percent of rape victims suffered from severe injuries, mental illness, or even death following rape.[47.] Primary-care reports indicate that as compared to nonvictims, women with a history of rape victimization present a wider range of symptoms across the entire body system with the exception of the skin and eyes.[48]

Rape victims are at greater risk of contracting sexually transmitted diseases (STDs), including HIV. Younger girls are particularly targeted for rape by men who want to avoid HIV infection. According to UNICEF, the global AIDS epidemic seriously threatens the lives and health of millions of women since women not only are vulnerable to men's sexual demands but also lack the negotiating power necessary to secure protected sex. Among the increasing number of poor women and girls who sell their bodies in order to survive, the risk of sexually transmitted disease is greatly multiplied. UNICEF estimates that four million of the ten million HIV infections worldwide in 1992 are among women. In some parts of Africa, as many as 30 percent of women of reproductive age are reportedly infected; and in Zimbabwe, HIV infection among fifteen- to nineteen-year-old girls is six times higher than in boys.[49]

In the United States, STDs occur in 4 to 30 percent of rape victims.[50] STDs that go untreated can lead to more serious reproductive-health consequences. For example, many of the former Korean "comfort women" had to be sterilized since their reproductive organs and urinary tracts were severely affected by STDs.[51] Inasmuch as rape victims are subjected to unplanned intercourse, they are usually unable to use contraceptive devices. As a result, rape victims often either become mothers of unwanted children or victims of black-market abortions.

From a cross-cultural perspective, relatively little is known about the psychosocial consequences of rape. Although a wide range of psychological complications have been reported in the literature, much of that which is reported focuses on Western populations and is discussed according to Western psychological standards and values. Be that as it may, a sample study conducted in the United States found that 60 percent of sexual assault victims experience sexual dysfunction three years after the assault. Even after many years following rape, victims have a two times greater risk of qualifying for ten different psychiatric diagnoses, including major depression, alcohol abuse, drug abuse, obsessive-compulsive disorder, generalized anxiety disorder, eating disorders, multiple personality disorder, borderline personality syndrome, and post–traumatic stress disorder.[52]

The most common syndrome associated with rape is post–traumatic stress disorder. PTSD sufferers show such symptoms as intense nervousness, difficulty concentrating, memory impairment, sleep disorders, emotional numbing, and intense reactions toward, and avoidance of, events that revive the traumatic experience. In some extreme cases, the psychological symptoms resulting from rape have included the development of trauma-induced psychoses.

The extent to which rape affects victims is influenced by a number of contextual factors. In some societies, a woman who has been raped is treated, not as a victim, but as a criminal. A study conducted in Bangladesh in 1989 found numerous cases involving women who were beaten, murdered, or driven to suicide because of the dishonor that their rape had brought upon their families.[53] A *New York Times* article reports that a twelve-year-old girl was given to an Ewe priest in Ghana to serve as a slave in order to atone for the rape that led to her birth.[54]

A similarly severe stigma is attached to children of rape victims in Rwanda. Up to five thousand children resulting from rape during the genocide were labeled as "child of hate and infant non-desires."[55] One woman who was ashamed of carrying the child of a Rwandan Hutu militiaman gave a false name at the hospital and left the infant behind after giving birth. The child had been conceived during a rape committed by the same man who had slaughtered her parents and brother.[56]

In countries like Fiji, the Philippines, Thailand, Mexico, and Peru, the culturally accepted resolution of rape is sometimes to legitimize the union of the woman and her rapist through marriage.[57] This is believed to preserve the family honor. In societies where virginity is highly valued, rape can become tantamount to a social murder.[58] Indeed, owing to the extent of its impact not only on the victim but also on whole communities, rape is sometimes used to restore a threatened hierarchy. In India, for example, gang rape has been a commonly used method of demoralizing opponents and crushing protest movements.[59]

Clearly, the consequences of rape for individuals and for communities are profound and far-reaching.

Sexual Harassment

A dimension of sexual abuse that has received relatively little attention on a global scale is the problem of sexual harassment of women and girls in schools and workplaces. Nevertheless, studies from a variety of contexts reveal that sexual harassment is a serious and pervasive problem. In Germany, the United Kingdom, Tokyo, Tanzania, and Asia, sexual harassment in the workplace has been identified as a serious problem for well over 60 percent of the women surveyed.[60] Despite its pervasiveness, until recently, few countries had established legal provisions for the protection of women from this insidious form of violence. In the United States, which was the first country to establish laws against sexual harassment, no legal definition of sexual harassment existed until 1980 when the U.S. Equal Employment Opportunity Commission (EEOC) issued guidelines prohibiting attempts to extort sexual activity by use of subtle or explicit threats of job-related consequences.

The EEOC guidelines noted that there are two forms of sexual harassment for which employers will be held responsible: quid pro quo harassment, in which the terms and conditions of employment were made conditional upon sexual favors; and sexual harassment that resulted from the creation of a hostile work environment. Sexual harassment was defined by the EEOC as unwelcome "sexual advances, requests for sexual favors, and other verbal or physical conduct of a sexual nature," wherein any of three criteria is met: (1) such conduct interferes with an employee's work performance by creating an intimidating, hostile, or offensive work environment; (2) submission to such conduct is either implicitly or explicitly used as a basis of an individual's initial or continued employment; or, (3) acquiescence to sexual requests serves as a criterion in employment-related decisions. Since the EEOC guidelines were established, numerous studies and lawsuits have established the widespread nature of sexual harassment in the United States.[61]

In his report on the occurrence of rape against women in the military, for example, Gary Warner notes that a woman serving in the U.S. Army is 50 percent more likely to be raped than a civilian.[62] Similarly, women serving in other male-dominated institutions, such as police and fire departments, construction companies, and manufacturing industries, are more likely to be subject to gender-related violence and abuse than are women serving in occupations with longer histories of female involvement.

The Thunder Bay (Canada) Committee on Sexual Harassment conducted a study in 1980 in which women were asked if they felt sexual harassment to be a serious problem: 83 percent said yes. Similarly, a 1981 Women in Trades questionnaire revealed that 92 percent of the respondents felt that they had been sexually harassed. In British Columbia, Canada, 90 percent of the unionized women surveyed indicated that they had experienced sexual harassment; and in the United Kingdom and several other regions of the world that record such data, sexual harassment is recognized as both a persistent and a serious problem.[63]

Cyberporn and the Sexual Exploitation of Children

Although rape, sexual slavery, incest, and sexual harassment have been long-established threats to the development and well-being of the world's children, a problem that has only recently emerged on the world scene is the exploitation of children through the Internet.

The proliferation of child-pornography trafficking has created an anonymous "pedophile superstore." These pornographic industries not only abuse children in the making of their materials but also contribute to a growing trend of sex-related violence against children and youth by family members. In the mid-1980s dealing in child pornography became illegal in every Western nation. Nevertheless, the U.S. Department of Justice estimates that at two billion to three billion dollars a year, child pornography continues to be one of the world's largest and most successful cottage industries. In the United States alone, more than a million children have been filmed undergoing various forms of sexual abuse and exploitation.

The largest source of commercial child pornography is Denmark. Denmark became the world's leading producer of child pornography when, in 1969, it removed all restrictions on the production and sale of any type of pornographic material. "The result," notes Tim Tate, "was a short-lived explosion in adult pornography, and the birth of commercial child pornography."[64] In his work, Tate links the global spread of child pornography to two men: Willy Strauss, founder of *Bambina Sex*, the world's first child-pornography magazine, founded in 1971; and Peter Theander, founder of Colour Climax Corporation and the producer of a short, professionally made pornographic film series entitled *Lolita*. *Lolita* depicts the sexual abuse of prepubescent boys and girls. Although Danish law at the time rendered the work of Strauss and Theander legal, by 1979 when Denmark finally banned the production and sale of child pornography, it had already become such a financial success on the international market that it has proven to be nearly impossible to bring its spread under control.

That child pornography contributes to the sexual victimization of children is unquestionable. Not only does the production of child pornography necessitate the sexual abuse and exploitation of children, but also child pornography merchants encourage their customers to "find" children with whom new pornographic materials can be produced. One of the most successful publishers of child pornography, Joop Wilhelmus, often encouraged his customers to send him photos from their pedophile collection so as to ensure his magazine's survival: "This magazine can only exist if you help us! Send us photos from your collection."[65] According to Tate, Wilhelmus also provided his readers a venue for advertising for both child pornography and child sexual partners.[66]

Despite the spread of child pornography throughout the Western world, the children most vulnerable to exploitation in this way are poor children of color. The number of children from "developing nations" appearing in pornographic photographs and films is escalating. In addition, throughout the world, poor, runaway, homeless, and refugee children are most likely to be depicted in dehumanizing and sadistic scenes because their compliance with such treatment is often linked with their survival. Commenting on the intersection of race and poverty in child sexual exploitation, Liz Kelly notes:

> The use of black children from the 'Third World' in commercially produced child pornography . . . demands further investigation. Is it only that children are easier to procure where physical survival is a daily struggle, where children have to work from an early age? What role do racism and Western economic and cultural imperialism play in this particular form of sexploitation? . . . While the picture of a white child might induce momentary guilt in the white Western consumer through a connection to his own children, this possibility is removed when the children are black. Even the outrage of white non-consumers of pornography often turns on what is being done to 'our' children, i.e. white children. Black children are thus not only 'non-persons' to the white Western consumer (and some of their critics), but also 'non-children'.[67]

In 1985, U.S. Attorney General Edwin Meese III appointed a commission on pornography. In service to this commission, and in his role as the surgeon general of the United States, C. Everett Koop organized a panel of clinicians and researchers to examine what we know about the way that pornography affects the physical and mental health of people, and especially young children and adolescents. After a review of available research, these experts gathered for a weekend workshop to discuss their findings and were able to reach consensus on five points that are summarized by the surgeon general below:

> 1. Children and adolescents who participate in the production of pornography experience adverse, enduring effects. The participants were thinking of the sexual victimization of young people and the pathway that takes them from involvement in the production of pornography to their subsequent involvement in child prostitution.
> 2. Prolonged use of pornography increases beliefs that less common sexual practices are more common. This is similar to the conclusions reached elsewhere concerning violence and other antisocial activities. Repeated exposure to depictions of such activities tends to build up the impression in the exposed person's mind that people are doing such things more often than is actually the case.

3. Pornography that portrays sexual aggression as pleasurable for the victim increases the acceptance of the use of coercion in sexual relations. I am certain that this kind of pornography is at the root of much of the rape that occurs today. Impressionable men—many of them still in adolescence—see this material and get the impression that women like to be hurt, to be humiliated, to be forced to do things they do not want to do, or to *appear* to be forced to do things they really *do* want to do. It is a false and vicious stereotype that leads to much pain and even death for victimized women (emphasis in original).

4. Acceptance of coercive sexuality appears to be related to sexual aggression. This statement, in a sense, completes the circle. In other words, if a man sees a steady stream of sexually violent material in which the victim seems to enjoy the treatment, he begins to believe that coercion and violence are acceptable in sexual relations. And then he may well take the next step: He may convert this attitude into behavior and himself become the perpetrator he has been watching or reading about in pornography.

5. In laboratory studies measuring short-term effects, exposure to violent pornography increases punitive behavior toward women. This statement is obviously impossible to prove by controlled ethical experiments. However, the workshop participants felt that this fifth and final consensus statement could be safely drawn from the experimental and survey data already available.[68]

U.S. National Child Sex Offender Registration Laws

The last several years have witnessed a significant increase in the passage of national laws intended to protect children and youth from child sex offenders and "sexual psychopaths." Awareness of the need for such laws grew significantly in the 1980s when, in the United States, sexual assaults committed by repeat sex offenders began to gain national attention. In one of the most tragic cases, Earl Shriner, who had been released on bail pending trial for an alleged rape in 1989, lured a seven-year-old boy from Tacoma, Washington, into the woods where he raped the child, stabbed him, cut off his penis, and left him to die. Despite his condition, the young boy did not die but was found wandering through the woods, covered in blood, nude, and in shock. When Shriner was arrested later that day, the community was outraged to learn that he had been arrested several times before for a variety of sexual offenses committed primarily against young girls.[69] In response to a campaign spearheaded by the young boy's mother and supported by the community, the Washington State legislature passed an act requiring the registration of convicted child sex offenders. This was the first such law to be passed in the United States.

When a year later an eleven-year-old boy named Jacob Wetterling was abducted near his Minnesota home and never found again, public sympathy for Jacob and his family led to action on the federal level. Congressman Jim Ramstad of Minnesota sponsored a bill requiring national registration of released sex offenders. However, as Ramstad's bill was under consideration, a ten-year-old boy named Zachary Snider was molested and murdered by a released child sex offender in Indianapolis, and Megan Kanka was murdered and raped by a convicted child sex offender in New Jersey. Thus, while Ramstad's legislation was being passed on the national level, "Megan's Law" and "Zachary's Law"—which were similar to the Washington State legislation—were under consideration on the state level. Following this pattern, as of January 1996, forty-six states have passed child sex offender registration laws.[70] Sex offender registration laws received strong legislative support, not only because of the heinous nature of the crimes described above, but also because of testimony rendered before the U.S. Congress concerning the likelihood that most sex offenders would rape and molest again. According to one report, 74 percent of imprisoned child sex offenders had already been convicted of a similar crime. In addition, research reports presented before the Congress suggested that the typical sex offender will molest more than one hundred children in his or her lifetime.[71]

In 1994, as part of the federal crime bill, Congress passed the Jacob Wetterling Crimes against Children and Sexually Violent Offender Registration Act. By requiring all states to establish a child sex offender registration system by 1997, this act was intended to encourage the creation of a national database. Those states that did not establish a registration program were in danger of losing 10 percent of their federal funding for crime prevention.[72]

The primary purpose of child sex offender registration was to have a list of child sex offenders available should a child be harmed or prove missing. Such a registry would decrease the likelihood that a pedophile could abduct a child, move to a new area where they are not known, and go undetected. By having information on the whereabouts of all offenders, the most likely suspects could be quickly identified and traced. Furthermore, some hoped that child sex offender registration would have a deterrent effect.

Sex offender registration laws in all states are similar in that they each require a convicted sex offender to notify law enforcement when he or she is paroled in a state or takes up residence there. Beyond this, there is variation. Some states mandate lifelong registration of offenders; some vary the period of registration according to/on the basis of the number and type of offenses. Most states require an offender to register anew whenever he or she changes addresses. In some states release of the identity of the offender is prohibited, while in others law enforcement officials may render public notice when a convicted sex offender has been released into the community and may also publicize the offender's street address.[73]

To be in compliance with national standards, offenders convicted of one of the following offenses must register: kidnapping or false imprisonment of a minor, criminal sexual conduct toward a minor, use of a minor in a sexual act, solicitation of a minor to engage in prostitution or any form of sexual conduct, and any act that is a sexual offense against a minor.[74] Anyone who has been convicted of one of these acts must register with the appointed state agency for a minimum of ten years and within ten days of relocating to a new state. For those who have already been convicted of a violent sexual offense and who have been diagnosed with a mental illnesses that may predispose them to commit future assaults, the designation "sexually violent predator" may be applied. An individual so designated is required to register for life and must confirm his or her address to the appropriate authorities every ninety days.

Despite widespread public support for sex offender registration laws, they continue to face constitutional challenges. Michelle Earl-Hubbard has argued that these laws may violate the Eighth Amendment, which prohibits cruel and unusual punishment; that they may violate the offender's right to due process; that they may have untoward and unintended consequences such as a deleterious impact on the effectiveness of sex offender treatments. Others express concern about whether the resources exist for such laws to be effectively enforced.

Another type of law designed to protect the community from repeat sex offenders is covered under the Sexually Violent Predator's Act (SVPA), which was first passed by the Washington State legislature in 1990. This act permits the indefinite civil commitment of a person who is designated a sexually violent predator, even after completion of the crime-related prison term.

According to Andrew Horwitz, the SVPA is a revised version of a previously repealed law referred to as the "sexual psychopath statute." First passed in Michigan in 1937, the sexual psychopath statute was written in response to a growing sense of the spread of sexual violence throughout the country. By the 1960s, almost all U.S. states had enacted sexual psychopath legislation, but by the 1970s, the same states had begun to repeal these laws. Horwitz explains that the demise of sexual psychopath legislation could be attributed most significantly to widespread disillusionment with the concept of criminal rehabilitation and expanding popularity of retributive sentencing.[75] Under the earlier sexual psychopath legislation, the principal aim was to rehabilitate those suffering from sexual psychopathy so that they would pose less risk to society upon their release from prison. The new act, however, is focused less on treatment and more on punishing offenders and protecting the public.

The Sexually Violent Predator Act defines those acts that are "sexually violent" and specifies those acts that may be labeled "predatory acts." In the most general sense, predatory acts are acts "directed towards strangers or individuals with whom a relationship has been established or promoted for the primary purpose of victimization."[76] Although such legislation may be necessary, limiting the definition of a sexual predator in this way precludes inclusion of the overwhelming majority of individuals who commit sexual crimes against children. In most cases, children are not victimized by strangers but by known family members and friends.

As is the case with sex offender registration laws, as well as with sexual psychopath legislation, sexually violent predator acts have been subject to considerable criticism. Chief among the criticisms is the effort to link this legal designation to a diagnostic condition that has no clinical significance and no known treatment. The American Civil Liberties Union has described SVPAs as "an exercise in lifetime preventive detention disguised as voluntary psychiatric treatment."[77] The principal concern here is that prosecutors and courts may have too much latitude in detaining an individual indefinitely once he or she has been convicted of any sexually violent crime. Although the law also requires that offenders show evidence of future dangerousness and mental abnormality to be committed under this act, civil libertarians worry that neither mental abnormality nor future dangerousness can be reliably established.

Another criticism lodged against these acts by some is that they endeavor to disguise punishment in the rhetorical garment of rehabilitation. This semantic device, critics charge, enables the indefinite imprisonment of offenders without the usual concern for justice and equity in sentencing. Finally, many have objected to SVPAs because they suggest that they exacerbate therapeutic problems among those seeking treatment for sexual offenses while serving time under the statute. Convicted offenders, one clinician noted, may perceive the law as both "arbitrary" and "excessive." It thus becomes difficult to establish a positive therapeutic relationship between the offender and therapist because of the former's bitterness. Notwithstanding these concerns, the first constitutional test of Washington's Sexually Violent Predator Act, brought before the U.S. Supreme Court on behalf of Leroy Hendricks, a man convicted of taking "indecent liberties" with two thirteen-year-old children, resulted in a 5–4 decision to uphold the act.

Moral and Spiritual Dimensions of the Problem: The Challenge of Self-Mastery

Consider the following dream:

> Last night I dreamed of a blood-sucking creature—part bug, part animal—which crawled along the floor, as does a cockroach or a lizard. I knew intuitively that it was dangerous, and that if left alive, would suck the blood from its victim, leaving it lifeless and without spirit. I was its intended victim and knew that only I could slay it. Although it moved rapidly, I was able to step on it with my foot, smashing part of it into the floor and releasing from it a white, foamy substance that belied its dangerous nature. But when I smashed a part of it, it had the ability to turn its head upon itself, and biting itself, to restore its body to health. Thereupon, it would continue its struggle to drink of the blood of my life. Several times I did slay it; and several times it brought itself back to life. But I persisted and I smashed it again and again. When I had smashed it several times, I smashed it yet

again, and beheld that in an instant, it had become a brown slipper—a comfortable shoe that I could wear. Inside the shoe there was again the white, foamy substance, but it had become a warm, soft cushion.

This dream, uncommon perhaps in the details but recognizable in form, symbolizes the archetypal struggle that everyone engages in to some degree with the lower self. The effort to master the lower self and to bring it under the stewardship of what the ancients referred to as the higher self is a recognizable motif in every culture across time. Islam commands this struggle when it prescribes jihad, or holy war; and while jihad is frequently invoked to justify acts of terrorism and violence, the jihad spoken of in the Qur'an may also be understood as a call to the holy war to conquer one's self. One who engages in jihad seeks to achieve a state of inner purity and self-mastery. Commenting on this fact, the Islamic Sufi mystic Bawa Muhaiyaddeen observed: "For man to raise his sword against man, for man to kill man, is not holy war. True holy war is to . . . cut away the enemies of truth within our own hearts. We must cast out all that is evil within us, all that opposes God. This is the war we must fight."[78] Buddhism, the Bahá'í Faith, Christianity, Hinduism, Judaism, the Zoroastrian faith, and the moralists of the humanistic school all address this struggle, as it is a universal one without which civilization is impossible. In the world's mystic, philosophical, and religious literatures, stories and parables abound about the tests that are related to self-purification and self-mastery.

In the *Republic,* for example, Plato is engaged in discourse with those who do not understand the necessity of this struggle and who therefore say that the best in life is to do injustice without penalty, while the worst is to suffer injustice without being able to take revenge. Inasmuch as the state would be poorly run if people committed injustice without fear of punishment, Plato's detractors affirm that the whole purpose of law is to prevent injustice by providing threats and punishments to those who would otherwise be unconstrained in pursuing their passions. To illustrate the force of their popular, albeit misguided, argument, Plato draws upon the mythic story about the power that the ancestor of Gyges of Lydia possessed:[79]

The story goes that he was a shepherd in the service of the ruler of Lydia. There was a violent thunderstorm, and an earthquake broke open the ground and created a chasm at the place where he was tending his sheep. Seeing this, he was filled with amazement and went down into it. And there, in addition to many other wonders . . . he saw a hollow bronze horse. There were windowlike openings in it, and, peeping in, he saw a corpse, which seemed to be of more than human size, wearing nothing but a gold ring on its finger. He took the ring and came out of the chasm. He wore the ring at the usual monthly meeting that reported to the king on the state of the flocks. And as he was sitting among the others, he happened to turn the setting of the ring towards himself to the inside of his hand. When he did this, he became invisible to those sitting near him, and they went on talking as if he had gone. He wondered at this, and, fingering the ring, he turned the setting outwards again and became visible. So he experimented with the ring to test whether it indeed had this power—and it did. If he turned the setting inward, he became invisible; if he turned it outward, he became visible again. When he realized this, he at once arranged to become one of the messengers sent to report to the king. And when he arrived there, he seduced the king's wife, attacked the king with her help, killed him, and took over the kingdom.

Let's suppose, then, that there were two such rings, one worn by a just and the other by an unjust person. Now, no one, it seems, would be so incorruptible that he would stay on the path of justice or stay away from other people's property, when he could take whatever he wanted from the marketplace with impunity, go into people's houses and have sex with anyone he wished, kill or release from prison anyone he wished, and do all the other things that would make him a god among humans. Rather his actions would be in no way different from those of an unjust person, and both would follow the same path. This, some would say, is a great proof that one is never just willingly but only when compelled to be. No one believes justice to be good when kept private, since, wherever either person thinks he can do injustice with impunity, he does it.[79]

In defense of his "virtue is its own reward" perspective, Plato devotes the *Republic* to demonstrating that the virtuous life is one in which the elements of the soul are properly coordinated; that such a life is healthy and is characterized by wisdom, courage, moderation, and justice; and that a life adorned by such virtues is one in which true happiness can be achieved. Only when this fundamental principle of human life is understood, affirmed Plato, will the inner psychological order of the individual and the outer social order of the state attain felicity.

Plato advances this thesis by invoking two metaphorical devices. The one that we will examine here is of a single being, a "multicolored beast" that is an amalgam of different animals, some of which are gentle and some savage. These animals represent the various aspects of the human personality but are joined together such that anyone who sees only the outer covering and not what is inside will think that it is a single creature, a human being. Plato is in discourse with his student, Glaucon:

> Then, if someone maintains that injustice profits this being and that doing just things brings no advantage, let's tell him that he is simply saying that it is beneficial for him, first to feed the multiform beast well and make it strong; and second, to starve and weaken the human being within, so that he is dragged along wherever either . . . leads; and third, to leave the parts to bite and kill one another rather than accustoming them to each other and making them friendly.
>
> Yes, that's absolutely what someone who praises injustice is saying.
>
> But, on the other hand, wouldn't someone who maintains that just things are profitable be saying, first, that all our words and deeds should insure that the human being within this human being has the most control; second, that he

should take care of the many-headed beast as a farmer does his animals, feeding and domesticating the gentle heads and preventing the savage ones from growing; and third, that he should make the lion's nature his ally, care for the community, and bring them up in such a way that they will be friends with each other and with himself? . . . In light of this argument, can it profit anyone to acquire gold unjustly if, by doing so, he enslaves the best part of himself to the most vicious? If he got the gold by enslaving his son or daughter to savage and evil men, it wouldn't profit him, no matter how much gold he got. How, then, could he fail to be wretched if he pitilessly enslaves the most divine part of himself to the most godless and polluted one and accepts golden gifts in return for a more terrible destruction than Eriphyle's when she took the necklace in return for her husband's soul?[80]

Plato's purpose is to show that human nature is an amalgam of qualities and that when an individual cannot regulate his own passions and must be regulated wholly by a force outside of the self (such as the force of law and threat of punishment), the noble and rational part of the self becomes enslaved, atrophied, and incapable. Furthermore, inasmuch as health, in any system, requires the proper balance and regulation of constituent forces, and health is a precondition of human happiness, such enslavement, while perhaps allowing for the uninhibited pursuit of pleasures, precludes the possibility of achieving a sense of inner peace and well-being. To the contrary, a life pulled in different directions by the force of desire is one that leads to various forms of torment, regret, shame, degradation, and a dulling of the human sensibilities.

Echoing Plato's observation more than three thousand years later 'Abdu'l-Bahá wrote that one of the most essential attributes of a truly learned individual was that he "opposes his passions." In the *Secret of Divine Civilization,* a document written with an eye toward rehabilitating the civil forces of society, he says that to oppose one's passions "is the very foundation of every laudable human quality . . . the impregnable basis of all the spiritual attributes of human beings . . . the balance wheel of all behavior, the means of keeping all man's good qualities in equilibrium." He continues:

For desire is a flame that has reduced to ashes uncounted lifetime harvests of the learned, a devouring fire that even the vast sea of their accumulated knowledge could never quench. How often has it happened that an individual who was graced with every attribute of humanity and wore the jewel of true understanding, nevertheless followed after his passions until his excellent qualities passed beyond moderation and he was forced into excess. His pure intentions changed to evil ones, his attributes were no longer put to uses worthy of them, and the power of his desires turned him . . . into ways that were dangerous and dark. . . . The primary purpose, the basic objective, in laying down powerful laws and setting up great principles and institutions dealing with every aspect of civilization, is human happiness; and human happiness consists only in drawing closer to the Threshold of Almighty God, and in securing the peace and well-being of every individual member, high and low alike, of the human race; and the supreme agencies for accomplishing these two objectives are the excellent qualities with which humanity has been endowed.[81]

In the Mathnaví of Rumi the story is told of four evil birds that, once put to death, are transformed into four birds of goodness. The allegory refers to the human quest to subdue our evil passions and qualities and to replace them with qualities that reflect the good. Of all the passions few appear to be as challenging to regulate properly as those associated with human sexuality. And while these challenges have been with us for all of human history, the liberties and excesses of the modern age have rendered it clearer now than perhaps ever before that our individual and collective well-being is dependent upon the proper expression of humanity's legitimate sexual needs.

Since the appearance of Freud's important work on the untoward consequences of sexual repression, many have come to identify the failure to vent the sexual impulse freely as either pathognomic of neuroses or indicative of a puritanical ethic. Commenting on the influence of Freud's ideas, Constance Chen, author of a biography of an early feminist, Mary Ware Dennet, observes:

> Freud's theories first hit American intellectuals and professionals at a Clark University lecture in September 1909. The radicals went on to portray a distorted view of Freud to a receptive audience. When Freud stated that repression of the libido led to pathological symptoms of 'neurosis,' the bohemians took this to mean that the libido demanded regular and constant expression in explicitly sexual terms—with no limits set. Repression led to illness; mental health required an active sex life. As psychology replaced religion as the new arbiter of human behavior, mental health and illness became the new metaphors for good and evil. Thus, to be 'good,' one had to be mentally healthy, one had to be sexually active. Since human beings were poly-morphously perverse, sexual activity did not have to be limited. . . . This take on Freud burst asunder all past restraints.[82]

Among those who were to become advocates of such a perspective was Arno Plack. "Man's aggressiveness is not original," wrote Plack, "but has been learnt only through frustration of his impulses; and only when his sexuality is no longer suppressed and he is allowed to live out his spontaneous instincts to the full can he achieve true fulfillment."[83] For many like Plack, it is clear that Freud's work rendered human sexual behavior equivalent in purpose and form to sex among primates. When, however, human sexuality is disconnected from a network of metaphysical values, others easily become mere outlets for the expression of impulses and urges.

At the height of Freud's popularity, Pitirim Sorokin, the founder of the School of Sociology at Harvard, warned about the danger of an emerging sensate culture. Sensate mentality, Sorokin wrote, is founded on the conviction that what we see, hear, taste, and smell is alone real and of value.[84] Within such a worldview, a commitment to supersensory, metaphysical values is viewed as arising from superstition, and the sensory organs are said to provide the sole and supreme measure of the validity of experience and the value of ideas. An extension of this perspective is reflected in the postmodern notion that all values are human constructions that reflect nothing more than the personal proclivities of those who happen to be in power. The resulting eudemonic philosophies, Sorokin suggests, give birth quite naturally to indulgence-based societies. In such societies, human beings are rendered equivalent in value to all other objects. They may thus be used in the same way that other objects are used. Under these circumstances the only legitimate constraint on what can or cannot be done is the threat of legal sanctions. Sorokin writes:

> If a person has no strong convictions as to what is right and what is wrong, if he does not believe in any God or absolute moral values, if he no longer respects contractual obligations, and, finally, if his hunger for pleasures and sensory values is paramount, what can guide and control his conduct towards other men? Nothing but his desires and lusts. Under these conditions he loses all rational and moral control, even plain common sense. What can deter him from violating the rights, interests and well-being of other men? Nothing but physical force. How far will he go in his insatiable quest for sensory happiness? He will go as far as brute force, opposed by that of others, permits. His whole problem of behavior is determined by the ratio between his force and that wielded by others. It reduces itself to a problem of the interplay of physical forces in a system of physical mechanics.[85]

3

Physical Abuse

Battering

Wife beating, the most common form of family violence, poses a threat to the quality of women's lives in nearly every culture and society on earth. It occurs with regularity in approximately 85 percent of all cultures and is severe enough to cause death or permanent injury in most of the societies in which wife beating is present.[1]

Murray Straus reports that out of 47 million couples in the United States, "in any one year approximately 1.8 million wives are beaten by their husbands."[2] More recent data suggest that the number may be closer to 18 million.[3] Of these, between 2,000 and 4,000 are beaten to death.[4] In India, spousal abuse often takes the form of wife burnings or "dowry deaths." The United Nations reports that in 1985 alone there were 999 documented cases of dowry deaths. These rose to 1,319 in 1986 and to 1,786 in 1987.[5] Data from Peru reveal that 70 percent of all reported crimes consist of women who have been battered by their partners;[6] and in Canada, Bangladesh, Kenya, and Thailand more than half of all females murdered were killed by family members.[7] Referencing these statistics, Bunch and Carillo noted that "domestic battery figures range from 40 percent to 80 percent of women beaten, usually repeatedly, indicating that the home is the most dangerous place for women and frequently the site of cruelty and torture."[8]

As the most common source of injury to women, battering poses one of the most serious risks to women's health worldwide. In the United States, for example, 22 to 33 percent of all visits to the emergency room are for the treatment of symptoms arising from abuse.[9] A similar pattern is observed in the developing countries, where battering tends to be underreported. In Papua New Guinea, 18 percent of all urban wives surveyed had sought hospital treatment for injuries inflicted by their husbands.[10] A three-month surveillance survey in Alexandria, Egypt, found that domestic violence accounted for 27.9 percent of all visits by women to area trauma units.[11] Similarly, a study in China found that

6 percent of all deaths and serious injuries in Shanghai were the result of domestic violence.[12]

Battering can have differential physical consequences on women depending on their preinjury health. In developing countries where many families live below the poverty line, women are often malnourished and overworked. As a consequence, they are less capable of withstanding ongoing abuse without severe consequences.

Battering has severe consequences on the reproductive health of women as well. Women who are battered are weakened and are less prepared, either mentally or physically, to make important sexual decisions. This renders them more susceptible to rape, unwanted pregnancies, and sexually transmitted diseases. Battered women are also more likely to be at risk of having miscarriages. Indeed, many battered women report intentional changes in the pattern of beating during pregnancies. While their upper body parts were the most frequent targets of attack prior to pregnancy, after pregnancy blows are directed toward the stomach or genitals.[13] As a result, battered women run twice the risk of miscarriage and four times the risk of having a low-birth-weight infant. Their babies are forty times more likely to die within the first year of life.[14]

The psychological consequences of battering are at least as pernicious as the physical consequences. A study of nine hospitals in Beirut indicated that psychological disturbances were reported more frequently than physical injuries among women seeking medical care.[15] Chronic exposure to abuse can often lead to abuse of painkillers, illegal drugs, or alcohol. Reports of studies conducted in the United States show that spousal violence is the strongest predictor of alcoholism in women, even after controlling for other contributing factors such as income, violence in the family of origin, and having an alcoholic husband.[16] Battered and abused women are also at increased risk of suicide. In the United States battered women are five times more likely to attempt suicide than nonbattered women.[17] One-fourth of suicide attempts by American women and one-half of all attempts by African American women are preceded by abuse.[18]

The World Bank predicts that of the healthy years of life lost to women in China, 30 percent are lost to suicide.[19] The same study cites a 1985 report by the World Health Organization that found that in Sri Lanka, the rate of death due to suicide among young women between ages fifteen and twenty-four is five times that due to infectious diseases and fifty-five times the rate due to obstetric-related causes. Of course, the lives of battered women are most often taken by those who abuse them. Data from around the world indicate that domestic violence is a major risk factor for murder of and by women. In 1992, 70 percent of all women murdered were killed by a male intimate. Between 1979 and 1982 in Papua New Guinea, 73 percent of all women murdered were killed by their husbands.[20]

Domestic Violence in Lesbian Relationships

In recent years we have seen a significant increase in same-sex partnerships in the West. These relationships frequently entail the same problems of domestic violence that have characterized many heterosexual relationships. Although few studies to date have examined the prevalence of domestic violence among lesbians, the relatively few that have been done indicate that domestic violence occurs at approximately the same rate in same-sex partnerships as it does in heterosexual unions. For example, comparative studies have found that approximately 27 percent of heterosexuals and 25 percent of lesbians have been physically abused by their partners in committed relationships.[21] Another study involving 43 heterosexual, 43 lesbian, and 39 gay couples found no significant difference in the prevalence of partner abuse among couple types. Overall, studies have indicated that anywhere between 22 and 46 percent of all lesbians have been in physically abusive relationships.

The data collected thus far would thus suggest that lesbians may be as susceptible to various forms of violence as are women in heterosexual relationships. As is the case in abusive heterosexual relationships, verbal abuse appears to be the form of violence evidenced most frequently among lesbians. One study of violence involving a sample size of 284 lesbian women found that 90 percent had been verbally abused by an intimate female partner; 31 percent reported one or more incidents of physical abuse; and 11.6 percent had experienced some form of severe physical violence, which included kicking, biting, and/or hitting with fists or other objects.[22]

Another study, involving a larger sample size of 1,142 self-identified lesbians who attended the Michigan Women's Music Festival in 1985, found that 47 percent of the respondents had themselves inflicted verbal, emotional, and/or psychological abuse, while one-third had perpetrated a combination of physical and psychological abuse. Less than 7 percent of the perpetrators reported having sexually abused their partners.[23]

One major difference in the pattern of violence observed between heterosexual and lesbian relationships is that in the latter, the power base sometimes shifts. In this way an individual who had been victimized in a previous relationship sometimes became the perpetrator in another. Half of the victims of abuse in the study cited above reported having been the source of abuse toward another partner.

High prevalence rates of violence among lesbian couples has led to the development of theories of domestic violence that question gender disparity as an important root cause. One such theory has been proposed by Island and Letellier.[24] In highlighting the failure of feminist theories to address same-sex violence, Island and Letellier have suggested that battering is best understood as a behavioral phenomenon rather than a gender-related issue. However, the conceptual framework that they propose in defense of their thesis suffers from an inability to explain the disproportionate number of male perpetrators of violence in heterosexual relationships worldwide and across history.

The data on violence among lesbians have inspired integrative approaches to explaining the primary sources of violence in same-sex relationships. These approaches suggest that individuals may learn abusive patterns through a combination of direct instruction, learning through observation (such as exposure to films and other media), and patterns of reinforcement wherein violence proves effective in achieving desired outcomes; a history of having gotten away with abusing one's partner without notable legal or social consequences (such as in heterosexual relationships where culturally ingrained patterns of sexism may bestow upon males special immunities for their acts of violence against women and in homosexual relationships where societal disdain for gays and lesbians can provide special protection for batterers); and personal choices leading to abuse on the basis of cost–benefit analyses or levels of emotional maturity.

One very powerful psychological tool used by some lesbian and gay batterers to maintain abusive relationships is the threat of "outing" to family, landlords, employers, or other groups. Same-sex violence is thus more likely to be sustained in circumstances where victims do not report abuse for fear of exposure of their socially proscribed sexual orientation.

As is the case with accounting for prevalence rates of violence among heterosexuals, only those analyses that give due regard to a multiplicity of factors are likely to be adequate. For example, patriarchal value structures that validate the use of force to secure various forms of subordination are implicated in many forms of interpersonal violence. Inherent in patriarchy is the supposition that violence and the threatened used of force are legitimate means of maintaining social order. As a result of people's having been nurtured within such a worldview, patterns of dominance and subordination may come to characterize the value systems of large numbers of people, regardless of their specific gender and/or sexual orientation. The potential or actual use of force to maintain power inequities can have particularly adverse consequences in gay and lesbian relationships, since partners cannot always rely upon either the law or the community to provide the same degree of support for their rights that heterosexual couples expect.

In addition to those sociopolitical factors that shape a people's worldview, social learning and family dynamics can also have important effects on prevalence rates of violence among lesbians and gays. According to the social learning perspective, violence is a way of coping that one learns through observation and experience, particularly within the family. The pervasiveness of violence in homes throughout the world inevitably influences what children learn as appropriate behavior and proper means of conflict resolution. Qualitative and quantitative studies of gay male and lesbian perpetrators of domestic violence have tended to find histories of abuse in childhood. In addition, as has been found among heterosexuals, lesbians exposed to sexual violence by a relative or nonrelative and those who had been physically and emotionally abused by parents have proven to be more likely to experience physical violence and other forms of violence in their current relationships.

Particular personality traits are also associated with violence in lesbian relationships. These personality traits, however, are commensurate with those found among heterosexual men who batter. Lesbian batterers, like heterosexual batterers, are more likely to abuse alcohol or drugs, feel powerless, and tend to be overly dependent and jealous. In addition to the presence of alcohol and drug abuse, lesbian batterers may, in general, suffer from higher rates of borderline personality disorder than do members of the general population.

Despite the prevalence of domestic violence in lesbian relationships, professional and social support for victims remains out of reach for many. Numerous factors contribute to the paucity of support for battered lesbians. Lesbian victims, for example, may be reluctant to report their experiences of abuse for fear of contributing further to negative stereotypes that detract from their struggle for social justice and societal acceptance. Lesbians may be justified in their reluctance to expose violence in their relationships for fear of intensifying homophobic attacks. Societal misconceptions regarding violence in lesbian relationships also prevent effective action. One such misconception is that lesbian domestic violence is unlikely since men tend to be the primary perpetrators of violence. Another factor contributing to maintenance of the problem is the tendency to underestimate the severity of partner abuse that is possible in lesbian relationships. Many falsely believe that same-sex abuse is not likely to be as severe as abuse perpetrated by a man against a woman.

Clearly if women are to be protected by human and civil rights laws that guarantee freedom from all forms of violence and abuse, violence perpetrated against women in lesbian relationships cannot be ignored by the human rights community. It is especially important that human rights law give special consideration to the problem of violence in lesbian and gay relationships because victims in these relationships may be particularly disinclined to bring their concerns before those who have responsibility for doing something about it.

Violence against Domestic and Migrant Workers

In addition to spousal abuse, violence committed against female domestic and migrant workers is a growing problem in many countries. In Asia and the Middle East, where unemployment and poverty are soaring, women are often compelled to seek employment abroad. Migrant domestic workers are especially vulnerable to abuse because, upon leaving their home country, they are deprived of their rights as citizens. Many also work as illegal aliens. As such, they often cannot appeal to authorities against their abusers. Commenting on the ineffectiveness of law to protect these women, the UN's Special Rapporteur on Violence against Women notes:

> In many countries with large migrant worker populations, there exist a variety of formal and informal legal and social structures that conspire against women domestic workers. Non-existent and ineffective laws and enforcement mechanisms exacerbate violence by creating a situation in which women domestic workers are vulnerable, [and] lack protection and rights. . . . Commonly, recruiters or the employers confiscate the passports of domestic workers, restricting their mobility within the country, as well as prohibiting their departure from the country.[25]

According to published reports, rape and physical assault of Asian women employed as maids in Kuwait, the United Arab Emirates, Saudi Arabia, Malaysia, and Singapore are both common and brutal. Sinhala Bolasi, for example, is a twenty-year-old Sri Lankan woman who was held captive by her employer who raped her. Following the rape, the employer allegedly threw Sinhala off a balcony several stories high; her fall resulted in broken ankles. Subsequent medical examination revealed that Sinhala had sustained internal injuries, had suffered lacerations to her labia and rectal area, and had a tear that extended from her vagina to her anus, which suggested that she had been raped by someone who had used a sharp object.[26] Although they had been informed by hospital officials of her injuries, Kuwaiti authorities took no action against Sinhala's employer.

Abuse of domestic workers is not confined to the Middle East. NGOs have documented more than two thousand cases of ill treatment and abuse of migrant domestic workers in the United Kingdom. Documented forms of abuse include withholding wages, food deprivation, forced modifications of contracts, denial of access to medical and health services, imprisonment in the home of the employer, interception of letters and calls from home, and violence of a physical and sexual nature.[27] Similarly, in Central and South America the exploitation and abuse of female migrant and domestic workers has been well documented. In Chile and Colombia, for example, rural female migrant workers serve as seasonal laborers in the fruit and flower industries. Not infrequently, these women are forced to work very long hours, under dangerously unhealthy conditions, and often under exposure to high levels of pesticides that have been banned in northern countries. The high number of birth defects, cancer cases, and deaths that result from such exposure is well known.[28]

Conceptualizing Domestic Violence as Torture

Among the most important developments in human rights law in recent years is the effort to conceptualize domestic violence against women and girls as acts of torture. Feminist legal scholar Rhonda Copelon maintains that "the most common and dangerous form of gender-based violence—the battering and sexual abuse of women by their partners . . . must be understood as torture, giving rise to obligatory international and national responsibilities."[29] According to Copelon, two obstacles preclude the recognition of domestic violence as torture: first, the public/private dichotomy that is an integral part of international law recognizes as acts of torture only public acts of violence that are perpetrated by the state, or by agents acting on behalf of the state; and second, the tendency to trivialize violence against women, along with its relegation, no matter how widespread or egregious, to the domestic sphere, precludes assessment of the responsibility of the state in its perpetuation and prevention. To appreciate the progress inherent in conceptualizing domestic violence as torture, it is necessary to examine the concept of torture as articulated in human rights law.

Since the human rights atrocities associated with the rise of Nazism, the Universal Declaration of Human Rights, the International Covenant on Civil and Political Rights, and the Geneva Conventions have all prohibited torture. Article 1 of the United Nations Convention against Torture defines torture as

any act by which severe pain or suffering, whether physical or mental, is intentionally inflicted on a person for such purposes as obtaining from him or a third person information or a confession, punishing him for an act he or a third person has committed or is suspected of having committed, or intimidating or coercing him or a third person, or for any reason based on discrimination of any kind, when such pain or suffering is inflicted by or at the instigation of or with the consent or acquiescence of a public official or other person acting in an official capacity.[30]

According to Copelon's analysis, the elements of torture include: (1) severe physical and/or mental pain and suffering; (2) intentional infliction of that pain or suffering; (3) specified purposes for inflicting pain and suffering; and (4) some degree of official state involvement, whether that involvement is active or passive. While torture may include ancient, traditional methods (such as the thumbscrew, near drowning submersion in foul water, cigarette burns, etc.), torture inflicted upon women frequently includes sexual violence, such as circumcision, forced sex with animals, fellatio or anal intercourse, multiple rapes, and the forcing of instruments or animals into the vagina. According to the UN convention, torture may also include efforts to "obliterate the personality of the victim or to diminish his physical or mental capacities, even if they do not cause physical pain or mental anguish."

Highlighting parallels between widely recognized acts of torture and common acts of domestic violence against women, Copelon demonstrates first that the techniques used by torturers throughout the world are quite similar to techniques commonly used by batterers in the home:

Batterers manipulate and create stress in much the same way as official torturers. . . . [W]omen are isolated from family, friends and others, which is a form of "house arrest." They are subjected to verbal insult, sexual denigration and abuse. The lives of their loved ones are threatened and they are made to fear the loss of their children. . . . In both domestic and official contexts, women often experience rape and sexual abuse as the most degrading aspects of their experience. . . . [T]he mental suffering women endure as a consequence of living in a battering relationship is, as with torture, profound.[31]

Having established that domestic violence satisfies the first criterion of torture (i.e., that it involves severe physical and/or mental suffering), Copelon sets out to demonstrate that the pain inflicted on battered women also satisfies the second criterion (i.e., that it is inflicted intentionally and is against the will of the victim). These criteria (1) enable ascription of culpability to the aggressor; (2) distinguish torture from accidents and disease; and (3) separate torture from treatments where pain is accepted in the expectation of attaining some greater good.

Addressing the question of intentionality, Copelon demonstrates, as have others, that domestic violence is generally not the result of a loss of control. Rather, numerous studies have shown that batterers engage in violence in an effort to achieve a premeditated state of affairs; that they often plan their attacks; that their targets are generally limited to their female partners, their children, pets, and inanimate objects; and that they are able to exhibit impulse control in contexts that are external to the domestic sphere:

Indeed, the notion that battering is simply an impulsive letting-off of steam reflects the depoliticization of domestic violence against women. This perspective, which treats battering as simply an individual problem of personal or family dynamics, obscures the underlying and purposive gender dynamic of domination and subordination. The human rights focus must be on the perpetrator's accountability in order to counter the traditional complicity of law and custom in giving men license to vent their violent "impulses" on women.[32]

The third criterion of torture is that pain or suffering must be inflicted for one of several specified, illegitimate purposes: to obtain information and/or to punish; to intimidate; to obliterate the personality of the victim; and/or as an act of discrimination. For the present discussion, it is sufficient to point out that the political or social purpose of torture is often to suppress or discriminate against a specific group or whole society. Gender-based violence fits the requirement of discrimination because it is both society-wide and global; furthermore, it is perpetrated against victims because of their status as women. "Thus gender-based violence should be recognized as an international human rights violation for two reasons: it violates the rights of women as persons entitled to integrity, security and dignity, and it constitutes discrimination against women by maintaining both the individual woman and women as a class in an inferior, subordinated position."[33]

Among the most significant factors traditionally invoked to distinguish intimate violence from acts of torture is that domestic violence is privately rather than publicly inflicted. As such, some have questioned whether states or states parties ought to be held accountable for domestic violence just as they are held accountable for other human rights violations. As has been noted by Burgers and Danelius, the expectation is that with private acts of violence, "the normal machinery of justice will operate . . . and prosecution and punishment will follow."[34] Torture, by contrast, precludes the possibility of seeking justice by appealing to the state. Also, according to Copelon, torture presumes that the victim is in custody, whereas victims of domestic violence are not; state-sponsored brutality is presumed to be greater than brutality administered by batterers in the home; and use of the term "torture" to refer to the behavior of individuals who are acting on their own behalf, rather than as agents of the state, "threatens to dissolve the boundaries of human rights law and dilute the meaning of torture."[35]

Copelon confronts each of these objections, demonstrating, first, that victims of domestic abuse are frequently held in both physical and psychological captivity by the use of overt acts of violence as well as by threats of even greater force should attempts at escape be made; second, that the failure of many governments to punish batterers and marital rapists adequately renders appeals to the state for redress an untenable solution for most women; third, that the frequency, duration, and intensity of pain and humiliation meted out by batterers at least equals, and often exceeds, the violence and brutality evidenced by state-sponsored torturers.

The consequence of conceptualizing domestic violence as torture in international law is that it obligates the state to ensure that such acts do not occur by enacting both preventive and prosecutory measures that are sufficiently effective to ensure that women, as a class, are no more vulnerable to domestic abuse than others. Such preventive measures would no doubt include vigorous educational and training programs directed at law enforcement personnel, the general public, and children throughout their development. Furthermore, both states and individuals may be held responsible under the international torture conventions, irrespective of the attitude toward domestic violence that may obtain in a particular region, nation, or community.

The Impact of Gender-Based Violence on Children

In an effort to torture and control their partners further, many battering husbands or boyfriends also abuse the children.[36] Indeed, in the United States, children who live in homes where violence occurs are themselves abused or neglected at a rate 1,500 percent higher than the national average.[37] Furthermore, testimony before the U.S. Senate Judiciary Committee has revealed that the most serious cases of child abuse requiring emergency-room treatment tend to be extensions of the battering rampages directed at the child's mother.[38] In Portland, Oregon, a city not known for particularly high levels of social pathology, 40 percent of child fatalities occur in homes where there is adult domestic violence. Thus, even in relatively stable communities, the safety and well-being of children is significantly compromised by violence in the home.

Even when children do not directly experience physical or sexual abuse, the impact of witnessing gender-based violence upon the lives of children can be profound and long-lasting. Each year, approximately three million to four million children witness violence between their parents in the United States.[39] Given the global nature of domestic violence, it is reasonable to estimate that worldwide, in any given year, tens of millions of children will witness serious violence perpetrated against their loved ones in their homes.

Children who observe their loved ones being battered or abused often suffer from anxiety, uncontrolled aggression, poor self-esteem, psychosomatic illness, impaired problem-solving skills, and/or severe mental illness. When Pynoos and Eth explored children's responses to witnessing violence against their mothers, they found that many of the children manifested the full range of symptoms generally associated with post–traumatic stress disorder. PTSD is a severe anxiety syndrome first identified in war veterans. It is characterized by sleep disturbance, severe anxiety and phobic responses, hypervigilance, worry, emotional incontinence, violent dreams, and reenactment of the traumatic event(s) throughout the day. In Pynoos and Eth's studies, children who witnessed their mothers being seriously injured or killed would sometimes reenact these events as they played.[40]

In their study "The Effects of Systematic Family Violence on Children's Mental Health,"[41] Laura McCloskey and her colleagues found that the degree of reported violence in the home may serve as a predictor of children's mental health. In concluding their findings the authors write: "Our study suggests . . . that wife abuse sets the stage for paternal child abuse, with children caught in the crossfire of marital combat. They are used for purposes of retaliation and control in adult relationships. The psychological problems which ensue are debilitating and could be long-lasting."[42] More specifically, they found that children from violent homes are at greater risk for abuse by others outside of the family; that while in their sample child-directed physical abuse was rarely accompanied by sexual abuse, spousal abuse was clearly linked to the sexual abuse of the child; that it is common for children of battered women to witness extreme forms of violence in the home, including attempted murder and rape; and that abuse tends to occur across relationships so that fathers who batter their wives are more likely to hurt and abuse their children.[43]

In addition to first- and secondhand victimization, children who live in violent homes do not generally receive the kind of nurturance that is important for healthy development. If the central purpose of parenting is the preparation of young people for maturity, family violence renders the achievement of such a goal a near impossibility. While it is certain that many people who grow up in violent homes are able to achieve a healthy state of psychosocial maturity, many others suffer from significant, lifelong impairments that preclude the actualization of their full potential.

In the last three decades, many researchers have explored the "cycle of violence" or the "intergenerational transmission of violence." For example, Cathy Widom has examined criminal records for a group of children who were abused or neglected during childhood to determine whether such children are likely to be at increased risk for arrest as juveniles or young adults. Not surprisingly, Widom discovered that a childhood history of physical abuse predisposes survivors to violence in later years. In addition, victims of childhood neglect are at increased risk to engage in later violent criminal behavior.[44]

In a subsequent study of 908 adults who had been subjected as children to abuse (physical or sexual) or neglect, Widom found that individuals who experience any type of maltreatment during childhood are more likely than people who were not mistreated to be arrested later in life. Of those who were abused or neglected in childhood, 27 percent were arrested as juveniles. By contrast, only 17 percent of subjects who had not been abused or neglected were later arrested as juveniles.[45] Childhood abuse and neglect also appear to contribute to the incidence of drug-related offenses. Approximately 14 percent of the subjects in Widom's sample who were abused or neglected as children were later arrested for drug offenses as adults, as compared with only 9 percent of the comparison group.[46]

A developmental analysis of the impact of family violence suggests that the effects will vary depending upon a number of interrelated factors, including the child's age, gender, temperament, and cognitive maturity. The work of Erik Erikson, for example, suggests that a child who is exposed to serious, ongoing violence in early infancy is not likely to develop a sense of trust in the world or in other people. Such children are apt to experience the world as fundamentally dangerous and unpredictable. Children who experience serious violence in their middle years may experience chronic levels of shame and self-doubt, or perhaps a sense of incompetence that is incongruent with their actual abilities.[47] Extrapolating from the work of developmental psychologists Egeland and Sroufe suggests early exposure to abusive situations may impair children's sense of autonomous problem-solving skills, their formation of healthy peer relations, or even their ability to modulate their own physiological arousal.[48]

In all societies, according to developmental psychologist Laurence Steinberg, the psychosocial requirements of adulthood revolve around three sets of tasks, those involving love, work, and citizenship: "The mature adult is expected to have the capacity to form and maintain caring and gratifying relationships with others (including, but not limited to, mates and off-spring); the skills, motives, and interests necessary to contribute to and take pleasure in society's activities of production and leisure; and the values and concerns necessary to contribute to the well-being of the community."[49] If children are to develop such capacities, they must first resolve a series of preparatory psychosocial issues. Perhaps chief among these are the issues associated with the capacity for intimacy and interpersonal responsibility, including, according to Steinberg, "the capacity to form satisfying emotional attachments to others that are characterized by sensitivity, mutuality, responsibility and trust."[50] Children who are exposed to family violence do not easily develop these capacities; thus, they often grow up to form relationships with others that are stormy, unstable, violent, and brief.

Clear connections have been established in recent years between childhood social relationships and adult mental health. Unpopular children, for example, are more likely to be found in mental health settings as adults. Indeed, peer rejection, which is commonly associated with aggressiveness in boys and low self-esteem in girls, may be more deleterious than low achievement in its long-term impact. Since elevated levels of aggressiveness in boys and low self-esteem in girls are among the most common effects of family violence, violence in the home may continue to impede an individual's well-being decades after the abuse has ended.

Developmental psychologists such as Smetana and Kohlberg have suggested that children acquire knowledge of the social world by observing the interactions of others.[51] Inasmuch as the moral, psychological, and societal aspects of social cognition can be seriously distorted by exposure to violent situations, abusive families are likely to impair the way that children actually view and feel about themselves and the people with whom they associate. In their comparative study of abused and nonabused children, for example, Camras, Grow, and Ribordy discovered that abused children are less competent than nonabused children in properly identifying emotion-related facial expressions. Specifically, abused children sometimes showed greater difficulty discriminating between a happy expression and an angry one.[52] In his explication of this finding, Shirk comments: "Abused children may be less frequently exposed to positive expressions of affect and as a result have more trouble discriminating expressive cues of happiness."[53]

Children who are unable to distinguish a happy expression from an angry one are also likely to manifest serious deficiencies in the capacity to show empathy. According to Norma Feshbach, a prominent researcher in the study of empathy, empathy requires three interrelated skills: the ability to distinguish among different affective or emotional cues in others, the ability to assume the perspective and role of another, and the ability to experience an emotional reaction to another person's experience.[54] An unknown writer put it more plainly by defining empathy as "your pain in my heart." Children who commonly experience abuse, or who witness others being abused, must learn to protect themselves from the emotional consequences of watching themselves or those whom they care about being hurt. At minimum, this self-protection requires that they not allow themselves to feel the full range of emotions associated with being human.

A series of observational studies by George and Main revealed that, as compared to nonabused children, abused toddlers showed greater aggressiveness toward caretakers and were more likely to avoid their age-mates.[55] George and Main also discovered that when abused children were exposed to a distressed playmate, the abused children manifested either little concern or actual hostility. Similarly, Howes and Espinoza found that abused children, in contrast to nonabused children, tended to respond more aggressively to signs of distress evidenced by peers.[56] These data would suggest that exposure to abusive situations not only may impair children's ability to empathize with others but also may actually render them more likely to respond with anger toward those who are in distress.

That this pattern of reacting to others in distress may predispose abused children to becoming abusive themselves is supported by studies that show abusive adults are less empathetic than nonabusive adults. Indeed, when Frodi and Lamb exposed a group of child abusers to videotaped scenes of crying and smiling infants, the abused group had greater difficulty discriminating between crying infant scenes and smiling infant scenes. Furthermore, when observing the videotapes of crying infants, subjects from the abused group tended to display more anger and less sympathy.[57]

Beyond these indirect effects, parenting styles associated with abusive families are usually either authoritarian or neglectful.[58] Authoritarian households are described as high in psychological and physical control but low in warmth. While this harsh pattern of parental involvement may lead children to comply with family rules, it does not facilitate internalization of ethical principles. Thus, children who are exposed to authoritarian parenting are likely to do what is right only as long as they are monitored. Neglectful parenting, by contrast, leaves children vulnerable to whatever influences they may happen to encounter. Neither approach to parenting will result in optimal outcomes with respect to adult development.

Of course, escalating levels of child neglect and abuse must be understood not only as sequelae of gender-based violence but also as consequences of increased levels of poverty and hopelessness in underdeveloped communities around the world. Indeed, Garbarino and his colleagues have found high correlations between child maltreatment rates and depressed socioeconomic conditions.[59] Inasmuch as frustrations induced by economic and sociopolitical powerlessness may serve as strong contributors to aggression, no comprehensive strategy to reduce or eliminate family violence can ignore this dimension.

PART II

CULTURALLY SANCTIONED
FORMS OF VIOLENCE

4

Culture, Traditional Practices, and Gender-Based Violence

Several patterns of culture-specific forms of gender-based violence occur in many parts of the world. These include female genital surgery or "circumcision," dowry burnings, "honor" killings, acid attacks, and female infanticides. Recognizing the interface between cultural practices and gender-based violence, the United Nations Development Fund for Women (UNIFEM) notes that although violence against women cuts across national, ideological, class, race, and ethnic boundaries, nevertheless, "the forms of violence are often culturally determined." UNIFEM further notes that "specific programmes to counter these must be developed both at the local and national levels."[1] Currently available figures indicate the extent and seriousness of these culture-specific practices.

Honor killing, for example, is an ancient practice in which men kill female relatives in the name of family honor for forced or suspected sexual activity before, or outside of, marriage—even when such women and girls have been victims of rape. In 1997, in one province of Pakistan alone, some three hundred women are estimated to have been killed to protect an individual's or family members' honor. According to 1999 estimates, more than two-thirds of all murders in the Gaza Strip of Palestine and the West Bank in Jordan were most likely honor killings. In Jordan, there are an average of twenty-three such murders per year. Thirty-six "honor" crimes were reported in Lebanon between 1996 and 1998, mainly in small cities and villages. Reports indicate that the offenders are often less than eighteen years of age and that in their communities they are sometimes treated as heroes. In Yemen, as many as four hundred honor killings took place in 1997, while in Egypt there were fifty-two reported honor crimes in the same year.

In her analysis of culture-specific forms of violence against women in Pakistan, Yasmeen Hassan observes that the dual constructs of women as the property of men and women as the standard-bearers of a family's honor set the stage for culturally sanctioned forms of violence against Pakistani women:

> The first assumption of *"woman as incapable"* (which translates into and is mir-
> rored by the economic, social, and political powerlessness of women as a group)
> reinforces the male right to control women. Women become the property of their
> male relatives. The dehumanization that results from the status of women as
> property makes atrocious forms and degrees of violence against women possible.
> The second assumption of *"woman as sexual"* tends to excuse aggressive male
> behavior towards women by blaming women for exciting men by their presence.
> . . . [T]he concept of a powerful female sexuality that threatens social order man-
> dates that this sexuality be kept under strict control. Social control over female
> sexuality is not guaranteed by simply veiling women. Women are viewed as irra-
> tional and untrustworthy. Because women have a will of their own, they may try
> to subvert controls on chastity that are achieved by veiling. Consequently, women
> must be deterred from defying the system through devious means and this de-
> terrence is achieved by linking women's behavior to the honor of the family. Thus
> arises the concept of *"woman as honor."* The fact that a woman is tied to her fam-
> ily's honor facilitates violence against her because to forgive an "errant" woman
> would bring dishonor on her male relatives and jeopardize their ability to hold
> their heads up in society. The fact that a man has lost control over his women im-
> plies a loss of masculinity that is more costly to the man than the woman's life.[2]

Acid attacks, which are meant to disfigure a woman, occur for any number
of reasons, ranging from a delayed meal or a rejection of a marriage proposal to
a perceived insult when a woman rebuts an indecent or unwelcome advance
from a man. In Bangladesh, between 1996 and 1998 reported acid attacks increased four-fold, from forty-seven to more than two hundred.

Female infanticide is the killing of a girl child within weeks of her birth.
Bride burning occurs when husbands or their relatives engineer an "accident"
(frequently the bursting of a kitchen stove) when they feel that the obligatory
marriage dowry (gifts from the in-laws) is not enough. In the sections that follow, we examine, in some detail, the nature of, reasons for, and consequences
of these culturally sanctioned forms of violence against women and girls.

Female Circumcision/Female Surgery

High rates of genital surgeries performed on millions of girls throughout the
Sudan, Ethiopia, Mali, Egypt, Sierra Leone, India, and other countries, most
often without anesthesia, have begun to stir the conscience of the world.[3] Female genital surgery (FGS), also referred to as female circumcision and female
genital mutilation (FGM), is painful and often life threatening. Postsurgical
complications may include hemorrhaging, shock, acute urinary retention, urinary tract infection, septicemia, fever, tetanus, pelvic infections, dysmenorrhea,

cysts and abscesses, painful intercourse, and death. It is estimated that as many as one hundred million women and girls worldwide have been subjected to genital circumcision. Furthermore, approximately six thousand additional girls and women are subject to this practice each day.[4] A *New York Times* article reported on the plight of one African woman who fled her homeland in an effort to escape this practice:

> Fauziya Kasinga says she fled her homeland of Togo at age 17 to avoid the tribal rite of Female Genital Circumcision and an arranged marriage as the fourth wife of a man nearly three times her age. When she arrived at Newark International Airport, she felt sure that she would find sanctuary in a country that "believed in justice." Instead she passed her 18th and 19th birthdays behind bars. First immigration officials took her to the Esmor detention center in Elizabeth, N.J., where she describes being shackled in chains at times, denied sanitary napkins and put in an isolation cell. Last June, she says, she was tear gassed and beaten during a melee at Esmor detention center, where immigration authorities later concluded that guards had abused detainees. After the Esmor uprising, she and many other asylum seekers . . . were sent to prisons in Pennsylvania, where she has been strip searched and locked in a maximum security cell with an American convict. . . . "I feel empty, mute," Ms. Kasinga said Friday in a barely audible whisper. . . . "I keep asking myself, What did I do to deserve such punishment? What did I do?"[5]

What Is Female Genital Circumcision?

Female genital circumcision is a cultural practice involving the excision of various parts of the genitalia of girls and young women. There are three major forms of female genital circumcision that differ in their level of severity:

- Clitorectomy (or the sunna) involves partial or total removal of the clitoris.

- Excision involves the removal of the clitoris and the labia minora.

- Infibulation (or the pharonic form) involves the complete removal of the clitoris, the labia minora, and the inner surface of the labia majora. This is followed by stitching the vulva together so that only a small opening is preserved in the vagina to allow for the passage of urine and menstrual blood.[6] Infibulation is, by far, the most serious and most prevalent form of the practice.

Prevalence of the Practice of Female Genital Surgeries

The World Health Organization (WHO) estimates that in 1994, a total of 114 million girls and women worldwide endured some form of the surgery. WHO also estimates that an additional 2 million girls per year are exposed to the practice.[7] Most girls undergo the operation between the ages of four and ten. FGS is practiced in twenty-six African countries and a few Asian countries, as well as in small immigrant populations in Europe, Australia, Canada, and the United States.[8] While infibulation is practiced in Somalia, Djibouti, the northern part of Sudan, some parts of Ethiopia, Egypt, and Mali, excision and circumcision are practiced in the Gambia, the northern part of Ghana, Nigeria, Liberia, Senegal, Sierra Leone, Guinea, Guinea-Bissau, Burkina Faso, parts of Benin, Cote d'Ivoire, parts of Tanzania, Togo, Uganda, Kenya, Chad, the Central African Republic, Cameroon, and Mauritania.[9]

How Is FGS Performed?

Circumcision is frequently performed by laywomen who inherit the role of circumciser. Traditional birth attendants, grandmothers, or sometimes village barbers who do not have any formal surgical training may also be involved. In some cases the procedure is performed using inadequate tools—such as dull razor blades or kitchen knives—under poor lighting and septic conditions without anesthetics or antiseptics.[10] More recently, according to Nahid Toubia, medically trained midwives and nurses have begun to take over the practice from traditional birth attendants and have thus played an important role in legitimizing the practice: "They use their prestige and knowledge of antisepsis, local anesthesia, and sterile suturing to win over the more affluent clientele from the traditional birth attendants."[11] Similarly, doctors—who maintain that they can reduce the health risks associated with this practice—have begun to take over this lucrative market from midwives. A summary of data derived from a family survey of circumcision among rural women in southern Somalia appears in table 1.[12]

During infibulation, the two sides of the vulva are sutured together by thorns or catgut, and a small opening is left for passage of urine and menstrual blood by the insertion of a tiny piece of wood or reed. The FGS operation is followed by a procedure where a mixture of herbs, earth, cow dung, and ashes is sometimes rubbed on the genital area to stop the bleeding. Afterward, the incision may be treated daily with native soap, palm oil, Vaseline, kerosene, or even engine oil. To prevent reopening of the wound, the girl's legs may be bound together.

Female genital circumcision endangers the lives of female children by directly threatening their reproductive and psychological health. One study found that more than 80 percent of the women who underwent FGS reported some form of medical complication as a result of the procedure. Side effects of the procedure often include severe pain, hemorrhaging, shock, wound infections, abscesses, ulcers, septicemia, tetanus, gangrene, and death. Furthermore, for some women, a long-term consequence of infibulation is hematocolpos (acute retention of urine and menstrual blood). This condition can lead to

**Table 1   Summary Data from Survey
of Rural Somali Women's Attitudes
toward Female Circumcision**

Descriptor	% (N = 589)
Type of circumcision	
Pharonic (infibulated)	98
Sunna (noninfibulated)	2
Uncircumcised	0
Person who performed circumcision	
Traditional midwife	43
Grandmother	30
Trained hospital nurse	24
Others	3
Equipment	
Machete	70
Scissors	17
Knife	9
Razor	5
Sewing material	
Cleaned thorns (dwarf acacia tree)	70
Needle	30

chronic pelvic infections, back pain, dysmenorrhea, infertility, and urinary tract infections. These medical conditions may also cause offensive odors that can result in ostracism of these girls and women.

Another common long-term complication of FGS is the formation of dermoid cysts, which can sometimes grow to be quite large, thus disfiguring the individual. A number of reports suggest that FGS can also result in the formation of keloids, which are irregularly shaped, progressively enlarging scars that develop owing to the formation of excessive amounts of collagen in the corium during connective-tissue repair. This form of disfiguration not only creates anxiety but also causes sexual intercourse and labor in childbirth to be unusually painful.

Some of the immediate consequences of the practice of female genital circumcision include hemorrhage, shock due to blood loss and pain (intensified by the absence of anesthesia), septicemia (blood poisoning), wound infections (due to the use of unsterilized, nonsurgical instruments), tetanus, pain on urination leading to urine retention, and trauma to the adjacent tissues such as the rectum and the urethra.[13] These problems can be exacerbated when professional treatment is unavailable. Wounds often fail to heal quickly because of recurring infections and irritation from urine or rubbing when walking. Anemia caused by hemorrhaging and malnutrition may also contribute to a failure to heal.[14]

A study of 105 Somali women found that 87 percent of circumcised women suffer from urine retention, 84 percent reported pain, 81 percent had fever, 74 percent were "very sick," 66 percent had bleeding problems, 52 percent mentioned slow healing, 45 percent fainted, and 35 percent mentioned foul-smelling discharge resulting from circumcision.[15] In addition to immediate postoperative complications, there may also be long-term effects on the reproductive organs affecting girls well into adulthood. Kidney problems can arise as a result of urinary problems; and, as a result of recurrent urinary tract infection, urine may be deflected into the peritoneum. Constant urinary soaking of the peritoneum may lead to bacterial growth and bladder infection that can spread to the uterus. Such infections can also result in bladder and kidney stones, as well as infertility.[16]

Long-term obstetric complications—such as obstructed labor—may also result from female circumcision. Scars formed from excision may prevent elasticity, thereby contributing to delayed labor, prolonged second-stage labor, and uterine inertia. In the absence of a traditional birth attendant to cut through the infibulation, large tears can result that may contribute to the death of both the mother and her child.[17] In the case of miscarriage, the fetus may be retained in the uterus or birth canal, thereby further endangering the life of the mother. Delay in labor can lead to the formation of obstetric fistulas as in the case of early pregnancy. In addition to their adverse effects on the internal reproductive organs of the woman, fistulas may also lead to incontinence.

Female circumcision also affects female sexuality. In her explication of its potential impact on the expression of female sexuality, Nahid Toubia, one of the foremost authorities on FGS and the first female surgeon trained in Sudan, observes:

> It would be difficult for any child above infancy not to associate circumcision with some diminution of sexual desire; the message and the act appear to be interrelated. With infibulation, in particular, the radical shaving off of all sensitive tissue plus the folding away of the vagina can be seen as a metaphor for the denial of a woman's sexuality and the locking up of her reproductive capacity with a chastity belt made of her own flesh. . . . Because women who have had either type of operation are likely to become sexually frustrated, they may no longer seek sexual contact with their partners. Ultimately, they become sexual objects and reproductive vehicles for men. This role conflicts with the social requirement that a woman be sexually desirable and pleasing to her husband, especially if sexual pleasing requires her to show that she, too, is enjoying the sexual experience.[18]

Upon marriage, the bride who has been infibulated may experience painful and often unsuccessful sexual intercourse as her husband tries to penetrate through the narrow opening. Two to three months of repeated trials might be necessary to penetrate the woman. There are reports of men who have become impotent due to fear of failure to penetrate.[19] Often penetration is made possible by defibulation of the genitalia either by the husband or by the circumciser, leading to further injury, infection, and painful coitus. Painful coitus also results from cases in which some of the nerves that supply the vulva are accidentally bundled together during the procedure and are trapped in scar tissue.[20] Thus, surgical alteration or removal of the clitoris not only may impair arousal but also may render any tactile stimulation of the clitoris painful.

The highest rates of maternal mortality are in countries where female genital circumcision is practiced. One report found that in Sierra Leone, Guinea, Somalia, Ethiopia, and Eritrea, where the practice is common, the highest maternal mortality rates are reported. Of course, maternal and fetal mortality rates are high in many of these countries not only because of female circumcision but also because of the shortage of medical facilities and staff. For example, there are four thousand Sudanese doctors in Britain, compared to only one thousand in Sudan; there are more Ethiopian doctors in New York City than in Ethiopia.[21] Even when circumcised women have access to medical care, proper gynecological examination may be precluded owing to an inability to insert a speculum to allow a cervical smear to be taken or to fit an intrauterine contraceptive device. Difficulty of examination during pregnancy can also lead to incorrect monitoring of the stages of delivery and fetal presentation.[22]

Circumcision may well result in psychological distress for many women and girls. However, the extent to which it does has not been carefully explored. In most countries where FGS is practiced, women are culturally prohibited from expressing concerns regarding their sexuality, so that any medical complications resulting from the surgery, as well issues related to the capacity to experience sexual arousal, are not subject to discussion. Despite the paucity of data related to the psychological impact of this practice, some psychosomatic and mental health problems have been observed in women who have undergone circumcision. For example, mood and thought disturbances, sleeplessness, recurring nightmares, appetite changes and weight loss or excessive weight gain, panic attacks, mood instability, diminished capacity to concentrate and learn, and post–traumatic stress disorder have all been reported.[23] According to Toubia,

> thousands of women come to the OB-GYN outpatient clinics with vague chronic symptoms which they metaphorically interpret as originating from the pelvis. These women are perceived by doctors and the hospital authorities as great nuisances and a drain on the system since they have no medically detectable pathology. Sitting for hours listening to them, it soon becomes clear that the vague symptoms of general fatigue, loss of sleep, backache, headache, pelvic congestion, uttered in a depressed, monotonical voice, are a muted cry for help for a much more deeply felt pain. With little probing, the women talk about fear of sex, the threat of infertility after infection and fears about the state of their genitals.[24]

Why Is the Practice of FGS Supported?

Female circumcision serves several important functions in the societies in which it is practiced. As a number of human rights activists have recently noted, these functions need to be more fully appreciated and understood by those who advocate its eradication. "Eradication efforts must be empathetic, not alienating," notes Toubia, "Some of the defensiveness and anger expressed by Africans is caused by the manner in which opposition to FGS has been expressed. The people of the countries where FGS is practiced resent references to 'barbaric practices imposed on women by male-dominated primitive societies,' especially when they look at the Western world and see women undergoing their own feminization rites. Both the message and the facts about FGS will be lost if advocates use the language of superiority—the language of the colonizer or slave holder."[25]

For example, the very concept of a healthy and ordered community has been linked with the maintenance of cultural practices like FGS. Such practices have been passed down from generation to generation because they have become an important part of adolescent initiation rites. These, in turn, are seen as critical for producing responsible adults for the community.[26] In Sierra Leone, for example, a woman who is not initiated in this manner will not be respected. To the Sande women, she will remain a girl socially even though she may be a woman biologically.[27] Additional reasons for practicing FGS include the effort to follow religious demands—and although neither Judaism, Islam, Christianity, nor any other established religion prescribes it, in the minds of many people, female circumcision has come to be seen as an integral part of religious observance. Those who would be persuaded to give up female circumcision are thus likely to do so only when it is clear that abandonment of such an age-old tradition is not equivalent to abandonment of cherished religious or sacred values.[28]

In addition, for many young girls and their families, circumcision provides access to a sense of belonging that is denied to those who eschew the practice. One Somali woman explains:

> When girls my age were looking after the lambs, they would talk among themselves about their circumcision experiences and look at each other's genitals to see who had the smallest opening. If there was a girl in the group who was still un-infibulated, she would always feel ashamed since she had nothing to show the others. Every time the other girls showed their infibulated genitals, I would feel ashamed I was not yet circumcised. Whenever I touched the hair of infibulated girls, they would tell me not to touch them since I was 'unclean' because I had not yet been circumcised and shaved. After the infibulation the girls' hair is shaved and washed in a special way as a rite of purification, but my hair was dirty.[29]

A reason commonly given for female circumcision is the preservation of female chastity by making sex physically impossible. The practice is thus seen by both men and women as an important means of maintaining morality and preserving family and cultural honor. It also meets men's demand for wives who come as virgins and who remain faithful. Other commonly invoked functions of female circumcision include elevating the sexual pleasure of men; rendering women "clean" by removing those parts of the female sexual organs that are considered dirty and impure; and exposing young women to the preparatory pain that serves as a metaphor for the pain of childbirth.[30]

Efforts to Eradicate Female Circumcision

The global campaign to eradicate female circumcision has focused on legal remedies and approaches that seek to change attitudes at the grassroots level. According to Layli Miller, several Western nations—including Canada, France, the Netherlands, Belgium, and Switzerland—have laws that prohibit FGS as a form of child abuse. However, only five countries where the practice of FGS is prevalent have legislated against it.[31] Sudan passed a law that rendered FGS illegal in 1956; and the Egyptian legislature banned only certain forms of FGS, allowing those practices that remove "only part" of the clitoris to continue.

Miller points out that although FGS has been outlawed in Britain for ten years, not a single person has been prosecuted under British law. Some of the reasons cited by Miller for the ineffectiveness of the British law are that the practice is not addressed from a culturally sensitive perspective; children who undergo circumcision are not usually willing or able to testify against their parents and/or relatives; and those who practice FGS often see the law as an insensitive attack on their culture and thus often see themselves as victims who would sacrifice anything to preserve their culture rather than as criminals who have transgressed the law.

In countries like Egypt where FGS is outlawed and banned in public hospitals, the practice has simply gone underground. According to Miller, legal action, especially by those nations that practice FGS, could achieve its potential at the state level only if the communities who perform the procedure are made more acutely aware of its illegality, practitioners are made to suffer its legal consequences, and indigenous or native opponents of FGS are readily protected against retribution and are aided by the state.

In the United States, Minnesota and North Dakota are alone in having passed laws criminalizing FGS. The laws of these two states render the practice a felony: "Whoever knowingly circumcises, excises, or infibulates, in whole or in part, the labia majora, labia minora, or clitoris of another is guilty of a felony," reads the law. "Consent to the procedure by a minor on whom it is performed or by the minor's parent is not a defense to a violation of this subdivision."[32] The Minnesota law also requires the commissioner of health to carry out educational and outreach activities in immigrant communities that practice FGS so as to inform them of the health risks and the penalties associated with the practice.

In recent years, the international human rights community has begun to argue that inasmuch as female circumcision is imposed largely upon children and poses serious threats to their physical and mental health, the practice of FGS is in violation of children's human rights. In support of such a position, human rights activists invoke article 24(3) of the Children's Rights Convention (CRC). Article 24(3) requires nations to take all appropriate measures to abolish those traditional practices that are detrimental to the health of children, and article 19 proscribes any form of child abuse. In addition, article 37 proscribes exposure of children to torture and to cruel, inhuman, or degrading treatment, while article 16 acknowledges and protects a child's right to privacy. FGS, it is suggested, violates each of these CRC provisions.

Although one of the chief architects of the international effort to eradicate FGS, Toubia warns that comparisons between FGS and child abuse must not go too far: "It is very important to differentiate between the motivations for FGS and those for child beating or sexual abuse," she notes. "FGS is undertaken with the intention of 'normalizing' a girl, to make her equal to her peer group, whereas child abuse isolates a child, and subjects her to the whims of an adult."[33] According to Toubia, in regions of the world where FGS is widely practiced, approaches that are likely to be most effective are ones that send a clear message of disapproval from government and professional bodies but that also seek to educate affected populations about the personal and global consequences of the practice and to encourage their compliance with national and international human rights law through consultation and persuasion.

In addition, Toubia recommends that agencies concerned with public health develop policy positions on FGS as a risk factor for the sexual, reproductive, and psychological health of women and girls. International human rights organizations should declare the practice of FGS to be in violation of fundamental human rights, and doctors, nurses, midwives, and relevant professional associations should be encouraged to take strong positions against it while also passing clear regulations that prohibit their members from engaging in it. In countries where FGS is practiced by immigrant minorities, Toubia advocates that penalties on practitioners be harsher than those imposed upon practitioners who work in countries where the practice is pervasive. Also, activists and legislators are encouraged to give due regard to the impact of penalties in countries where the scarcity of trained health personnel is already acute. Finally, Toubia maintains that the global campaign to eradicate FGS cannot hope to be successful if it does not address the social and economic injustices that compel women to submit to such practices as a means of social acceptance and access to fundamental necessities such as family, employment, and community. "If women are to be considered as equal and responsible members of society," she writes, "no aspect of their physical, psychological, or sexual integrity can be compromised."[34]

Notwithstanding our conviction that female circumcision is a harmful practice that requires the attention of the international community, we close this section by quoting from Ellen Gruenbaum's sensitive and insightful book, *The Female Circumcision Controversy: An Anthropological Perspective*. We close this discussion with Gruenbaum because she brings to the subject a degree of insight and sensitivity that we both admire and seek to emulate:

> Whatever condemnation people might feel for those who perpetuate human injustices or cause harm with their actions needs to be tempered by an understanding of their purposes. Enculturation, life experiences, and spiritual beliefs contribute to human actions over which reasonable people will differ. So it is important to understand people's reasons for their actions. Is an action based on love and a desire to do the right thing? Or is it defined by anger, hatred, or evil and destructive intent?
>
> High mortality rates have wrenched so many infants and children from their African mothers. Clean water, immunizations, economic opportunities, and the cessation of warfare are certain routes to ameliorating this suffering. Yet the world wears cultural blinders about the causes of poverty that make if difficult to understand how to prevent these tragedies of child deaths and stunted lives. Are we inured to the suffering of poverty? Is it easier to focus on female circumcision because it seems so much starker and occurs as a single event? . . . We need dialogues about priorities. Is ending the pain of female circumcision high on everyone's list? Or is it perhaps lower on the list than clean water, economic opportunities, clinics and schools? In struggling to understand the insider's view, are we at risk of succumbing to meta-twaddle, failing to take up the sword in an important crusade? Or is seeing the spectacular kaleidoscope of human experience the prerequisite for a calmer, more effective human movement toward a future vision of a healthy life on this planet?

The Nature and Prevalence of Dowry Murder

Dowry murder, also known as bride burning or dowry death, is the murder of a woman who is set on fire by her husband or in-laws for the purpose of keeping the dowry that the woman has brought into the marriage. By burning his wife, the husband can remarry and obtain another dowry. In India, dowry consists of gifts that are presented to the groom and his family by the bride's family; in addition, dowry commonly covers the marriage expenses and provides household goods for the newlyweds. The bride's family is customarily expected to give gifts on various occasions, especially upon the delivery of the bride to her in-laws' residence, her new marital home. The most common form of dowry murder involves pouring kerosene on a woman and setting her on fire. Since many homes in India have kerosene-fueled stoves, those who commit the murder may attribute the death to a cooking accident.

Dowry and the Indian Economy

In her study of the social power of women, Carol MacCormack found that two economic variables are consistently correlated with women's social and economic status. The first is the amount of labor women provide in production, while the second is the extent to which women control the product of their labor. MacCormack's research revealed that women have low status in agricultural societies where plowing (which is mainly performed by men) accounts for the larger part of the total task. In such cases women are restricted to the less valued domestic sphere and are often considered burdens. In wetter climates, where land is tilled by hoe cultivation, women provide 50 percent or more of the labor and are more valued in their homes and communities. In such societies, families invest more in the care of female children.[36]

MacCormack goes further to note that the system of dowry as a marriage transaction is prevalent in areas where women do not participate in agriculture (for example, in the northern part of India where tractors and other technologies are controlled by men), while bride price is common in parts where women are active both in the household and in the fields (for example, in the southern part of India where rice is produced in large quantities). This pattern clearly indicates that the prevalence of dowry murders in India, as well as female infanticide and neglect, correlates with the perceived economic value of women.[37]

The Cultural Significance of Dowry

Initially, the practice of dowry payment in the Hindu custom was intended to help provide for daughters, who were traditionally excluded from real property inheritance and could inherit only movable goods. Thus initially the material interests of the in-laws were excluded from the transaction. Since in the Indian patriarchy daughters stay with their parents only until they are given to their husbands and their in-laws in marriage while sons bring their wives to their parents and become the family caretakers, girls are considered burdens to the family—extra mouths to feed with no future payoff. As a result, the in-laws demand heavy payment from the bride's family in exchange for relieving them of their burden. "You have to pay dowry," noted one Indian woman, "or nobody will marry your daughter."

The dowry provided by a bride's family is often regarded as additional income not only for the newlyweds but also for the groom's extended family. "Indian officials say families of every religious, social and economic background are turning increasingly to dowry demands as a means to escape poverty, augment wealth or acquire the modern conveniences they once never heard of but now see advertised daily on television. . . . [T]he demand for dowry has become a lever for extorting money and goods from a bride's family for years after the wedding. If her family does not comply, she frequently is subjected to cruelty, physical abuse and often death."[38]

Although the intense desire to break from poverty and the desire to emulate the upper castes may explain the practice of dowry burning among the lower castes, it does not explain why highly educated and affluent families demand higher dowry and are engaged in the crime of bride burning just as much as the lower classes. In the upper classes, dowry seems to serve the purpose of preserving the high class and status of the groom's family by choosing a bride who can afford to meet the demands. In the lower and middle classes, however, dowry serves the purpose of elevating the economic status of the groom's family.

Dowry murders persist, in part, because the legal system is ineffective in stopping the crime. For example, although the Prohibition Act, which makes taking and giving dowry punishable by imprisonment for a minimum of six months was passed in 1961, it actually discourages the family of the bride from reporting the murder of their daughter for fear that they will be prosecuted for having given dowry in the first place. Furthermore, many police officers as well as other law officials are corrupt and are thus not trusted by victims and their families: "In many instances, policemen have been known to refuse to enforce laws against dowry murder because they themselves do not want to give up demands for dowry as a source of income from their sons."[39]

In addition, law officials are easily bribed by the groom's family to disregard criminal evidence and to terminate investigation: "Doctors stated that the police did not take the crimes seriously and usually spent their time on 'more important' things. Often when the police did come, and the burned woman stated that she was set on fire by her in-laws, the police were hesitant to record the declaration before speaking to the in-law. . . . The police do not immediately collect evidence for these cases because they wait to be bribed."[40] Beyond this, the fact that very few women actually survive an attempted dowry murder encourages continuation of the practice. Burning using kerosene not only proves to be an inexpensive means to murder but also rarely leaves a trail of solid evidence. What evidence does remain is easily attributed to accidental fires that result from cooking. Also, a number of studies show that the few women who survive attempted murder are not willing to testify against their husbands and in-laws for fear of retaliation. Since it is rare to find law officials who refuse bribes and successfully prosecute dowry criminals, survivors often choose to remain silent about their experiences.

Court cases in India, which are infamous for their delay, can drag out up to a decade before a verdict is reached. A woman who is accusing her husband and in-laws of attempted murder may well face tremendous danger during the long interval of court proceedings. What is more, it is not socially acceptable for a married woman to live with her parents, and thus she is often forced to return to her husband and in-laws. As a result, those few survivors are discouraged by the legal as well as the social system from pursuing justice.

Women's inferior position in Indian society also contributes to their silent victimization. As has been noted, women are not entitled to inheritance from their parents. Once married, they are forced to live with their in-laws, and the value of the bride is often measured by how much dowry her parents are willing to pay for her. If the amount does not meet the demands of her husband and her in-laws, she may become the victim of psychological and physical torture. Furthermore, since many women have little say in deciding when and whom they will marry, many are vulnerable to marriage at a very early age, when they can least defend themselves from abuse. Also, since at the time of marriage husband and wife are typically strangers to one another, it is easier for the husband to make aggressive and threatening dowry demands with emotional detachment.

Added to these difficulties is the fact that an Indian woman's identity revolves around her position as a wife. A woman who is single at old age or a woman who runs away from her husband is a disgrace to her family. "It is socially unacceptable for a bride to return to her parents' household. Indian women are expected to marry and stay married, and, apart from a few shelters established by charities or women's groups, there are virtually no alternative living arrangements. Even for female professionals who could afford to rent their own apartments, there are few landlords who would rent to single women."[41]

Because social norms discourage divorce, the husband can threaten to reject his wife or, worse still, threaten to kill her if her parents refuse to meet his dowry demands. Thus, a female child is sometimes resented for the financial burden she imposes on her parents, and she often cannot support them in their old age. As a result, her devaluation contributes to her vulnerability to lifelong victimization. As an infant, she faces the risk of infanticide, as a child she faces neglect, and as a bride she faces dowry abuse. When an Indian woman gives birth to a baby girl, her visitors sometimes sympathize with her.

Most families who engage in the practice see themselves as justified in committing female infanticide as the only possible way to escape the burdens of finding a husband, paying a dowry, and bringing a girl child into a male-craving society where she is not welcome. A family who gave their second little girl cow's milk mixed with five sleeping pills they had bought from a pharmacist in town recalls the incident: "For a month, we cried every day. We felt bad, but bringing up girls is very difficult nowadays." The father said that he has borrowed and saved for his first girl's dowry since the day she was born. He will ask the same amount in dowry when his ten-month-old son is married. A second daughter would ruin the financial stability of the family. It would mean borrowing money equivalent to a year's household income. Without dowry, no one will marry the second daughter, and as an unmarried woman, she will be shunned for life.[42]

Upper-class families who face no financial problems still engage in sex-determination tests and are more likely to abort the pregnancy if the fetus is a female. A mother of two daughters who was deciding to abort her third child were it a girl noted that the reason behind her decision was not that she and her husband couldn't afford another girl, or that they didn't love their daughters, but rather, that "Our society makes you feel so bad if you don't have a son. Especially when I go for parties, people say, 'how many children?' and I say, 'Two girls,' and they say 'oh, too bad, no boy.' And I feel bad."

When women escape dowry murder, they still cannot escape their husbands. Thus, often when a woman survives burning by her in-laws, she will be forced to return to her husband and his family. She will not reveal their crime for fear of retribution. Despite all the evidence that shows the act to be intentional, the police will take her word that it was an accident.

The Role of the Legal Culture

The impact of the legal culture cannot be overlooked, as it is "the legal culture that provides the impetus for the use, abuse, or avoidance of the law."[43] If India's legal culture or the legal cultures in many parts of the Middle East are disinclined to protect women from dowry murder, honor killings, and acid throwing, a proliferation of laws, however much needed, will not be a sufficient remedy. There are, as has been noted, three dimensions to a legal culture: the outer form or legal structure of a community; the inner dimension, or philosophical and moral principles that animate and support that structure; and the actors within a legal and/or social system that embody in their acts the degree of their commitment to the standards of ethics embodied in the abstract principles that animate the legal and social system of which they are a part.

The outer aspect of a legal culture is utilitarian and consists of mechanisms designed to facilitate the application of a community's body of laws; the inner is abstract and reflects those community-wide values that the laws of a community are designed to embody, protect, and advance. The legal culture and social fabric depend, therefore, upon a people's internalized, fundamental values. When the fundamental values of a culture are understood to be in harmony with violence against women and girls, violence will be perpetrated in the belief that in this violence the values of the social order are protected. If, for example, village dwellers believe that severe punishment of real or suspected infidelity on the part of a woman is necessitated by Islamic law and values and that male family members are thereby justified in their assaults against women, international legislation that fails to address this perception on the local level cannot possibly be effective.

In the absence of an interrogation of the actual or perceived values that the law presumes to protect, laws become relatively impotent against certain forms of abuse. Underlying the failure of India's legal culture to protect against dowry burnings, for example, is not only a set of legal institutions that fail to protect the rights of women but also a deeply held set of values that place the lives of women below that of the material advantages that accrue to those who are willing to burn women for financial gain. In this respect, dowry burnings in India are animated by the same materialistic values that encourage the abuse and exploitation of women and girls throughout the world for profit. These values, as much as the nature and application of India's gender-related laws, require the public's consideration.

James Wolfensohn, president of the World Bank, spent two days in 1998 meeting with spiritual leaders from nine major world religions to discuss how spiritual and material development are interrelated. This historic meeting, known officially as the "World Faiths and Development Dialogue," was held in London in February 1998 and included high ranking officials from the Bahá'í Faith, Buddhism, Christianity, Hinduism, Jainism, Judaism, and Islam. Convened by Wolfensohn and the archbishop of Canterbury, the consultations have been described by several sources as "ground-breaking" and "remarkable." "For the first time in contemporary economics," noted the director of the International Consultancy on Religion, Education, and Culture (ICOREC), "the role of religion in development was not just publicly acknowledged or even acclaimed, but brought into a partnership with one of the largest . . . secular organizations in the world."[44]

One participant in the proceedings described development as "an organic process in which 'the spiritual is expressed and carried out in the material.'" Meaningful development, he continued, "requires balancing the seemingly antithetical processes of individual progress and social advancement, of globalization and decentralization, and of promoting universal standards and fostering cultural diversity. In our increasingly interdependent world, development efforts must be animated by universal values and guided by a vision of world community."[45] For much of humanity's history, many of the benefits conferred by material development have been exacted at considerable cost to the well-being and development of women and girls. The murder of women for dowry is one of the most visible examples of how the struggle for material development—in the absence of a concern for spiritual and moral development—may result in atrocities that are difficult to regard as indicative of progress. The call for a new "global ethic" that respects and protects cultural diversity, while at the same time promoting the safety, dignity, and development of each individual person, represents significant progress in international human rights discourse. We turn, in the following chapters, to an exploration of the issues and concerns that animate this movement.

PART III

EFFORTS TO ERADICATE
GENDER-BASED VIOLENCE

5

The Role of Education

The program of action articulated at the International Conference on Population and Development (held in Cairo, Egypt, in September 1994) identifies education as among the most important means for imparting the skills, knowledge, and self-confidence women need to participate fully and equally in development processes. On the most basic level, there is an urgent need to improve literacy rates for women and girls in many parts of the world. While in most countries of Latin America, the Caribbean, and southeastern Asia basic literacy rates for women aged fifteen and older have increased significantly over the past several decades, very high rates of illiteracy continue to prevail in northern and sub-Saharan Africa and southern Asia. Among older women and women living in rural areas, illiteracy is especially high. In those countries that have begun to collect such data, the illiteracy rate for young women in rural areas is typically two to three times higher than in urban areas. Furthermore, illiteracy rates among women over twenty-five years of age are characteristically twice or more those of young women aged fifteen to twenty-four.[1]

While some of the factors limiting women's access to education are structural (e.g., the need for subsistence agricultural labor in rural areas, better job prospects and wage rates for men, galling poverty in many parts of the world that renders education of either boys or girls a practical impossibility), significant barriers to the education of female children are attitudinal. Women and girls are routinely denied access to education out of fear of the impact of too much freedom for females, a preference for investing in sons, and traditional stereotypes that continue to raise questions about the usefulness of educating girls. Nevertheless, a significant body of research shows that when women and girls are given access to education, it is among the most effective of all means for raising the level of health, education, and prosperity for the entire population. As the Bahá'í International Community notes:

> For twenty-five years, the span of a generation, the data have been available to document the correlation between a variety of crucial development indicators and

the education of girls. From reductions in infant mortality, fertility, and the incidence of AIDS to improvements in the environment, it has been amply demonstrated that it is the mother's education that makes the difference and that the positive effects increase with every additional year a girl stays in school. When all the benefits are taken into account, educating girls yields a higher rate of return than any other investment that can be made in the developing world.[2]

The promotion of greater access to educational opportunities for women and girls would go far not only in reducing vulnerability to abuse and exploitation but also in bringing about fundamental improvements in the quality of life for everyone. There are three types of education: material, human, and spiritual.[3] Each of these forms of education plays a role in securing human development and well-being. In this chapter we explore the nature and role of material, human, and spiritual education in the global campaign to eradicate gender-based violence.

Material Education

Material education is concerned with knowledge that is necessary to safeguard and improve humanity's physical well-being and health. Material education thus concerns itself with nutrition and hygiene, the procurement of food and shelter, and the micromanagement of limited resources within the context of the family. Women and men who have access to material education are more likely to do a better job protecting themselves and their children from communicable diseases, are apt to understand and employ basic sanitary practices, are more likely to seek pre- and postnatal care when it is available, are more likely to take steps to protect against unwanted pregnancies, and are conversant with available remedies for common ailments.

The obvious benefit of material education is that it confers upon its recipients a greater number of healthy and productive years. For instance, in many parts of the world infant mortality has declined significantly over the last few decades—in large part owing to better control over major childhood and communicable diseases, widespread improvement in maternal health services, and greater access to nutrition. Thus when members of a village, community, or city have knowledge about the basic care of infants and children, as well as access to those resources necessary to apply this knowledge, the physical, emotional, and economic burdens upon all are significantly reduced.

Among adolescent girls, the greatest risks to reproductive health are sexually transmitted diseases (STDs), early childbearing, unwanted pregnancies, and unsafe abortion. A lack of knowledge and inadequate access to services to prevent unwanted pregnancies and to prevent and treat STDs thus result in compromised health for millions of teenage girls in both developing and developed nations.

The importance of material education is rendered particularly salient when data on deaths related to communicable diseases are disaggregated by region. For example, among women and men in developed areas, communicable diseases account for only 5 to 6 percent of all deaths. In sub-Saharan Africa, by contrast, 70 percent of female and male deaths are attributable to this single factor. While much of this disparity can be accounted for by differential access to effective treatments, a great deal of it is also the result of inadequate education of primary caregivers—most often women—in disease prevention.[4]

Human Education

Human education encompasses those systems of knowledge that are necessary to promote the development of civilization and that are essential to humankind as distinct from the animal world. Mathematics, the sciences and arts, commerce, government, and the humanities are among those areas of knowledge encompassed by human education. In many parts of the world, men have prevented women from participating fully and equally in the benefits conferred by exposure to such education. Thus the number of women who are given opportunities to cultivate their capacity to undertake high-level studies in governance, science, mathematics, engineering, theology, and philosophy is relatively low. Furthermore, when women are given access to higher education, major obstacles continue to prevent many from translating their high-level education into social and economic advancement.

For example, while women tend to be well represented in the health and teaching professions in many countries, hierarchical patterns of occupational segregation in these fields continue to lead to inequality between women and men at both the top and bottom levels. Indeed, as was pointed out recently by the United Nations, both the health and teaching professions have large numbers of positions at the bottom of the status and wage hierarchy, and these are the levels at which 90 percent of the women in these professions practice. "As salaries and prestige increase going up the hierarchy," noted the UN, "the number of positions decreases and men's participation increases."[5]

In the health sciences in the West, for example, women's roles have been traditionally limited to lower-paid levels of employment such as nursing, while men have enjoyed the higher-paid, higher-status positions such as physician and hospital administrator. In Eastern Europe, where communism led to rapid increases in the number of women who were given access to advanced training in the health professions, a different pattern emerged. As women began to fill the highest ranks within the health professions, these professions were increasingly devalued by the Communist governments, and men began to abandon them to pursue better opportunities with greater prestige. The result was that women continued their work in these fields "but under rapidly deteriorating conditions and declining status and pay."[6]

Similarly, in the teaching profession women are overrepresented at the elementary and secondary school levels, while men continue to occupy the highest ranks as university and college professors. This disparity remains even in those fields (such as psychology) in which the majority of students at all levels are women. Furthermore, with notable exceptions—such as the Caribbean (Trinidad and Tobago), Bulgaria, Jamaica, Mexico, Israel, Sri Lanka, Spain, Kuwait, and Qatar—the number of women in scientific and technical fields at the college and university level continues to be very low. A global campaign to promote the advancement of women in those fields necessary for the maintenance and development of civilization not only would lead to a substantial increase in the world's knowledge pool but also would give women the confidence and skills required for full and equal participation in reshaping the structures and processes of civilization as we embark upon a new millennium.

The international right of women and girls to education has been established in a number of UN documents. The 1979 Convention on the Elimination of All Forms of Discrimination against Women was the first legally binding instrument designed to secure this right. Prior to this, UNESCO (the United Nations Educational, Scientific and Cultural Organization), which was established in November 1945, affirmed in its preamble that "the education of humanity for justice and liberty and peace [is] indispensable . . . and constitute[s] a sacred duty which all the nations must fulfill." That body further called for "full and equal opportunities for education for all" and urged member states "to collaborate in developing educational activities and to advance the ideal of equality of educational opportunity without regard to race, sex, or any distinctions, economic or social."[7]

The responsibility of states to ensure access to education for all people is also affirmed in article 26 of the Universal Declaration, which states that "everyone has the right to education." Article 1 of the Declaration on Education "recalls that education is a fundamental right for all people, women and men of all ages" and that "every person—child, youth and adult—shall be able to benefit from educational opportunities designed to meet their basic needs."[8] The role of education is said to be the full development of the personality, as well as "strengthening respect for human rights and fundamental freedoms; promoting understanding, tolerance and friendship of all nations, racial or religious groups; furthering the activities of the United Nations for maintaining peace; and promoting respect for parents."[9]

Momentum toward ensuring equal access to education for women and girls has accelerated. As has been noted by Margaret Galey, education has emerged as an important theme of Human Rights Day, International Literacy Day, the International Day for Eliminating Racial Discrimination, International Women's Year (1975), the International Year for Human Rights (1968), the International Year of the Child (1979), the International Literacy Year (1990), the UN Decade for Women (1976–1985), and the recently ended UN Decade for Human Rights Education.[10] In addition, the number of world conferences convened specifically to address equality of access to education for women and girls has increased dramatically. These include the World Conference on Education for All, sponsored by UNESCO, the United Nations Development Programme, UNICEF, and the World Bank; the World Human Rights Conference, which stressed the need for equality of access to education; the International Conference on Population and Development; and the Children's Summit. All affirmed that education of women and girls is among the most important means of empowering women so that they can participate more fully in development and governance.

To be sure, one of the most important dimensions of the problem—yet to be addressed on either the national or the international level—is the crisis in public funding for education. In many technologically advanced nations, access to quality education continues to be dependent upon the wealth of parents and the wealth of the country or neighborhood where one happens to live; in rural settings, lack of access to books, basic computer resources, and adequate classroom space hampers the ability of teachers to provide the most rudimentary access to education for millions of students. This crisis has been chronicled in a number of books over the last two decades and should become as much of a part of the human rights movement as is the right to be free of various forms of violence.

Spiritual Education

As Hossain Danesh noted in his address to the International Symposium on Strategies for Creating the Violence-Free Family, spirituality may well be the most misunderstood and rejected aspect of human nature:

> Some equate spirituality with religiosity or emotionality. Some consider spirituality to be the equivalent of being superstitious or illogical, while others consider spirituality to be found in artistic expression alone. Still others consider anything beyond their comprehension to be spiritual. There are, of course, other perspectives as well. Spirituality does have some of the qualities found in these various definitions; yet, spirituality is a far more complex and comprehensive reality. In fact, spirituality is the core reality of being human. It refers to the human power of consciousness and our ever-present search for meaning and purpose. Spirituality connects the past, the present, and the future. It places our sense of mortality and immortality into a comprehensive framework and allows us to face death from the perspective of existence rather than annihilation. Spirituality connects us with the Source of all creation and, in the process, enables us to become creators ourselves. Spirituality makes it possible for us to be both unique and united, thus

removing, once for all, the dichotomous mindset that has brought and continues to bring such destruction and sorrow to the life of humanity. Spirituality is the force of transcendence and the source of transformation.[11]

Without tapping into the deep reservoir of humanity's spiritual potential, it would be impossible to transcend the past and to set in motion the processes necessary for bringing into being a new form of social order that is devoid of exploitation and violence. In this chapter, and throughout the chapters that follow, we explore the concept of spirituality, the nature and function of spiritual and moral education, and their role in the global campaign to eradicate gender-based violence.

The Concept of Spirituality

Awareness of, and concern for, the spiritual dimensions of existence is uniquely human. By this is meant that only humans concern themselves with the non-material aspects of life. On the most basic level, spiritual concerns are embodied in our attraction to that which is perceived to be good, beautiful, and true. We seek the good, not only because that which is good brings pleasant feelings, but also because it attracts us in the way that the gravitational pull of the earth attracts those things that belong to it. Indeed, we may pursue that which is thought to be good, even at considerable cost of comfort and personal well-being. We are attracted to the good because we belong to the good and cannot really be at peace unless we come to rest in it. As humans, we want our lives to be in harmony with the good; we generally want it said of us that we are reflections of the good; and when we are healthy and mature, we wish our days to be spent in promoting that which is good. Humanity's attraction to the good is embodied in the universal human concern for values.

Every society seeks to impart to its children its values, not only as a strategy for protecting the social order, but also because we believe that by adhering to values, the inherent potentiality of our children—that which is fundamentally good in them—will best be realized. Values are thus taught in every society as part of the humanizing process. Our concern for spirituality is thus a concern for those transcultural, transhistorical values that would redound to the fullest development of human potential. When we speak of the cultivation of spirituality, we are speaking, in part, of the creation of the moral context in which human development can most effectively take place.

In their materials designed to promote the cultivation of moral leadership, the University of Núr in Bolivia observed that in 1987, when the World Health Organization evaluated the effectiveness of the first decade of its global plan to provide "Health for All by the Year 2000," the evaluation concluded that the failure of the first decade of the plan was "not for lack of scientific knowledge, nor for lack of appropriate administrative models, nor for lack of financial resources, but rather for lack of moral leadership at all levels in the ministries of health throughout the world."[12] They went further to note that success proved impossible because of the absence of a moral leadership sufficiently committed to the values of social justice, equity, and participation that underlie the plan, the unavailability of a moral leadership sufficiently committed to sustained efforts in the struggle for bringing about the budgetary and structural changes required for setting up primary health care service systems for the most needy, and the lack of a moral leadership that was willing to assume the personal risks inherent in dealing with resistance to change. The university concluded that it is not often money or organizational competence, or even knowledge, that is lacking to better the world, but the necessary qualities of moral leadership.

According to the world's spiritual traditions, there are certain moral conditions without which human development is nearly impossible. Among the most important of these moral prerequisites are truthfulness and trustworthiness, compassion and love, a commitment to social justice and equity, purity of motive, and freedom from inordinate desire. Patience and perseverance would also seem to be critical, as would respect and consideration for duly constituted authority, and the ability to work and to strive in harmony with others. The cultivation of these social goods, or virtues, has been seen as important throughout the ages and across all civilizations. It is the eternality and cross-cultural nature of their importance to human life that lead us to regard virtues as spiritual qualities, without which human civilization is impossible.

A global program of spiritual education would seek to cultivate these social goods on local and international levels as part of a general scheme to increase human capital and capacity. The goal would be to assist humanity to recognize and apply the core spiritual truths that have animated all the world's major faiths and to use the virtues that arise in application of these truths as a fulcrum with which to raise the status of women and girls, as well as the general standard of community life across the planet.

In addition to a concern for the good, spirituality also expresses itself in the human concern for truth or knowledge. As has been noted by the moral theorists Nagouchi, Hanson, and Lample, an innate desire for knowledge motivates each human being to acquire an understanding of the mysteries of the universe and its diverse phenomena, both on the visible and invisible planes. An individual motivated by a thirst for knowledge, observed Nagouchi, Hanson, and Lample, approaches life as "an investigator of reality and a seeker after truth."[13]

While we agree with the postmodern observation that truth is always relative rather than absolute, we depart from postmodernist thinking in affirming that the relativity of truth results, not from its state, but from ours. In other words, truth is always relative to us because we necessarily approach it with the limitations of human consciousness, human maturation, and human needs and concerns. As human consciousness matures, and as our instruments for investigating reality advance, we naturally come to recognize that what we once regarded as true requires modification, and sometimes even outright rejection. In addition, as the number and diversity of truth seekers who are given voice expands, what we understand as truth must necessarily undergo change. Nevertheless, it is our striving to attain an apprehension of truth that has inspired both our scientific and our religious quests throughout the ages. The spiritual hunger for truth is reflected in our disdain for those who wittingly distort the truth for personal gain; it is reflected in our dissatisfaction with our own selves when we fail to be truthful; and it is manifested in the vast personal and collective resources that we expend in the search for truth as we explore the natural, social, and spiritual worlds.

Spirituality is manifested in our capacities of heart or feeling. These emotional capacities reflect themselves most potently in our longing for connection with other human beings, with our quest for union with God, and with our striving to surround ourselves with that which is beautiful. Indeed, it is an attraction to beauty—the beauty of an object, an idea, an act—that, in many cases, activates our will and motivates us to work and to strive so that we might be the creative authors of beauty or manifest beauty in the quality of our own lives. When we speak of spirituality, we are thus speaking, in part, of the heart's attraction to beauty. We are suggesting that when it is properly developed, the attraction to beauty may serve, not only as an aesthetic lens with which to view the world, but as a guiding light or standard whereby individuals may judge their own work and behavior. Attraction to beauty, noted Nagouchi, Hanson, and Lample, "manifests itself in love for the majesty and diversity of nature, the impulse to express beauty through visual arts, music and crafts, and the pleasure of beholding the fruits of these creative endeavors. It is also evident in one's response to the beauty of an idea, the elegance of a scientific theory, and the perfection of a good character in one's fellow human beings. On another level, attraction to beauty underlies the search for order and meaning in the universe, which extends itself to a desire for order in social relations."[14] We suggest that a program of spiritual and moral education will want to cultivate humanity's natural sensitivity to beauty, as the cultivation of such sensitivity may serve as an antidote to the vulgarity in interpersonal relationships that is so much a part of the violence and exploitation that we have chronicled in the foregoing chapters.

A spiritually informed process of moral development must also assist individuals to distinguish between superficial and lasting goals. This quality is necessary because the accomplishment of worthwhile objectives commonly requires self-sacrifice. Self-sacrifice is achievable when one's goals are aligned with that which is greater than one's self. Thus one is able to work for personal and collective improvements that are both meaningful and enduring. As we will discuss in the next chapter, the ability to sacrifice what is of lesser value for that which is of greater value is at the heart of all moral and spiritual development. Without this capacity, human progress, whether moral or material, is impossible.

A healthy process of education leads to the development of the spirit of service. The perfection of one's self naturally finds expression in efforts to serve others; and one's endeavor to serve others enhances the refinement of one's own capabilities. In this way, the motivation to contribute to an ever advancing civilization is not externally imposed; rather, it arises within the individual and is inextricably bound with opportunities for continued personal growth. In the words of Nagouchi, Hanson, and Lample, "Helping others and helping oneself become two aspects of one process; service unites the fulfillment of individual potential with the advancement of society and ensures the integrity of one's sense of moral purpose."[15]

Invocation of the need to foster a sense of individual moral responsibility for society invites discussion of the moral responsibilities that rest upon the social order as well. Indeed, any campaign designed to improve humanity's moral and spiritual condition that fails to address the social order is inadequate. For this reason, we turn briefly to a discussion of the social dimension of moral and spiritual development here and return to a fuller discussion of this theme in a subsequent chapter.

Spiritual Development and the Social Order

Any society or social group is determined by two things: first, the personal qualities of the individuals who make up the collectivity and, second, the formal structure of the group. Thus, any society = people (individuals) + structure. Social structures arise from implicit and explicit agreements, covenants and conventions according to which the collectivity is seen to have certain goals and certain norms. Goals determine the purposes of group activity, and norms establish the rules that govern group activity in the pursuit of group goals.

In particular, social structures define a certain number of roles or functions that an individual may play in the pursuit of group goals. Whenever an individual plays a specific role in the group, she must conform to the norms established by the group for that role; she is not free to perform the function according to her strictly personal proclivities alone. Also, simply being a member of the group is in itself a role, and there are (explicit or implicit) general group norms that apply to all group members. Thus, the total effect of group structures is to establish the group as a social organism having a collective personality (or group identity) and with the individuals as its cells. We suggest that just as individuals can possess moral and spiritual qualities and capabilities, so also can such qualities be embodied in institutions and in social structures. Indeed, the very process of imbuing institutions with moral qualities is one of the most important dimensions of human social evolution over time. On the collective level, the most important moral quality to be developed is justice.

Practically speaking, the existence of group structures and norms means that relationships within the context of a given group have at least three components: (1) a personal component in which two group members relate purely in terms of their personal identities, independently of group norms and goals; (2) a functional component in which two group members relate on the basis of their respective roles within the group; (3) a global component that derives from the relationship each group member has to the group as a whole.

As we will show in the chapter that follows, altruistic love and reciprocal friendship would be the natural moral basis of the purely personal component of a group relation. However, the functional and global aspects of group relations bring into play other principles, which are primarily related to the concept of social (rather than purely individual) justice. Social justice involves, on the one hand, *rights,* meaning that the group norms recognize what an individual is allowed to do in a given context, and, on the other hand, *obligations,* which determine what the individual is required to do in the given context. Social justice is established whenever both rights and obligations are respected and observed by everyone.

Of course, in any given case, and depending on the nature of group norms and goals, social justice may have either much or little to do with *authentic justice,* which we define as *the knowledge and implementation of what is appropriate to the satisfaction of legitimate human needs and the development of human spiritual potential.* A given social system therefore has a moral value that is greater or lesser depending on the degree to which the justice of the system approximates authentic justice. A social system that approximates authentic justice to a greater degree than another is said to be a "more just" system than the other. Thus, in the same way that we strive to approximate pure altruistic love in our individual relations, we should strive to have our social systems approximate pure justice to the greatest possible degree. A program of moral development that focuses on the cultivation of social institutions will thus be animated by a concern for authentic morality that has as its object the creation, maintenance, and evolution of authentic justice.

From the point of view of authentic morality, the worst possible social configuration is anarchy—the total absence of any social order whatever—because such a situation leads eventually (usually quite quickly) to rampant power seeking and the complete domination of the less powerful by the more powerful. Anarchy is, so to speak, a process of negative natural selection in which the very worst elements of society and of human nature come to the fore. For instance, anyone who tries to practice altruistic love in such a system will be quickly victimized, enslaved, or killed. She may maintain her own moral integrity, but her moral superiority will have no effect on the system itself, nor will it guarantee her physical survival.

In other words, order itself has a positive moral value, however imperfect a particular system may be when compared with other possible systems. However, once an order is established, it is the moral duty of every member of the society to strive to increase the justness of that order. We thus have a first principle of group relations: *In group relations, we should always act in such a way as to increase the justness of the group structure.*

The problem with this principle, in its present form, is that it has logical content but no substantive content. It does not tell us what are the features of a social order that may serve to render it more just than it is. This brings us to the question of the moral value of the purposes and norms of a society: what should be the goal of a society and how should a just goal be justly pursued?

The commonly received answer to this question in the West is that society exists primarily as a marketplace, as an arena for economic activity. Crudely put, the principle of a market society is that whatever helps the economy is good and whatever hinders it is bad. It then follows that if certain social norms and structures are painful or oppressive to a segment of the population (e.g., women, minorities, or citizens of another nation) but are nonetheless good for the economy, then the painful and oppressive features of the system must be endured. This degree of unjustness in the system represents "the price we pay" to have a healthy economy that will presumably be of more long-term benefit than a less healthy economy based on a more just system of norms and values.

In any event, the usual assumption is that there is an unavoidable, intrinsic opposition between the good of the individual and the good of society as a whole. A consequence of this view is that most social systems are seen as a compromise in which a certain degree of individual self-realization must be sacrificed for the establishment of the social order. Authentic morality rejects this conception and holds that the underlying purpose of any social order is, or should be, to create a social environment that maximizes the spiritual growth and development of each member of the society. In other words, in our view, the moral value of a social order is precisely measured by the degree to which it facilitates the development of human spiritual potential. From this perspective, all other social goals and purposes, including economic development, are secondary, though perhaps legitimate in themselves.

In general the evidence of history would suggest that social structures based on cooperation, mutuality, and universal reciprocity are favorable to individual spiritual development, while structures that encourage power seeking, conflict, and competition are unfavorable. Thus, the principle that guides us in the elaboration of social structures is unity: those social structures that favor an increase in unity and cooperation are good, and those that favor competition, power seeking, and conflict are bad. We have a moral duty to strive to replace bad or defective social structures with good or better ones.

However, the process of change must also be just, because otherwise conflict and anarchy will ensue and the ultimate result will be a worse system, however good the initial intentions of the reformers. There must be a harmony of means and ends: moral ends cannot be obtained by unjust means.

Authentic unity is a "unity in diversity" that respects and encourages all creative and legitimate differences, not a uniformity that seeks to suppress individual difference. Indeed, it is not individual differences themselves that lead to conflict and competition, but rather a lack of tolerance toward such differences, which betrays our underlying insecurity and leads to the will to dominate the other.

A somewhat subtle but crucial logical distinction must be made here. It is not social structures but individuals who compete, seek power, or engage in conflictual behavior toward each other. The very existence of morality and moral questions depends upon the existence of individual free will. Otherwise, we could not be held responsible for our actions any more than a computer could be blamed for executing its program. Thus, in the final analysis, all questions of morality pertain to the individual in one way or another.

However, it is equally clear that the moral quality (justness or unjustness) of social structures has a powerful influence on individual moral choice. In the context of an overwhelmingly negative social environment, a few moral heroes will undoubtedly persist in pursuing moral authenticity, but the vast majority will be dragged down by negative influences instead of rising above them. Thus, the (positive or negative) moral value of a social structure is measured ultimately by the influence it has on individual moral behavior. As we will endeavor to show in the next chapter, *the justness or unjustness of a social order is reflected in the degree to which that order is favorable or unfavorable to the flourishing of altruistic love between its individual members.*

So when we say, as we have above, that there is no intrinsic conflict between the authentic individual good and the authentic social good, we are saying that a just social order is possible. In other words, there exist social structures that encourage and permit, and in no wise discourage or limit, the flourishing of altruistic love between individuals. Such a social order will be characterized by authentic justice and authentic love. We are now ready to formulate our full principle governing the moral relationship between an individual and a social group: *With respect to society or a social group, we should always act so as to increase the authentic unity of the collectivity.* A program of moral and spiritual development that has as its focus a social organization will thus want to work to increase the institutional capacity for cultivating authentic unity among group members.

Though succinctly stated, this principle is pregnant with meaning. Recalling the three components of group relations (personal, functional, and global), it means that, with respect to personal relationships within the group, we continue to act on the principle of altruistic love, and with respect to the functional and global components, we act to increase the justness of the system. In particular, if the goals and norms of the group are morally legitimate (which does not mean they are perfect), then we will show our support for the society by respecting socially established rights and accomplishing our socially required duties, whether specifically with regard to our role within the group or generally with regard to our relationship with the group as a whole.

What if either the goals or the norms of a group are not morally legitimate? Then, of course, we should not be a member of such a group. Indeed, we should strive to have no relationship with it whatsoever.

What if we have no choice but to be a part of a morally illegitimate society? Then we must still act as best we can to increase the justness of the social order and show forth altruistic love in our personal relationships. However, while recognizing that such an unjust order may be morally preferable to anarchy, we cannot compromise our moral authenticity to satisfy truly immoral obligations such an order may impose upon us. We can of course try to avoid a situation that would require us to break openly with the established authority. Such avoidance action is not cowardice but wisdom and moderation in the pursuit of unity. But when and if such a situation is forced upon us (e.g., we are required by social authority to act cruelly or unjustly toward another), then we have no choice but to refuse and to accept the social consequences of such a refusal. We then become a true martyr (true because we have not actively sought to provoke the persecution heaped upon us).

Some moral philosophers have sincerely argued that the threat of extreme social sanctions, such as torture, unjust imprisonment, or death, changes the overall moral equation and thereby relieves the individual of all moral responsibility if he acts immorally when under this kind of duress. If, for example, I am threatened with death as a consequence of a refusal to act immorally on behalf of an unjust social authority, then why should I not preserve my life so as not to deprive my wife and children of my support? Maybe someone else will commit the immoral act anyway and I will have sacrificed my life for no good reason (except, some would say, my stubborn moral pride).

From the point of view of authentic morality, the fault in this argument can be clearly seen as soon as one reflects that the person who survives by deliberately perpetrating an act he knows and judges to be immoral is not the same as the person who existed before the act in question was committed. The *apparent* choice involved in the dilemma of "save your life by committing this one act under duress, or die without having really changed anything" is no choice at all. You literally *cannot* preserve the person you currently are if you consciously perpetrate an immoral act. As soon as the act is committed, the moral self regresses (at least temporarily) to a lesser self that survives in your place. Thus, the only real choice in such a situation is between the survival of the authentic, moral self and the temporary physical survival of the body (which will eventually die in any case).

Of course, it is one thing to engage in all of these abstract arguments and analyses and quite another to have the courage actually to make such a morally authentic choice when in extreme circumstances. Indeed, everyone agrees that the existence of social duress considerably diminishes moral responsibility (but without entirely eliminating it, as we have seen). In other words, there is certainly an objective moral difference between someone who perpetrates an immoral act for purely selfish ends under normal circumstances and one who perpetrates the same act only under extreme duress. But recognizing this difference does not change the objective truth of the moral equation that dictates that we cannot maintain the same level of moral authenticity while deliberately perpetrating a morally reprehensible act.

Most people live their lives without ever facing such dramatic dilemmas as having to choose between moral authenticity and the preservation of physical life. Nevertheless, all human beings are daily faced with moral choices of various magnitudes, and everyone's moral courage is tested sooner or later. For example, the simple act of willingly incurring the rejection and disapproval of one's friends rather than compromising one's moral principles can take immense courage, especially if one must continue to live daily in the same milieu or within the same social system as do the friends in question.

But more important, it is not sufficient for moral authenticity that we refrain from moral compromise and avoid thereby becoming a cause of disunity or injustice in our group relations. Authentic morality requires that we become proactive *unifiers*—that we actively and dynamically seek to facilitate a continual increase in the degree of unity of those morally legitimate groups of which we are members. Social participation is thus an important and irreplaceable aspect of the process of authentic moral development. The moral challenge of overcoming injustice and disunity in group relations presents unique opportunities for spiritual growth that do not occur within the context of purely individual, one-to-one relations. The global campaign to eradicate gender-based violence will have to nurture and draw upon the spiritual and moral powers that develop as a result of the struggle to be an instrument of social justice.

6

The Authenticity Project

The first author's early training is in experimental psychopathology. Experimental psychopathologists try to create in the laboratory, often using animals, conditions that mimic the onset and development of psychological disorders in humans. My particular interest is in the impact of exposure to uncontrollable experiences on human health and development. To expose an organism to an uncontrollable experience is to render it helpless; and to be helpless is to be in a condition wherein our actions do not influence what happens to us. In such circumstances the outcomes that we experience are under the control of arbitrary or random forces.[1] Over the last three decades a great deal of research has been done on the impact of helplessness on individuals and groups.

In a typical helplessness experiment, the *triadic design* is employed. This design enables researchers to expose one group of subjects to unpleasant controllable events, a second group of subjects to unpleasant uncontrollable events, and a third group to neither uncontrollable nor controllable events. What is illuminating about the triadic design is that the subjects that are in the first two conditions (the controllable and uncontrollable conditions) are exposed to exactly the same amount of the aversive experience (for example, a loud buzzing noise) for exactly the same amount of time. When the subjects in the controllable condition figure out what they can do to turn off the noise, the noise goes off for the subjects in the uncontrollable condition as well. We say that the subjects in this latter condition are *helpless* because there is nothing that they can do to stop the noise. Their destiny, with respect to the noise, is determined wholly by the actions of another.

At early stages of a helplessness experiment, the subjects in all conditions will do all that they can to figure out how to avoid or stop the noxious stimulus. Sometimes they must solve a puzzle, or run through a maze, or jump over a barrier in order to turn off or avoid the noxious stimulus. In the uncontrollable condition, subjects are exposed to situations in which it is impossible for them to solve the puzzle, make it through the maze, or get over a barrier, but they do not know that the experiment is designed for them to fail. When subjects in this condition come to realize that their actions do not have an effect, they stop acting and begin to suffer the noxious stimulus passively. We have seen helplessness deficits develop in a wide range of species—including rats, cats, goldfish, cockroaches, and humans—and thus we know that controllability is fundamental to life at all levels of existence.

Controllability is vital to so many species because it is connected with the more pervasive and fundamental law of cause and effect. The operation of the law of causality is the manifestation of the principle of justice in nature. Because of the operation of this law, the natural world is rendered orderly and predictable. It is this order and predictability that renders the natural world a place wherein organisms can develop their inherent capacities. For organisms that have the cognitive capacity to prefer that some effects be realized while others are avoided, causes and effects take on hedonic value and may be experienced as rewards and punishments. The expectation of reward and the fear of punishment are critical in fueling human development and are major pillars sustaining the social world. It is for this reason that when the laws of a nation are arbitrary, discriminatory, or not upheld, the social order becomes chaotic, and the processes of human individual and collective development are significantly arrested.

When women and girls are exposed to ongoing forms of injustice, the development of their inherent capacities and the subsequent development of the inherent capacities of all human beings are significantly thwarted. This is the reason why the advancement of women's civil and human rights, using the instrumentality of law, has been so vital to the global campaign to eradicate gender-based violence and discrimination. However, justice is more than a legal condition. It is at once a *social process,* a *human virtue,* and a *healthy community goal.* The development and maintenance of justice thus requires more than a body of laws and more than the institutional arrangements necessary to apply and administer those laws. It requires, as the early Greek and Chinese philosophers knew well, a process of citizen cultivation and the refinement of human character.

In its most primitive usage, law derives its power to protect against anarchy and against civil and human rights abuses by the force of threat it imposes upon would-be transgressors. In its more refined manifestation, law evokes a sense of appreciation for the "rightness" or "goodness" of the social reality it seeks to protect. In the latter case, laws are obeyed not so much out of a fear of punishment as out of an awareness of, and an attraction to, the ultimate meaning and purpose in life that the law seeks to embody and advance. As has been argued by Harold Berman, "Law itself, in all societies, encourages the belief in its own sanctity. It puts forward its claim to obedience in ways that appeal not only to the material, impersonal, finite, rational interests of the people who are asked to observe it but also to their faith in a truth, a justice, that transcends social utility."[2]

Where people fail to apprehend the transcendent dimensions of law, the social order is jeopardized because people obey the law only insofar as they believe that they will not be forced to suffer the consequences imposed upon those who transgress it. Since many forms of violence and abuse directed against women and girls are perpetrated under the cover of night or behind veils of secrecy and corruption, a wholly legalistic approach to eradicating gender-based violence is likely to prove inadequate. It is for this reason that we believe a discussion of the psychological, moral, and spiritual dimensions of society must play an ever increasing role in prevention models.

Out of a legitimate concern for preserving freedom of conscience, a number of contemporary thinkers have argued against efforts to introduce moral or spiritual considerations into development or human rights initiatives. Others object on the grounds that these are private matters and ought not to be imposed by agents acting on behalf of the state. Important as these concerns are, we endeavor here to share an approach to moral development that is grounded in those universal human values already endorsed, either explicitly or implicitly, by the global community. Among these values is respect for the dignity and worth of all persons, irrespective of race, gender, religion, or culture, as well as the fundamental right of all persons to live free from any unnecessary pain and to realize their inherent potentiality as human beings. These universally recognized values provide the "social glue" and institutional arrangements that render families, communities, and societies viable over long periods of time. Where appreciation of these values is neglected or the instruments necessary for their dissemination do not exist, a crucible for the cultivation of various forms of abuse and exploitation is created. This chapter examines, in some detail, a model of moral development and of authentic human relationships that has been articulated by the Authenticity Project.

Overview of the Ethics of the Authenticity Project

The International Moral Education Project, also known as the Authenticity Project, has developed materials that hold considerable promise for promoting a global approach to moral and spiritual development. Founded by the mathematician and philosopher William S. Hatcher, the Authenticity Project grounds its approach to moral development in the assumption that the highest values that a civilization can promote are the cultivation of human consciousness and the development of authentic human relationships (see appendix E for the project's mission statement and a list of current members).

Moral education, according to the Authenticity Project, is impossible without first understanding the nature of value. There are, the group affirms, two types of value: *intrinsic* value, which is inherent in the properties and capacities of an entity; and *extrinsic* value, which is ascribed to an entity through personal subjective preferences and social conventions. The value of money, for example, is largely extrinsic, as money derives its value from a community of people who agree to accept it in exchange for other goods that may be necessary for life. Whenever a community withdraws its recognition of the value of its currency, that currency becomes literally useless. Its value is thus *extrinsic* to its inherent qualities and nature. Those things that are of *intrinsic* value, by contrast, derive their value, not by social agreement, but from their inherent qualities, properties, and potentialities. The sun is of value, for example, irrespective of any individual's opinion about it. Its value is inherent in the fact that it provides essential light and warmth to our biosphere.

Similarly, the value of the human person is inherent in the facts that persons represent the most complex, refined, and evolved entity in nature and that the maintenance and advancement of civilization—in all of its forms—depends upon the cultivation of persons. The protection and development of this value is the supreme objective of any legitimate social order. According to the Authenticity Project, the legitimacy of any system of government or cultural practice can be evaluated with respect to the extent to which it promotes the development and expression of the inherent potentialities of individuals and of the body politic. By contrast, those practices and policies that unduly jeopardize the realization of the inherent potential of human beings are in violation of the human person's inalienable right to become. Such a system has betrayed its legitimate raison d'être. According to the Authenticity Project, true morality consists in apprehending the inherent value of the self and others and in living in relationship in such a way as to afford the development and expression of humanity's full potential. The principal signs of authenticity in relationships are said to be justice and the presence of love and altruism. Nonauthentic relationships, by contrast, are characterized by conflict, disharmony, manipulation, cruelty, jealousy, exploitation, and so forth. "Altruistic love," the group writes, "is not just a feeling of emotional warmth towards others, but is an objective, attractive force that operates according to certain objective laws and principles. Moral education means learning these laws and principles so that we become ever more subject to the force of love in our lives. Morality, then, is *the pursuit of authentic relationships* or, stated more fully, *the process of developing our innate capacity to sustain authentic relationships.*"[3]

Inasmuch as the acquisition of the capacity for authentic morality requires continual, often painful self-evaluation, a number of strategies have been developed throughout history to transform basic morality into something that can be more easily achieved. For example, although one of the overarching goals of religion is to facilitate the achievement of authentic moral relationships, this goal is frequently transmuted in such a way that religion becomes primarily an ideology. When a religion becomes an ideology, its doctrines become the supreme value, and morality is conceived as their protection and propagation by all possible means. The error of ideologized religion, according to the Authenticity Project, lies not in seeking to propagate and advance certain doctrines but rather in exalting these doctrines above authentic relationships, thereby interchanging means and ends. As it is with ideology, culture-specific values and traditions are also frequently invoked in support of the continuation of practices that may be harmful to the equal participation, development, and/or well-being of subgroups such as women and girls within a culture. The continuation of such practices is inspired by the belief that cultural values are the only ultimate values and that these values are necessarily local and accidental, rather than intrinsic and universal. Inasmuch as this perspective renders all cultural values fundamentally equivalent, the argument is that each cultural group must be left free from outside interference in deciding the values that should animate community life.

Legitimate as is the concern for preserving a people's right to determine the nature and course of their own lives, the work of the Authenticity Project assumes that there are also intrinsic, universal values that derive from the universal nature and needs of all human beings—irrespective of race, culture, or historical time period. The global community is said to have a moral responsibility to safeguard these values, even when the parties concerned would prefer to operate free from external influence. To do otherwise would be to render the preservation of culture the supreme value, irrespective of the impact of culture-specific practices on the lives of human beings. The articulation of an international body of laws designed to preserve human rights is an explicit rejection of the assumption of absolute cultural relativity by the community of nations. At the same time, inasmuch as the adoption of a universal set of moral values on the local level is not likely to be realized unless large segments of the population are persuaded of their logic and necessity, the promotion of such values depends upon processes of education and persuasion. The Authenticity Project thus articulates its moral framework in such a way that the logic that it embodies is understandable and the moral capacities and skills that it seeks to impart can be acquired by those who are sincere in the desire to attain higher levels of moral development.

Basic Framework of the
International Moral Education Project

According to the Authenticity Project, everyone begins the journey of life from the same initial position: total unawareness and absolute unconsciousness. It is only after several years of life experience that humans slowly emerge from unawareness to awareness. The state of unawareness that characterizes the beginning stages of life is described as a *paradise of innocence*, in which all our needs are satisfied without any effort on our part. We are said to be unaware of our existence and unaware of the law of cause and effect by which autonomous individuals are able to act to satisfy their own needs and those of others. However, with the development of autonomy comes an increasing understanding of the law of causality. That is, we come to appreciate that certain actions on our part will lead to positive and productive consequences and that other actions, under the same conditions, will lead to negative and destructive consequences.

This understanding of the law of cause and effect, notes the Authenticity Project, is the "knowledge of good and evil" spoken of in the Book of Genesis in the Bible. Indeed, the Bible describes a mythical paradise of Eden as the beginning point for the human race as a whole. In Eden, as for the individual in the womb, all the needs of Adam and Eve were satisfied without any effort on their part. Their expulsion from Eden, the group affirms, is clearly a symbolic account of their awakening to self-awareness (e.g., that they were naked) and their confrontation with the law of causality. Moreover, just as Adam and Eve must face a world of pain outside their paradise, so each human being, once expelled from the blissful conditions of the mother's womb, must face a world filled with suffering that is both potential and real.

As we acquire greater autonomy in childhood and adolescence, we also increase our awareness of just how much pain and suffering this world can inflict on even the most fortunate of human beings. In the face of this realization, we may naturally have moments when we long to return to the Edenic paradise of ease and innocence. But of course to return to that paradise would be to lose our growing autonomy and independence, our mature sexual, intellectual, and physical powers.

We therefore conceive of a second, *adolescent paradise,* one where we have total freedom to act as we please—to seek gratification of all our desires and to indulge all our passions—but without there being any negative consequences. It is thus a paradise of complete freedom and total irresponsibility. Inasmuch as the very law of causality that allows us to gratify our desires or fulfill our needs also dictates that we will suffer whenever we seek such gratification or need fulfillment in an illegitimate manner, such a paradise does not, and cannot, exist. The more irresponsible our use of our freedom, the more suffering we bring upon our selves and others.

Misuse of freedom, according to the Authenticity Project, also incurs a decrease in autonomy. This loss of autonomy is experienced in the form of various unnatural dependencies or addictions, which render us prey to impulses that we find difficult or even impossible to resist. In the end, we may feel that we "cannot live" without continual sexual gratification, or drugs or alcohol, or the constant approval of others. In this way does the abuse of freedom lead to loss of freedom. Moreover, the satisfaction experienced from these temporary gratifications actually diminishes, even as we pursue them more desperately.

The only escape from this vicious cycle of the increasingly desperate pursuit of a steadily diminishing gratification is to replace it by a virtuous cycle of increasing self-mastery. The first stage of this virtuous cycle, according to the Authenticity Project, is to increase our autonomy (self-development) by gaining true and accurate knowledge of the moral law of cause and effect. We must truly understand what are the short- and long-term consequences of acting, thinking, and feeling in a certain manner. Once this knowledge is achieved, we then feel attracted to the goal of acting rightly, because we now know that this is what will produce our true happiness. This attraction to righteousness is the "love of the truth" so often spoken of in the holy scriptures of all religions.

This love of the truth, along with the "thirst after righteousness," gives us the energy to maintain a sustained motivation or intention to act in accordance with our (increasing) knowledge of the law of causality. Though we may not always act in accordance with our knowledge, the very striving to do so gradually produces an inner development—an inner freedom. This inner freedom is the hallmark of the autonomy that is the goal of moral development. Moreover, as a result of this pure striving, we gradually overcome our previously "uncontrollable" impulses and gain the power to act in conformity with the law of causality and thereby satisfy our needs in a legitimate manner. This legitimate satisfaction of our needs, both spiritual and material, results in genuine and enduring happiness.

There is thus a third paradise, the *paradise of autonomy and responsibility*. This paradise is attainable, and it brings a true and enduring happiness. By gaining accurate knowledge of the law of causality and then developing the inner freedom to act on the basis of this knowledge and in conformity with this law, we are able to satisfy all of our true and healthy needs in a legitimate manner. Moreover, to enter the paradise of autonomous responsibility, we do not have to renounce any of our mature capacities. We only have to learn to use them properly.

Thus, according to the Authenticity Project, the process of moral development is the journey from the irrational and untenable paradise of irresponsible freedom to the lasting and attainable paradise of responsible autonomy. The hallmark and end of this journey is said to be the capacity to sustain authentic human relationships that are characterized by the presence of love and justice.

According to the Authenticity Project, any two human beings (such as a husband and wife, an employer and an employee) have a deep need to relate authentically to each other. An authentic relationship becomes possible as soon as we have each recognized the intrinsic value of the other. This intrinsic value is embodied in the human personality, self, or soul and is expressed in each person's inherent capacities of knowing, loving, and willing. Mutual recognition of intrinsic value enables us to relate in a way that permits each of us to give priority to the legitimate needs of the other rather than to our own needs (whether legitimate or otherwise). Thus, the trademark of relational authenticity is sincere, unselfish love. Such altruistic love makes the other the *end* or *goal* of the relationship. That is, it honors the other as a human being (rather than as a mere instrument for the realization of our personal desires) and thus as a representative of the highest value in creation.

Whenever we give priority, however subtly, to our own (perceived) needs over the needs of the other in a relationship, this kind of relating is a manifestation of egotism and negates authenticity. In extreme forms it gives rise to manipulation, exploitation, competition, and the mutual search for dominance. In a nonauthentic relationship we each seek power—the power to compel the other to satisfy our needs. Thus, authentic relationships are said to be based on love and nonauthentic relationships on power.

The process of relating authentically is an *authentic dialogue* in which we exchange ideas (seek truth together), share emotions, and work collaboratively. Thus, whatever we bring to such a dialogue is used to establish an increasingly authentic relationship. When we relate nonauthentically, we bring only our needs, and the other becomes a means to their satisfaction. Hence, the pursuit of a nonauthentic relationship leads not only to the passive negation of authenticity but also to its active reversal: what was the end has now become the means to a lesser end.

We express our love for others by seeking to satisfy their legitimate needs because this helps develop their inherent potential (as well as our own). But this supposes that we have at least some ability to distinguish between legitimate (or proper) needs and unreasonably selfish desires. The knowledge and implementation of what is appropriate for the development of human potential is *justice.* Justice and love, according to the Authenticity Project, go together: love provides the motivation to serve the other, and justice provides the knowledge necessary for the proper and efficient implementation of this motivation.

Thus, authentic relationships involve not only sincere love for the spiritual reality of others but also valid knowledge of that reality. When love and justice express themselves in action, then we have all that is necessary for successful, ethically sound, and authentic dialogue. These conditions are those that characterize a state of interpersonal unity. The fundamental moral principle governing the interaction between the self and another individual human is, in the view of the Authenticity Project, articulated in the following way: *In relation to another human being, we should always strive to act in such a manner as to increase the actuality and potentiality of altruistic love.*

Such a principle suggests that we must consciously evaluate our actions and attitudes toward others according to whether such actions and attitudes are favorable or unfavorable to an increase in altruistic love. This evaluation of actions and attitudes is ongoing. It precedes a given action and is then applied again in a retroactive consideration of the actual consequences of the action. Both pre- and postevaluation of our actions are necessary. The preevaluation tends to assure that our motives and intentions are pure. However, we must realize that the human condition is such that we may fail in a given instance even if our intention was sincere. In such a case, it is not enough to say that we have sincerely tried and that is all one can expect of us. If we truly desire unity and harmony in our relationships, then we must correct our actions and attitudes until such harmony is actually achieved. We are not looking for (even legitimate) excuses for our failures. Rather, we are striving for genuine success.

But what if our postevaluation leads us to believe that failure truly is the fault of the other? To answer this question, the Authenticity Project invites a somewhat deeper examination into the essential nature of human relationships.

Love, Power, and Justice

As has been suggested, the Authenticity Project regards altruistic love as the fundamental principle of human relations. It further holds that this principle is implemented on the basis of an accurate perception and knowledge of the inherent value of ourselves and others. Human love has both an active and a passive component. The *passive* component of love expresses itself in our total acceptance of the other, without prejudgment or preconditions. The *active* component is our vital and proactive concern for the welfare of the other. Thus *love is acceptance plus concern.*

Though it may seem difficult to conceive at first, the two components of love are quite independent of each other. This is due to the extreme flexibility of human nature. Acceptance without concern is what is usually called *tolerance,* while concern without acceptance is *conditional love.* Tolerance occurs when we renounce the desire to change, convert, or dominate the other but have not yet developed the capacity to work actively for the improvement of his or her well-being. Conditional love means that, while we have recognized the spiritual potential of the other and are concerned for the development of that potential, we have not yet reconciled ourselves to what we perceive as his or her limitations.

Authentic love involves both components and is the goal toward which we are striving, but we can nevertheless appreciate the fact that any degree of love is better than its absence. On the one hand, tolerance is better than rejection or hatred, and in many situations of social conflict, the establishment of genuine tolerance is recognized by all as a significant achievement. On the other hand, parental love can sometimes be conditional. The mother and father may be sincerely concerned with improving the welfare of the child, and indeed may make many sacrifices to that end, but they may be unable to accept the child's limitations (perhaps because they perceive the child as an extension of themselves and thus the child's limitations as a reflection of their own).

Of course, there remains a fundamental problem. Given the fact that, for the most part, human relations are currently based on selfish interests rather than altruistic love, how are we to move from the present configuration to the intended one? This is the true problem of moral development. The Authenticity Project thus addresses the question of why selfishness and power seeking seem to predominate over love in human relationships.

One answer often given to this question is that we humans are intrinsically selfish and aggressive and we literally cannot be otherwise. Indeed, a number of materialist philosophers and scientists have actively propagated the view that we are genetically programmed to be selfish and aggressive, and that the best we can do in the face of this "fact" is to arrange our society so that the inevitable discharge of our ego-aggressive drives and impulses does the least possible social damage. The many historical examples of intraspecific aggression and human cruelty are frequently adduced as conclusive evidence of the thesis that humans are inherently and ineradicably selfish and aggressive. From this point of view, true altruism does not and cannot exist, and attempts to implement altruistic love as the basis of human relationships are doomed to failure.

Refuting this pessimistic view of human nature is easy once one understands clearly what the thesis really asserts. In the first place, no one doubts that humans are capable of the most extreme cruelty and aggression toward each other, as is proved conclusively by a mere glance at history or current events. What the materialistic thesis asserts is that humans are incapable of anything else (though aggressive motives may be sometimes cleverly disguised as sincere concern for others). However, the same history that is so replete with evil is also replete with examples of genuine altruism and self-sacrifice.

One powerful example is that of the Roman senator who, upon conversion to Christianity, deliberately sold himself into slavery to replace and thus free from slavery the only son of a (non-Christian) widow. Such a clear act of deliberate self-sacrifice cannot be reasonably interpreted as disguised selfishness or aggression. Beside this and similar dramatic examples (e.g., the example of the sacrifices of Martin Luther King Jr., Nelson Mandela, Mother Teresa, Mohatmas Gandhi, and so forth), there are such perennial examples as the daily sacrifices of mothers for their children in all cultures all over the world.

Indeed, some anthropologists, including Richard Leakey, have pointed out that the capacity for social cooperation and mutuality was the dominant factor —much more important than intelligence—in enabling early humans to survive and prevail against animal competitors that were physically superior to humans in every conceivable respect: strength, acuity of perception, fleetness of foot. Furthermore, Leakey points out, the operation of natural selection would take only a few generations to destroy any species that was genetically programmed for intraspecific aggression. One can hardly imagine a more negatively selective gene than one that predisposes those who carry it to destroy or be destroyed by all others who carry it. Thus, if there ever was such a species, it has long since disappeared from the earth, and it is certainly not, therefore, the human species.

The evidence of history has led the Authenticity Project to another basic principle of its program of moral development: *the human being is capable of both extreme cruelty and extreme altruism,* and thus any satisfactory theory of human nature and behavior will have to account for both these capacities. Since the materialistic thesis does not do this, it has been rejected by the Authenticity Project as unscientific (it does not explain the facts of human existence). How then can one explain the frequency and extent of conflict and aggression in human history?

One comprehensive answer to this question is to consider our history as a collective growth process, analogous to the process by which an individual gradually attains maturity by passing through successive stages of development. Humankind is currently experiencing its collective adolescence, the stage immediately preceding adulthood or maturity. Viewed in this light, our past is the history of our collective childhood.

For the individual, childhood is the period when one moves from a position of total weakness, dependency, and vulnerability to a position of relative strength and independence. The individual experiences this process as an accretion of power, and he may easily become preoccupied with the process of *acquiring* greater and greater power rather than the process of learning to use his power appropriately: gradually and subtly, the pursuit of power becomes the focus of his life.

In a similar manner, the collective childhood of humanity has been characterized by the pursuit of power, and this pursuit is the root cause of the prevalence of conflict and injustice in human history. Indeed, we inherit a history of injustice in which the strong have consistently dominated the weak: men have dominated women, more powerful tribes and nations have conquered and enslaved weaker ones, war has predominated over peace, physical and military power have predominated over intellectual prowess and social harmony.

Notice that what is deemed the cause of injustice is the *seeking* of power, not power itself. Without power we can do nothing, neither good nor evil. The error lies in pursuing power for its own sake—making power the end rather than the means of pursuing moral and socially productive ends. Indeed, each of us possesses a certain degree of power, but to use that power to establish our dominance over others is a moral and spiritual error. To pursue power is to misuse power.

We may of course misuse power without pursuing it. For example, we may harm someone by the exercise of our power even though we sincerely intend to do good (e.g., a surgeon who sincerely tries to heal but makes a professional mistake). Such misuses of power are an inevitable part of learning how to use power appropriately. But the pursuit of power for its own sake is always wrong, because the very intention is itself immoral, regardless of the external consequences.

This raises the question of the appropriate use of power. More specifically, inasmuch as power cannot command or create love, and inasmuch as love is the ultimate and legitimate object of human striving, it is reasonable to ask about the moral use of power. In particular, it is reasonable to ask how the exercise of power can serve the pursuit of altruistic love. The answer given by the Authenticity Project is that power can be used to create and establish justice. Once established, justice provides the conditions under which love can flourish. Thus, the moral use of power, in the view of the Authenticity Project, is the pursuit of justice.

According to the Authenticity Project, an act of injustice opens up three potential responses from the offended party. The first is to seek revenge; the person may use her power to make the offender suffer in the same way that she has been made to suffer. This is referred to as a "power response," and it is one that often appears the most natural to us given the history of power seeking we all inherit. Indeed, the power response is so spontaneous that it usually takes considerable self-insight and self-control to avoid it.

The second response is to do nothing, to suffer the injustice in silence. The offended party then becomes a victim, either because he is too weak to do otherwise or because he is too afraid to use what power he has to seek revenge. This is the "victim response."

The third response is to seek justice. This response can take a number of forms. On one end of the spectrum is the possibility of confronting the injustice and denouncing it openly. The other extreme is to oppose the injustice with active love. All of the subtle combinations of love and justice between these two extremes leave room for immense personal creativity in dealing with injustice. The third response to injustice is thus the "unity response," because it involves an appropriate combination of love and justice.

Once we have clearly understood what is involved, virtually every personal encounter with another, whether initially positive or negative, provides us opportunity for an original and creative response, a response that will take us a step forward in our moral development. However, we need some principle that will allow us to determine whether the unity response in a given situation should be more weighted in favor of justice or in favor of love. The Bahá'í philosopher, 'Abdu'l-Bahá, has provided the Authenticity Project with such a criterion:

> O ye beloved of the Lord! The Kingdom of God is founded upon equity and justice, and also upon mercy, compassion, and kindness to every living soul. Strive ye then with all your heart to treat compassionately all humankind—except for those who have some selfish, private motive, or some disease of the soul. Kindness cannot be shown the tyrant, the deceiver, or the thief, because, far from awakening them to the error of their ways, it maketh them to continue in their perversity as before. No matter how much kindliness ye may expend upon the liar, he will but lie the more, for he believeth you to be deceived, while ye understand him too well, and only remain silent out of your extreme compassion.[4]

In the perspective of the Authenticity Project, and according to the above criterion, our response to individual evil should be governed not so much by the degree of injustice perpetrated against us, or even by the other's active intention to harm, as by the educative effectiveness of our response. We must respond in a manner that maximizes the likelihood that the perpetrator (and others involved) will gain effective insight into the nature of his own moral condition.

According to the moral tradition initiated by the teachings of Jesus Christ, and reaffirmed by later philosophers and moral teachers, it would seem that in the majority of cases our response should be to oppose active love to provocative injustice. However, in cases that involve a deliberate attempt to deceive or manipulate others, confrontation and denunciation may be morally necessary. Also, if the unjust act of the other is directed not at us but at an innocent and weaker third party, then the moral equation changes. We can choose for ourselves to return good for evil, but we cannot impose our personal choice on others. Our moral duty to protect the innocent may thus require us to respond with justice when we would have chosen mercy had only we ourselves been the object of the unjust act.

Clearly, we may not know in the beginning whether we are dealing with a person who is a deceiver. Thus, a reasonable strategy seems to be to respond initially with kindness and compassion. If further encounters with the individual give us hard evidence or clear indications of an intent to deceive, we can then generate a response more weighted in favor of justice. But if we allow the "justice response" to become the habitual first response to any aggressive behavior on the part of others, then we will miss many occasions for our own spiritual development, and we will probably slip easily into the power response under the guise of seeking justice.

In the perspective of the ethics of authenticity, what renders the power response unjust, what renders it inappropriate for the offended to seek revenge for an undeserved hurt, is that revenge simply perpetrates another injustice in response to the initial one. Compounding injustice with another injustice will not reduce the incidence of injustice in the world, but increase it. The revenge response perpetuates a spiral of action and reaction that can continue for a lifetime, for generations, for centuries, for millennia (as has indeed happened in history).

The point is that *we cannot change or undo the past.* We can only change the future by acting, in the present, in a manner different from the past. Nothing can be clearer than the fact that if we continue to act today as we have acted until now, our future will simply be a continuation of our past. The revenge response, notes the Authenticity Project, seeks to undo the past by returning to an "even" situation in which we each have the same moral balance sheet toward the other. But this is simply impossible. If, for example, you have injured my pet dog, how can we say that for me now to perpetrate a similar act toward you will restore the balance? How can the pain you have caused me be measured or compensated by the pain I would then cause you?

Perhaps, for example, I am much more attached to my pet than you are to yours. What then? How much damage must I do to be certain of causing the same degree of pain you have caused me? I will have to examine your life, seek out your attachments and weak points, and deliberately perpetrate an act that causes you sufficient pain. But what if I overshoot the mark? In that case I now have a "pain debt" toward you.

Of course, in reality a revenge seeker never attempts to make such fine calculations. She simply maximizes the damage done in retaliation, in order to "show" the other that she is a force to be reckoned with. But, as we have seen, this only evokes a maximum response in further retaliation, and the spiral continues.

The justice response recognizes and accepts the fact that, however grievous the injustice initially perpetrated, the past cannot be undone. Rather, the justice response seeks to change what can really be changed, namely, the future. *Specifically, our personal response to an injustice committed against us by an individual seeks to maximize the likelihood that the individual in question (and/or others) will acquire a sincere motivation not to repeat the injustice in the future.* In some instances this is best done by confronting and denouncing the injustice, perhaps seeking social sanctions for the act. In other instances a response of active kindness on our part will more easily awaken the person to his moral condition.

The Authenticity Project embraces the foregoing view because the only thing that can produce long-term changes of behavior and attitudes in human adults is self-motivation. Indeed, the project notes that whereas the behavior of children can be changed through an appropriate combination of reward and punishment, adult behavior changes only when, as a result of certain life experiences, the adult acquires a sincere determination to change. The key to improving adult–adult relationships thus lies in our understanding that only we have ultimate control over our own behavior and that we have very little control over the behavior of other adults. This means that *the surest way to change a one-to-one relationship is to change our behavior in the relationship.*

This principle is more particularly true when it comes to long-term, intimate relationships. Suppose, for example, that you have a difficult, complicated relationship with your spouse. There is clearly mutual love, but, over the years, you have established a relational pattern in which you each have ways of "getting" the other. Whenever your spouse acts in such a manner, your response is to protest, "Why do you always have to do this [e.g., treat me like I was still a child, embarrass me in front of my friends, give me unwanted advice]?" And your spouse's most likely response will be to say that if you resent his obvious expressions of love and concern, then perhaps you do not really love and appreciate him as you should.

In overcoming such entrenched patterns, the Authenticity Project encourages realization of the fact that long-term relationships have a history in which each party seeks a certain "payoff" or outcome from his behavior. For example, it may be that the very reason your spouse treats you like a child is so that you will protest and then he can make you feel guilty about lacking appropriate love and appreciation.

In such a case, the most effective way to break the unhealthy pattern is for you to generate a *paradoxical response*. If you act completely differently from the past and fail to give the anticipated or expected response, then your spouse will be forced to act differently. If, to take a simple example, you do not protest but thank her for (unwanted) advice (not hypocritically, but because you truly appreciate the motivation behind it), then she can hardly criticize you for being unappreciative. She will be confronted with a new situation where, in any case, she *cannot* continue to act as in the past because the necessary behavior on your part is no longer present.

Thus, when a moral teacher such as 'Abdu'l-Bahá counsels us, for example, to "show forth abounding love" in return for "curses, taunts and wounding words," he is not telling us to become naïve victims of others' injustice. He is rather giving us the key to an appropriate response that will break entrenched patterns of injustice, establish new patterns of mutual harmony, and lead ultimately to our enduring happiness and well-being.

The bitter experience of continual conflict in our history should, at the very least, make us willing to try 'Abdu'l-Bahá's approach. After all, if we try it and don't like it, we can always return to the daily round of mutual criticism, struggle, and unhappiness to which we are already accustomed.

There is no doubt that generating the appropriate unity response in human relations takes considerable moral courage. For example, if our response to a particular act of injustice toward us is weighted in favor of mercy and kindness, others may well perceive us as weak and helpless victims. We may then be goaded into a power response because we feel it will elicit the approval of others, who tell us we have a "right" to seek revenge. Only our emerging moral autonomy will allow us to disregard such social pressures and to act in a deliberate manner according to principles we have freely chosen.

An alternative to the revenge variation of the power response is the "blame response." We claim we are ready to forgive and forget the past *provided* the other is willing to acknowledge the unjustness of his actions and ask our forgiveness. This may at first appear to be a love response, but it clearly contradicts the principle that we show to others "the utmost loving-kindness, disregarding the degree of their capacity, never asking whether they deserve to be loved."[5] After all, it is easy to love the lovable or the sincerely contrite; loving the unlovable is the real moral challenge. Indeed, it is in striving to generate a love response to injustice that we grow most toward moral autonomy and authenticity, which constitute the fundamental goal of our moral striving in the first place.

In any case, a love that sets preconditions is not altruistic love, because altruistic love is unconditional by its very nature. Our conditional love, though better than seeking revenge, is still an attempt to gain power over the other by forcing him to acknowledge our moral superiority. (In some instances it may even turn out that an unconditional-love response on our part was a crucial factor in finally leading the other to acknowledge his injustice.) More generally, the blame response is a power response because it still looks to the past, requiring that some sort of retro-corrective action take place as a precondition for changing the relationship. The true love response looks only to the future. No matter what the history of a relationship may be—no matter how fraught with injustice—the individuals involved are free to choose, *at any moment*, to change the future history of their relationship by acting differently toward one another.

Given the object of our discourse, it is reasonable to ask about the response that should attend a relationship characterized by physical and/or psychological violence. As we will discuss in the chapter that follows, researchers have recently described the *cycle of feeling avoidance* that often fuels the abuser's cycle of violence. Abusers in battering relationships typically experience feelings that overwhelm their perceived coping capacities, and a crisis ensues. The feelings that may precipitate the crisis include such feelings as shame, hurt, helplessness, fear, guilt, inadequacy, loneliness, weakness, incompetence, or failure. Inasmuch as these feelings are painful, ego-dystonic, and unacceptable, they generate a counterfeeling of defense. Defensive feelings may include blame and denial; making the other the enemy that must be attacked; asserting control over others; using alcohol, sex, or drugs to blunt awareness; or other kinds of escape that substitute for feeling and provide temporary relief in the short run.

Inasmuch as short-term relief reinforces the use of these defensive strategies, they are used more frequently and may become part of the abuser's personality style. Since they are not very effective for solving problems, they actually lead to increased difficulties in the relationship and an increased need to use them. Early in the relationship the abuser may feel genuine remorse because he wishes that he had responded differently; but because he lacks emotional skills, his response repertoire is limited to the strategies already used.

In this cycle of behavior, what the abused partner does or does not do has proven to be largely irrelevant. Whether she is forgiving, passive, resistant to the abuser, or placating does not appear to matter in whether she is likely to experience abuse. The abuser is in a cycle of his own construction that is usually broken only when an outside force that is more powerful than the abuser is brought to bear. Furthermore, while an abuser may be violent only in intimate relationships, he is usually controlling and abusive in other relationships as well because he lacks the emotional maturity that is required to be otherwise. It is this cycle of escaping one's own emotional insecurities by being abusive that often fuels the cycle of violence perpetrated by the batterer.

In such situations, the response that is the most productive of development is one in which the victim of abuse no longer makes herself available as a scapegoat for the abuser's moral failure. Inasmuch as a willingness to see one's self and to reflect upon one's own actions is an absolute precondition for moral growth and relational authenticity, the cycle of violence and victim blaming that often accompanies physical abuse renders such self-evaluation extremely unlikely. In these situations the relationship must be terminated unless and until there are clear and unequivocal signs that the abuser has chosen to relate to self and others in a wholly new mode.

To sum up the perspective of the Authenticity Project, thus far it has been affirmed that we inherit a history of power-seeking behavior that has created injustice and thereby reduced both the actuality and the potentiality of altruistic love in human relationships. The project affirms that we must reverse this pyramid and deliberately seek altruistic love instead of power, and that we can do this by using our power to establish justice. Once established, justice provides the conditions under which altruistic love can flourish and endure. In the past, we have sought power and sacrificed justice, and thus love, in the process. The challenge we face today is to seek unity (love and justice) and sacrifice (use) power in the process.

Thus, in the view of the Authenticity Project, *the conscious renunciation of the pursuit of power* is the key to establishing altruistic love in our relationships with others. Every time we are confronted with a situation in which we are tempted to generate a power response (or a victim response), we must strive instead to generate a unity response. The resistance we may feel to abandoning the pursuit of power is a measure of how deeply power seeking has become entrenched in our individual and collective psyche.

By its nature, power seeking creates asymmetrical relationships between people. I cannot have power and dominance over you at the same time and in the same way that you have power and dominance over me. This asymmetry leads to relational conflict. If you and I are each seeking power over the other in our interactions, then fundamentally we will be striving against each other, for we will each realize (perhaps instinctively or unconsciously) that only one of us can be successful. In the power game there are winners and losers, and this means that somebody will be unhappy in almost every interaction, because the loser's feelings of oppression and domination are experienced negatively by all human beings. Moreover, no one will be a winner in all situations, and winning itself is no protection against unhappiness: the consistent winner will be subject to increasing fear at the anticipation of possible future losses, and he will become the object of envy, jealousy, and periodic sabotage attempts on the part of others.

Thus, the relational asymmetry created by power seeking is the very antithesis of the relational authenticity that is the proper goal of true moral striving. The mark of authentic relationships is altruistic love, which leads to reciprocity, mutuality, and symmetry, not to asymmetry and dominance. Moreover, in a relationship based on authentic love, both parties experience positive feelings, for it is the nature of love that it benefits both giver and receiver. Love is the prototypical "win-win" relationship in which everyone is happy.

The pursuit of authenticity and love leads, therefore, to enduring happiness, whereas the pursuit of power is literally the pursuit of our own unhappiness. Yet, if we accept, albeit unconsciously, the collectivist notion of value, then we have no choice but to seek our value through the acquisition of power and status in society, because the only alternative is (so we think) the nonbeing of worthlessness, which no one can accept.

It is a fundamental truth of human nature that our actions and motivations are determined not by reality but by our perception of reality. Thus, even though it is objectively true that we each have an inalienable intrinsic value, if we are unaware of this truth, then we will act as if we do not have this value. It is only knowledge and awareness of our intrinsic value that enables us to develop the inner strength necessary to renounce the pursuit of power. If we feel that all value is solely a function of "social permission," we will never have the strength and courage needed for the kind of moral transformation called for here.

The Authenticity Project notes that we pursue power because we feel weak and vulnerable, and we think (perceive) that an accretion of power will make us strong and invulnerable. We consider ourselves weak because of what we do not possess, and we see power as the means to acquisition and possession. But the objective reality is that possession is an illusion. We possess nothing that unforeseen circumstances of life, beyond our control, cannot in an instant take from us. In particular, we did not create and do not possess our own intrinsic value. Rather, our intrinsic value is inherent in our being; it is what we *are.* Once we know this fully, the illusion of possession is destroyed forever, and the impulse to seek power recedes within us. We are freed from the tyranny of the power imperative.

In individualistic societies, which generally lack the notion of intrinsic value, we see the "supervaluation" of the special. In such a society, where all accept the individualistic notion of value, we can avoid the self-perception of worthlessness only by demonstrating special ability in some way. This is done primarily through *competition,* by constantly striving to outperform others and thereby demonstrate our superior ability in a given area of endeavor. Each time we "win" a competition by demonstrably outperforming another, we (and others) perceive an increase in our personal value.

In other words, since individualism lacks the notion of intrinsic value, it impels us to seek our value through competition in the same way that social constructivist views of human value incite us to seek our value through power and dominance. Just as power seeking is the underlying motif of constructivism, so competition is the underlying motif of individualism. Moreover, the two motifs are not mutually exclusive. In a sufficiently unspiritual society we can have the worst of both worlds: power seeking and competition.

Competition proceeds by a horizontal comparison of the performance of two different individuals at the same time. If we seek to determine which of the two of us is better at playing the violin, then we will each play before a similar audience at approximately the same time, and the comparison between our two performances will be the basis of a social judgment as to which of us is superior.

The logic of competition is, in some ways, similar to the logic of power seeking (though there are important differences as well). I cannot outperform you at the same time and in the same way that you can outperform me. Thus, like power seeking, competition leads to asymmetrical relationships and hence to relational conflict. However, winning a competition in a given area of endeavor does not necessarily confer any direct power or dominance of winner over loser. But in an individualistic society it does result in the attribution of a higher personal value to the winner than to the loser. This value differential means that losers will have a deflated and negative self-image (at least to the extent that they are unaware of their intrinsic value).

Thus when competition becomes the dominant mode of interaction in a society, relational authenticity and hence authentic morality are defeated. Individual members of the society become prey to immense stress. People feel alienated and alone, and they find it difficult to trust others and to communicate effectively with them.

If we live in such a society, we will tend to perceive ourselves as weak and vulnerable and will often be haunted by the fear that others may discover our weaknesses and use this knowledge against us. We will thus attempt to project an image of strength to others and to hide self-perceived weaknesses. This creates further alienation, hypocrisy, and ultimately self-deception as we strive to hide our weaknesses not only from others but also from ourselves.

In highly individualistic societies where competitive modes of interaction are prevalent (e.g., North America and Western Europe), the negative impact of competition on human relationships has been generally recognized and acknowledged, at least in recent years. Nevertheless, social philosophers continue to purvey the notion that competition is necessary to the pursuit of excellence. We are told that the stress, tension, and unhappiness resulting from life in an environment of continual competition are the price we must pay for excellence. Comparisons are frequently drawn between the (supposedly high) level of development in individualistic societies and the (presumably lower) level of achievement in less competitive societies. This perceived difference in development is held to demonstrate conclusively that competition is productive of, and necessary to, excellence.

In this way, the identification of the pursuit of excellence with competition has become gradually and uncritically accepted as an established fact. That this identification is false can be readily seen by a thoughtful analysis of what is involved in each of these endeavors.

On one hand, the pursuit of excellence proceeds by the vertical comparison of two different performances by the same person at two different times. If I can play the violin tomorrow better than I could today, then that is progress toward excellence. Whether, at any point in this vertical pursuit, I can play better than you is beside the point entirely. For example, if I have great native ability, it may be that I can easily outperform you without my making any real progress toward perfection.

On the other hand, competition is the lateral comparison between the performance of two different people at the same time. Thus, the vertical pursuit of excellence is orthogonal to the lateral pursuit of competition: the two endeavors are fundamentally different.

Of course it is possible that competitive comparison between two performances can stimulate each performer to pursue excellence, but this happens *only* when excellence is the conscious goal of each. Let us examine this in more detail.

Suppose I am striving to outperform you. What strategies can I deploy to achieve this goal? One strategy is to improve my performance over time (pursue excellence) so that I can eventually outperform you. But what if you are also striving to improve your performance? No matter how much progress I make, I have no guarantee that you will not make equal or greater progress so that I will never be successful in outperforming you.

Of course, if excellence is our goal, then there is no problem. The world will be better off with two excellent performers instead of two mediocre performers where one is recognizably better than the other. But if winning the mutual competition is my goal, then I will not be content with striving for excellence year after year only to see you continue to outperform me (because your performance is also improving).

Thus, the pursuit of excellence is not the optimal strategy for winning a competition. What better strategy is there? The answer is *sabotage.* Sabotaging your opponent's performance (and preventing her from sabotaging your own) will be a superior strategy for winning the competition. It takes much less energy than the pursuit of excellence, and the outcome is quicker and surer.

We can now understand clearly the fundamental difference between competition and the pursuit of excellence. On one hand, sabotage is always a reasonable strategy, and frequently the preferred strategy, for winning a competition. On the other hand, sabotage can never, under any circumstances, lead to an increase in excellence on the part of either the saboteur or the sabotaged.

Because it is a vertical pursuit, the seeking of excellence lifts us to a higher plane. But the lateral striving of competition leads us to work against others, not with them. It wastes energy we can apply to pursuing excellence, and it distracts us from the source of excellence—the intrinsic value of our capacities of mind, heart, and will—by focusing our attention on the weaknesses and vulnerabilities of others.

The moral difference between competition and the pursuit of excellence lies principally with our motivation. Pursuing excellence is a form of service to others and thus an act of humility, whereas the motive for striving to outperform others is most often a form of pride. Yet, the act itself (performing at a certain level) may be the same in both cases.

This illustrates the important fact that physical actions can be morally evaluated only in relationship to the underlying motive of the act. In isolation from their context, such acts do not have an intrinsic *moral* value (though they may well have objective social consequences). Thus, the roots of authentic morality lie within the recesses of our hearts, where our acts are conceived, and cannot be measured by external conformity to ethical rules alone.

It is sometimes said that striving for moral development itself constitutes an example of a morally authentic form of competition, contrary to the analysis of the Authenticity Group given above. However, this involves a confusion of two different notions of competition. If I succeed in serving you more than you serve me, it will hardly be the cause of feelings of depressed self-esteem on your part. This is an entirely different thing than the competition discussed above, which is a striving *against* others not *toward* them in service. Whenever we need to clarify in our minds the difference between the two notions of competition, we need only recall our initial definition of competition: striving to outperform the other with the goal of attributing to oneself a higher personal value than the other.

Striving toward excellence is a motivation that is not only morally superior to competitive striving but also more difficult to achieve, requiring as it does a considerably higher level of moral maturity. In the short run, it is much easier to incite motivation by competition than by the pure pursuit of excellence, and this is undoubtedly one of the reasons why the identification of the two pursuits has become so generally accepted as an established fact. Indeed, learning how to pursue excellence without giving in to jealousy toward others or yielding to the temptation to sabotage them is one of the challenges of authentic morality.

The Authenticity Project on Social Norms and Material and Spiritual Values

According to the Authenticity Project, prevalent competition is not the only negative consequence of an individualistic social milieu. Individualism's supervaluation of the special leads to a general devaluation of whatever is perceived as normal or ordinary. Indeed, in a highly individualistic society the worst insult that can be addressed to an individual is to say that he is "ordinary," because this means he has no special ability and thus no (individualistic) value.

Consider, for example, the individualistic societies of North America and

Western Europe, which give extremely high value to successful athletes and cinema actors, who are paid enormous sums to display their particular abilities and talents. Contrast this with the generally low value these same societies give to motherhood, which is devalued because it is ordinary: supposedly "anyone" can be a mother; it takes no special ability.

However, when viewed from the spiritual perspective of authentic morality, motherhood is the primary and most valuable role in society. Indeed, we can observe that even "ordinary" mothers give priority to the needs of their children over their own needs at virtually every instant from the birth of a child until it becomes an autonomous adult. Not only is this "common" degree of self-sacrifice an extraordinary phenomenon, it is the very foundation of society: if only one generation of women refused to play this role, it would be the end of the human race. Yet, our individualistic Western societies take the self-sacrifice of mothers for granted while laying immense social energy and resources at the feet of professional athletes and rock musicians, who perform no vital social function whatever. Indeed, the complete disappearance of these latter roles from society would be of little significance.

Moreover, as the case of mothers versus rock musicians shows, the very notion of what is normal or ordinary is extremely unclear. For example, let us imagine a society in which the capacities and achievements of a Beethoven or an Einstein are common currency: virtually everyone has the ability to write Beethoven's Ninth Symphony or conceive of the theory of relativity. In such a society, these abilities and achievements would be ordinary and thus taken for granted. If, further, the society was based on an individualistic value system, these now ordinary abilities would be less valued than those (of whatever nature) perceived as special or above the norm.

Science has shown that, in any stable population with random mating (any two individuals of the opposite sex are equally likely to mate), talents and abilities are normally distributed according to the well-known Gaussian or bell-shaped curve. What this means practically is that, whatever the norm of a given collectivity may be, the vast majority (about 68 percent) of the population will be normal. Thus, in a society where only the supernormal is valued, at most 10 or 15 percent of the population has any hope of demonstrating superior ability at a level sufficient to be perceived as special by the population as a whole. Thus, an individualistic value system guarantees that the majority of people will be devalued (and thus unhappy), *no matter how high the actual level of achievement of the majority of individuals may be.* This mathematical analysis of normality is the ultimate reductio ad absurdum of individualism as a viable moral system.

In light of the above analysis, one can legitimately wonder how indeed such a morally inauthentic value system could have become so widespread. Part of the answer undoubtedly lies in the confusion between competition and the pursuit of excellence that we have discussed above. However, another significant factor appears to be a similar confusion between spiritual (intangible) and material (tangible) values.

According to virtually all modern theories of economy, material (economic) values are based primarily on the principle of rarity: the rarer a material good, the greater its value. This leads, in turn, to what is held to be the fundamental principle governing human economic behavior, *competition for rarity.*

The logic of these principles derives from the fact that material values are diminished when they are shared. If I have an apple and must share it with you, then we will each have half an apple. Moreover, the greater the population that must share the apple (the rarer it is), the less each person's share will be and the greater the value attributed to the apple. Thus, there will be competition for possession of the apple and the control of its distribution (sharing).

The principle of competition for rarity does seem to describe accurately quite a bit of economic behavior, though modern, high-tech means of production have begun to undermine this principle. (Which would you rather possess: a very good computer that you need and is easily available for a few hundred dollars, or a precious stone potentially worth thousands of dollars but that is of absolutely no use to you?)

Be that as it may, the point is that this principle is totally false when applied to spiritual values because *spiritual values are multiplied and enhanced, not diminished, when shared.* If I have a good idea and share it with you, then we both have a good idea. The more the idea is shared, the more valuable it becomes. Or, if I have love and share it with you, then you will most likely respond in a loving manner, because love evokes love. Thus, material values are diminished when shared, whereas spiritual values are enhanced when shared.

Moreover, spiritual values (such as motherhood) are universal, whereas material values are local and limited. This means that the materialistic notion of normality simply does not apply to spiritual values. The more spiritual values are shared—the more "normal" or "ordinary" they become within a given society—the greater their worth. Thus, it is not competition but cooperation (sharing) that enhances spiritual values.

Of course, we can only share something we have in the first place, and this applies to spiritual values as well as to material values. We are thus led back to the notion of intrinsic value: each of us is naturally endowed with a personal source of spiritual values in the form of our inherent capacities of mind, heart, and will. Hence the awareness of intrinsic value, when coupled with the clear knowledge of the universality of spiritual values, completely alters the traditional logic of competition for rarity, transforming it into a logic of cooperation for universality.

We can now understand that the basic logic of individualistic competition derives in large measure from an inappropriate application to the spiritual realm of certain principles that do have a genuine (if limited) validity in the material realm. We have confused the merely general or mediocre with the universal and valuable. The material realm and the spiritual realm each obey certain laws and principles, but spiritual laws are not in all cases the same as material laws. A confusion between the two can result in an inauthentic moral system.

The relevance of the work of the Authenticity Project to the gender-related problems facing men and women around the world is readily apparent. Furthermore, the training and workshop programs developed by the Authenticity Project are designed to help individuals and societies to appreciate the dynamics underlying the pursuit of power and to consciously and willingly abandon such pursuits. The work of the Authenticity Project thus holds considerable promise in the global campaign to eradicate gender-based violence, exploitation, and abuse. We invite readers who are interested in a more detailed explication of the philosophical bases of the Authenticity Project to review Hatcher's 2002 book, *Love, Power, and Justice: The Dynamics of Authentic Morality.*

7

The Development of Emotional Competence

For those who may be skeptical of, or resistant to, approaches that emphasize psychospiritual growth, the emerging field of *emotional intelligence* also offers tools that might be employed in the global campaign to eradicate certain forms of gender-based violence. In our exploration of this work, we begin with a few definitions.

Leonard Berkowitz, one of the leading authorities on violence, has identified two distinct types of human aggression: instrumental aggression and emotional aggression. In *instrumental aggression* the perpetrator commits an assault in order to achieve objectives that are motivated by a desire to do more than injure the victim. For example, the motivation behind instrumental aggression may be to inflict pain on the target, to exert power over the victim, to establish a favorable identity, or to maintain dominance and control.[1] In Finkelhor's interpretation of data on family violence, for example, it is suggested that domestic violence serves most often to maintain men's dominance through force and is likely to be used most frequently in contexts in which the degree of inequality between men and women is most extreme.[2]

There is much empirical evidence for this point of view. In his widely cited study of ninety societies, for example, Levinson found that female economic inequality, when supported by male control in the household and a woman's inability to divorce, provided the strongest predictor of her vulnerability to violence and abuse. In another set of studies, Straus and Hornung et al. found that wide status differences between marriage partners was associated with a higher frequency of violence—especially if the man had a lower status than his wife.[3] Coleman and Straus sampled approximately two thousand couples, classifying them as male-dominant, female-dominant, or egalitarian. Their study revealed the lowest rates of violence among egalitarian couples.[4]

In their interviews with battered wives, Dobash and Dobash found that battering tended to occur when there had been a perceived challenge to the husband's control or authority, when there were unfulfilled expectations about domestic work, or when husbands felt possessiveness and sexual jealousy. In light of these findings, Dobash and Dobash concluded that males' use of violence in the home functions to establish or maintain power over the wife when her behavior becomes "unacceptable" or threatens the status quo.[5]

Although information about batterers is less extensive than information about the victims, data available from batterers in treatment groups suggests that the abuser's need to control or dominate his female partner is a significant and recurring theme. Lenore Walker has found that the typical batterer believes strongly in the stereotyped masculine sex role in the family, to such an extent that his entitlement to be obeyed and provided for allows him to deny the wrong inherent in the violence he perpetrates. Furthermore, it is not uncommon for the victims of violence to have internalized traditional beliefs about the relative status of men and women. Indeed, having accepted, perhaps even unconsciously, the rightness of inequality, many battered and abused women assume a great deal of responsibility for the violence perpetrated against them.

Yllo and Straus examined the relationship between violence and the overall status of women in different U.S. states. Using the legal, economic, educational, and political rights of women in each state as predictors, Yllo and Straus found a curvilinear relationship between these rights and marital violence. Where women's status was found to be low, there was greater violence. However, violence against women tended to decrease as status increased. At high levels of status, there was again an increase in violence. In addition, patriarchal norms in each state evidenced a linear relationship with marital violence: the more egalitarian the normative climate among men in that state, the lower the rate of violence against women in the home.[6]

A man is particularly apt to dominate using physical force when his partner is highly dependent upon him, either economically or psychologically. The 1975 U.S.-based National Family Violence Survey found that violence against wives was most likely to occur when both economic and psychological dependence were manifest. Thus, the greater the wife's psychological dependence on her husband, the greater the likelihood of minor forms of violence. By contrast, economic dependence was associated with much more severe violence. Approximately 4 percent of the women who were economically self-sufficient were reported to have been severely beaten, as compared to 7 percent of those women who were totally dependent upon their husbands for financial support. Reflecting upon their findings, the researchers concluded that wives who are highly dependent on marriage are not as able to discourage, avoid, or put an end to abuse as are women in marriages in which the balance of resources between husbands and wives is more nearly equal.[7]

Despite the undeniable role of instrumental aggression in many cases of domestic violence, there is a second type of aggression, referred to as *emotional aggression,* that may also account for a significant percentage of violent acts committed against women and children in the home. Emotional aggression results in violence that is perpetrated largely out of anger, frustration, or fear.

Like wild animals that attack on instinct, the perpetrator of emotion-induced violence may have no conscious objective in mind when acts of aggression are committed; such acts may arise largely out of poor impulse control and inadequately developed emotional skills. In *Aggression: Its Causes, Consequences, and Control*, Berkowitz describes the nature of this form of aggression:

> Aggressive actions can . . . be described in terms of yet another dimension . . . the degree to which the behavior is either consciously controlled or impulsive. Some attacks are carried out calmly, deliberately, and with a clear aim in mind. The aggressors know what goals they want to achieve and believe that their assaults have a good chance of paying off. . . . There are also times, however, when attacks are carried out with little thought—with little consciousness of either what might be gained beyond injuring the target or the costs that might be incurred. As several psychologists have put it, there is a short-circuiting of the normal evaluation process. Emotionally aroused aggressors usually have an urge to strike out at an available target. Whether because of intense emotional agitation within them and/or because of the nature of their personalities, some people don't stop to think of what might happen if they do hit their victims (physically or verbally). Their attention is focused primarily upon what they most want to do at that time—their aggressive purpose—and they don't consider alternative courses of action and the possible negative consequences.[8]

In close interpersonal relationships, emotional aggression accounts for a significant number of homicides. Indeed, as has been noted by the Centers for Disease Control, most murders in the United States occur between friends or family members during the heat of passion over relatively trivial disagreements. Quoting one veteran detective in Dallas, Berkowitz observes, "Murders result from little ol' arguments about nothing at all. . . . Tempers flare. A fight starts, and somebody gets stabbed or shot."[9]

Emotional aggression results primarily from the activation of primitive brain centers, such as the amygdala, which is part of the limbic system. The development of the neocortex in humans renders it possible to bring the automatic, impulsive, and aggressive reactions that arise from the activation of the limbic system under varying degrees of conscious control. The maturation of the structures of the neocortex alone, however, does not ensure that humans will acquire the capacity for conscious control over primitive emotional reactions. For such control to mature, humans must develop a set of intrapersonal and interpersonal skills that in the aggregate have come to be known as *emotional competence, emotional intelligence,* or *emotional literacy.*

At the heart of emotional competence is the capacity to recognize feelings when they emerge, to evaluate those feelings (i.e., to determine whether they are appropriate or warranted), and then to act based upon these postfeeling assessments. Aristotle captures this capacity well in his famous quotation on human emotions: "Anyone can become angry—that is easy. But to be angry with the right person, to the right degree, at the right time, for the right purpose, and in the right way—this is not easy."[10] This capacity to gain perspective on one's own feelings, to evaluate them, and to act only after such an evaluation requires the ability to delay the impulsive reactions that are triggered by the activation of the limbic system. In anger and rage reactions, the absence or poor development of this capacity can easily trigger violent and aggressive responses that result in injury to others.

The development of emotional intelligence begins in childhood and depends a great deal on a certain quality of parenting. But it is also conditional upon a variety of societal factors that we will explore in detail later. Concerning the role of parenting, a growing body of research has found that three parenting styles are most likely to lead to a failure to develop emotional competence in children. These parenting styles include the tendency to treat a child's emotional upset as trivial or bothersome; the tendency to notice the child's emotional responses to a situation but to be passive and laissez-faire in showing the child how to best respond to a situation that he or she finds upsetting; and the tendency to be contemptuous toward the child's feelings, showing little or no respect for them. By contrast, parents who foster the development of emotional maturity tend to take advantage of emotionally volatile situations by serving as a coach, a mentor, or a guide as their child struggles to deal with an emotionally challenging situation.

If parents are to be effective in this, they must possess a rudimentary degree of emotional intelligence themselves. If, for example, children are to learn how to distinguish among feelings such as hurt, anger, shame, and fear, they need to have exposure to models who are able to recognize their own feelings when they arise. Chronic exposure to parents who manifest only a narrow range of emotions (e.g., anger) is likely to lead to a constriction of emotional response among offspring. Similarly, children who grow up in families or communities that show little empathy toward them are not likely to have the capacity for empathy as they grow to adulthood. Emotional skills do not tend to develop in children unless they are taught.

Of all parenting styles, capricious parenting—parenting in which the child gets treated according to the parent's passing moods—is the one that appears to be most predictive of producing children who are the least able to understand and regulate their own emotional reactions. When punishments and rewards come to children not as a result of what they do but as a result of whether mother or father is in a good or bad mood, the outcome is often the development of children with emotional handicaps. Emotional disabilities that may result from capricious parenting include emotional constriction, feelings of helplessness and/or worthlessness, personality disorders, and depression. In addition, having had no reliable model from which to learn how to manage emotions, such children may naturally grow up to treat others according to their own shifting moods. Such an approach to relationships is chaotic and dangerous. Daniel Goleman provides an illustration of the distorting influences of capricious parenting:

> In the rough-and-tumble play of the day-care center, Martin, just two and a half, brushed up against a little girl, who, inexplicably, broke out crying. Martin reached for her hand, but as the sobbing girl moved away, Martin slapped her on the arm. As her tears continued Martin looked away and yelled, "Cut it out! Cut it out!" over and over, each time faster and louder. When Martin then made another attempt to pat her, again she resisted. This time Martin bared his teeth like a snarling dog, hissing at the sobbing girl. Once more Martin started patting the crying girl, but the pats on the back quickly turned into pounding, and Martin went on hitting and hitting the poor little girl despite her screams.[11]

Goleman goes on to explain how this disturbing encounter illustrates how being beaten at the whim of a parent's moods can warp a child's natural tendency for empathy. "Martin's violent response to distress at the day-care center may well mirror the lessons he learned at home about tears and anguish: crying is met at first with a peremptory consoling gesture, but if it continues, the progression is from nasty looks and shouts, to hitting, to outright beating. Perhaps most troubling, Martin already seems to lack the most primitive sort of empathy, the instinct to stop aggression against someone who is hurt."[12]

As we suggested in the previous chapter, two forces are necessary within families, schools, and communities in order to develop emotional competence. These forces are love and justice. The importance of justice to emotional development has been validated in thousands of studies extending across all higher-order species. Consider a simple experiment.

Some years ago, a group of researchers introduced a school of meat-eating fish known as piranhas to a school of minnows in a large fish tank in their laboratory. Since piranhas enjoy eating minnows, whenever minnows were put into the tank, they were eaten. One day the researchers placed a small, circular glass around the minnows so that each time the piranhas attempted to eat them, the predators would bump into the glass. After about a day of this, the researchers took the glass away. What they discovered surprised and amused them: the piranhas no longer attempted to eat the minnows. Their exposure to a situation in which their actions did not produce the desired results led to the extinction of the action even though the piranhas needed to eat the minnows to survive.

As we have explained, the law of causality establishes a relationship between the actions of organisms and the effects that they experience. If the outcomes that we experience are independent of what we do, we are in a situation that is uncontrollable and unjust. The ways that human beings cope with uncontrollability is to distort or blunt their emotional reactions, to interpret (and thereby understand) the uncontrollable experience by invoking a higher-order schema (e.g., to see it as part of a developmental process that will be better understood in the future), to distort their perceptions of what is happening to them, or to renounce the struggle to cope by giving up. The tendency to give up, to become helpless, withdrawn, and apathetic in the face of challenge is one of the most widely recognized consequences of *chronic* exposure to injustice.

The emergence of the body of literature on learned helplessness and hopelessness discussed in the previous chapter began to give researchers deeper insight into the interplay between emotions and cognitive processes. Inasmuch as this work has played an important role in the evolution of the idea of emotional intelligence, we will revisit it briefly here.

The importance of cognitive expectations and "cognitive styles" in the development of emotional deficits has been recognized for a long time. Most cognitive theories of depression, for example, characterize depressives as deeply pessimistic about their ability to control important outcomes in their lives. For example, in his well-known laboratory-based studies on depression, Seligman found that the cognitive expectation of future helplessness tended to result in the development of sad affect when animals and humans are faced with uncontrollable events.[13] Given the central role of the expectation of helplessness in the deterioration of subjects' mood, Seligman referred to his theory as the "learned helplessness theory of depression."

The notion of "learned helplessness" was first identified by Seligman and Maier and was used to describe the impaired escape-avoidance responses evidenced by dogs exposed to uncontrollable shocks in the laboratory.[14] Since these initial studies, research in the area of learned helplessness has included cats, goldfish, and rats (see Maier and Seligman 1976 for an extensive review of research on learned helplessness in animals).[15] More recently, researchers have documented the learned-helplessness phenomenon in humans.

The typical learned-helplessness experiment employs the triadic design in which one group of subjects receives controllable events; a second group, yoked to the first, receives uncontrollable events of equal intensity and duration as the first group; while a third group is exposed to neither controllable nor uncontrollable events. In Hiroto's classic human helplessness study, for instance, college students were exposed to either loud controllable noises or loud uncontrollable noises. A third group was not exposed to any noises. Subjects were then tested on a hand shuttle-box task in which noise termination was controllable by all subjects. Hiroto's findings are typical in that groups receiving controllable noises and no noises learned to terminate noises in the shuttle-box task, whereas subjects previously exposed to uncontrollable noises failed to terminate aversive noises during the task.[16]

According to the learned helplessness theory, learning that events are uncontrollable results in profound motivational, cognitive, and emotional deficits. The motivational deficit is characterized by the failure to initiate voluntary responses in situations in which an active effort to cope or resist will decrease the likelihood or degree of harm that the individual experiences. This deficit is said to arise from the expectation that responding is futile. Survivors of childhood abuse, for example, commonly note the chaotic and unpredictable enforcement of rules that they experienced in their homes. Regular exposure to random beatings, harassment, or unpredictable intrusions on one's privacy can result in the development of coping strategies that are passive and accepting of abuse. Such a response makes sense because if what we do has no effect on the abuse that we experience, doing nothing makes as much sense from a defensive perspective as offering resistance.

In her book on traumatic disorders that develop in adulthood as a result of childhood abuse, Judith Herman discusses the phenomenon of repeated victimization that has been observed by a number of researchers and clinicians. In her explication of the phenomenon, she notes that "repeated abuse is not actively sought but rather is passively experienced as a dreaded but unavoidable fate and is accepted as the inevitable price of relationship. Many survivors have such profound deficiencies in self-protection that they can barely imagine themselves in a position of agency or choice."[17] This loss of a sense of agency, of personal empowerment, is the central motivational deficit that attends exposure to uncontrollable aversive experiences.

The cognitive deficit that results from injustice and uncontrollability is manifested by difficulty in learning that responses do have an influence on outcomes when, in actuality, they do. The frequently traumatized child has fewer adaptive cognitive skills at her disposal for dealing with challenging situations. Cognitive coping strategies develop, in part, because they prove useful for helping us to avoid dangerous or painful situations. If the strategies that we use in childhood do not help us in this way, we abandon them for other strategies that often prove maladaptive once the abuse has ended.

The sadness and depressed affect that accompany learned helplessness derive from the awareness of one's impotence in the face of challenges and threats. The victim comes to expect that bad events are likely to happen and that there is nothing that she can do to prevent or avoid them. It is this expectation of uncontrollability for future events that maintains the deficits generally associated with helplessness-related pathologies.

Given the similarities between helplessness deficits and depressive symptoms, Seligman began to suggest that learned helplessness may model and explain the etiology and symptoms of at least some types of depressive disorders. The original learned helplessness theory, however, proved inadequate to account for either the chronicity or the generality of helplessness or depression. Hiroto and Seligman, for example, found that sometimes laboratory helplessness is general, while others found that it is circumscribed.[18] In addition, negative events were sometimes found to precipitate depressive reactions, while at other times they did not.[19] Thus, the question of what determines the chronicity and generality of depression and helplessness remained unresolved by the original theory.

Neither could the original theory stand up to the criticism that the expectation of uncontrollability is not sufficient to produce depression in humans, inasmuch as there are many outcomes in life that are uncontrollable but do not lead to sadness. Furthermore, the lowered-self-esteem characteristic of depressives and the tendency of depressed persons to attribute failure to personal shortcomings were not adequately addressed by the theory.

In a reformulation of the helplessness theory, Abramson, Seligman, and Teasdale argued that an individual's *attributional style* results in the development of helplessness deficits when they are faced with uncontrollable aversive events. Attributional styles are akin to personality traits that develop early in life and structure how people explain why bad things happen to them. People who explain undesirable events and outcomes in terms of global and stable characteristics (for example, I am stupid) are more likely to become helpless when faced with stressful life events than are individuals who explain the same events by invoking specific and unstable factors (for example, I didn't try hard enough). Moreover, Abramson and her colleagues hypothesized that when negative events are attributed to internal, as opposed to external, causes, the expectation of helplessness will be accompanied by lowered self-esteem.

Consider, for example, the person who has experienced abuse over an extended period of time. That person is likely to begin to think of that abuse as being somehow deserved. In fact, the abuse that children experience is often accompanied by statements that indicate that they are being punished because of something that they have done or failed to do. When victims of injustice and abuse attribute the abuse to something about themselves, they have internalized the source of the abuse and are thus more likely to lose self-esteem and to be vulnerable to the motivational and cognitive deficits that are described above. However, as Janoff-Bulman has found, in an ironic way, self-blame for abuse can also be adaptive.[20] The logic is that if the way that you are treating me is due to something that I have done, then perhaps I can change what I do in the future and thus avoid the undesirable treatment. The problem with such a strategy, however, is that it seldom leads to actions that enable victimized persons to avoid the abuse. They thus end up blaming themselves for events over which they actually have little or no control. The self-blame, low self-esteem, and motivational deficits that accompany chronic exposure to abuse may help explain why it is often difficult for many abused adults to leave violent relationships.

Concomitant with the *cycle of violence* invoked to help explain women's behavior in abusive situations, researchers have recently begun to describe the *cycle of feeling avoidance* that often fuels the abuser's cycle of violence. Painful feelings that under healthy circumstances would promote personal reflection and growth overwhelm the batterer's perceived coping capacities, and a defensive cycle of violence, intended to serve as an escape from psychological pain, ensues. The feelings that precipitate violence may include actual or anticipated shame, feelings of helplessness, the perception of incompetence, or the fear of failure. Inasmuch as these feelings threaten to cast the self in a negative light, they often precipitate the activation of relatively primitive defenses. Among these primitive defenses is violence.

Having been reinforced by the short-term relief conferred by these defensive strategies, they tend to be used with greater frequency and thus become an integral part of the abuser's character or personality style. In a remarkable synthesis of studies from a wide range of fields, Roy Baumeister demonstrates that a diversity of human pathological conditions may result from attempts to escape painful self-awareness.[21] Because this pattern of responding is so intimately related to emotion-driven violence, it deserves to be examined more carefully.

For most living organisms, development is fueled by exposure to threats and challenges. Consider an example from the plant kingdom. A few years ago scientists developed a self-contained ecosystem that they named Biosphere II. All was well in Biosphere II except for one problem that puzzled the scientists for quite a while. The problem was that the trees in Biosphere II, though growing tall, could not stand upright. After numerous studies, one of the researchers was struck by the realization that in this totally enclosed ecosystem, there was no wind. Since saplings acquire the strength to stand by resisting the wind, the lack of exposure to wind during their early development rendered these saplings incapable of fully functioning as adult trees.

In a similar way, human beings acquire emotional and psychological strengths by encountering psychosocial and emotional challenges in childhood and youth. When these challenges occur in situations of love and justice, and when we confront these challenges with the help of competent models, we acquire psychological robustness and emotional competence. These strengths are needed to face the more difficult challenges that attend the responsibilities of adulthood. When we confront adult challenges without these skills, our responses are often childish, maladaptive, and ineffective. Indeed, it is the incongruence between what is expected of him and what he perceives himself capable of doing that often fuels the cycle of maladaptive responding so characteristic of the emotion-driven batterer.

Furthermore, if your self-concept is that you should be more competent and more in control than you actually are, when situations make it clear that you lack the qualities that you are supposed to have, you can react by trying to better yourself or by diverting your attention away from yourself and onto something or someone else. When the batterer, for instance, makes the faults of someone else the focus of his concerns, he diminishes the chances that he will acquire either much-needed self-knowledge or the skills needed to turn self-awareness into more effective coping strategies. By escaping responsibility for his own emotional, psychological, and spiritual development, the batterer becomes more and more incapable and subsequently more dependent upon force and violence to feel effective or secure. Such a person is in a vicious cycle that can be exited only if new capacities for dealing with stressful situations are acquired.

Relatedly, some years ago psychiatrists began to identify a clinical condition known as *alexithymia*. Alexithymia is characterized by the inability to put words to feelings and has proven to correlate with difficulty controlling emotions and impulses to act, impairments in the ability to cope with stressful situations, and the pathogenesis of psychosomatic illnesses (such as heart disease, strokes, and high blood pressure). Graeme Taylor, one of the pioneers in alexithymia research, identified four deficits that are generally associated with it: (1) difficulty identifying feelings, (2) difficulty describing feelings, (3) difficulties in emotional processing, and (4) externally oriented thinking. Further, as Taylor notes, people are not either alexithymic or nonalexithymic. Rather, they manifest the trait to varying degrees, with men tending to be more alexithymic than women.

Related research designed to explore how people tend to cope with stressful situations has led to the identification of three general coping styles: problem-focused or task-oriented coping; emotion-oriented coping; and avoidance-oriented coping. People who employ a problem-focused strategy tend to approach stressful situations by reflecting upon their previous experiences with problems and drawing upon that experience in order to craft adaptive responses to the current situation. Those who employ an emotion-oriented coping strategy use an avoidance-oriented style that diverts attention away from the actual problem onto nonrelated processes, such as bodily aches and pains, or into anger and aggressiveness. The avoidance-oriented approach is reflected in the tendency to self-distract by eating, watching television, procrastinating, shopping, and so forth. Taylor's research has shown that people high in alexithymia are more likely to use emotion-oriented coping than those low in alexithymia. That is, when faced with stressful situations, they tend to become angry or engage in various strategies of denial.

Complementing the work on alexithymia and coping, some clinicians and researchers also developed an interest in the therapeutic benefits of "emotional awareness" and "psychological mindedness." Patients who were high in emotional awareness also tended to be psychologically minded; that is, they were both generally aware of their emotions and able to express them. These patients turned out to be the best candidates for psychotherapy because speaking enabled them to gain deeper personal and interpersonal insight, which could then be translated into change.

Emergence of concern for the development of emotional competence has also come out of a body of socially focused theoretical work on optimal human functioning, human aggression, and violence. This work, whose most notable contributors include (among others) Pitirim Sorokin, Erich Fromm, Christopher Lasch, Viktor Frankl, Alfred Adler, and Abraham Maslow, suggests that any prescription for the development of psychologically healthy human beings must take account of the special qualities and concerns that distinguish human life, as well as the larger social context in which we come of age.

In one of his most important theoretical works, *The Anatomy of Human Destructiveness* (1973), Fromm explores the factors that distinguish human aggression from aggression in other animals. Fromm notes that while defensive aggression is biologically adaptive, and may thus have the same neurophysiological bases in both animals and humans, the incidence of defensive aggression is many times greater in humans than in animals. This is owing to the fact that while animals perceive as threat only clear and present danger, humans, being endowed with the capacity for foresight and imagination, tend to react not only to present threats but also to threats that they can imagine might emerge in the future. In addition, humans are capable not only of foreseeing real dangers in the future but also of being persuaded and brainwashed into believing that dangers exist where they do not. Thus the range of real or imagined stimuli against which we can react with defensive violence is potentially infinite. Fromm writes:

> Man, like the animal, defends himself against threat to his vital interests. But the range of man's vital interests is much wider than that of the animal. Man must survive not only physically but also psychically.... First of all, man has a vital interest in retaining his frame of orientation. His capacity to act depends on it, and in the last analysis, his sense of identity. If others threaten him with ideas that question his own frame of orientation, he will react to these ideas as to a vital threat. He may rationalize this reaction in many ways. He will say that the new ideas are inherently "immoral," "uncivilized," "crazy," or whatever else he can think of to express his repugnance, but this antagonism is in fact aroused because "he" feels threatened.
>
> Man needs not only a frame of orientation but also objects of devotion, which become a vital necessity for his emotional equilibrium. Whatever they are—values, ideals, ancestors, father, mother, soil, country, class, religion, and hundreds of other phenomena—they are perceived as sacred. Even customs can become sacred because they symbolize the existing values. The individual—or group—reacts to an attack against the "sacred" with the same rage and aggressiveness as to an attack against life.[22]

Earlier we observed that the successes thus far achieved in the global campaign to grant equality of status and opportunity to the women of the world has generated, in many individuals and groups, a counterreaction that has led to a more pervasive use of violence against women in the home and community. We characterized this violence as "instrumental" in nature, inasmuch as it appears to function to keep women from enjoying the same opportunities as are seen to "belong" to men and boys. Fromm's thoughtful analysis, however, raises the possibility that even instrumental forms of violence may have an irrational component that can be addressed only when the deep, unconscious commitments that animate our responses to the perception of threat are addressed.

Making sense of emotion-driven aggression, notes Fromm, requires also that we appreciate the human need for a sense of direction in life. Without goals to strive for that transcend the self and that equip the human personality with a sense of meaning and purpose, humans tend to become bored, depressed, and angry. These feelings, in turn, can fuel processes of interpersonal violence and destruction that are more savage in the human world than in any place else in nature.

In his insightful analysis of this phenomenon, Fromm notes that human and animal organisms need a certain minimum of stimulation. Indeed, as we have already explained, it is largely in responding to the excitation and challenges provided by the world that all organisms develop. However, with respect to humans, it is critical to distinguish between two types of excitement-inducing stimuli: those that stimulate *active* responses, and those that render the person a passive recipient of the impact of the stimulus. While the former invite the individual to become actively interested in them by producing a "drive" or a certain manner of striving to see and discover ever new aspects of the stimulus, the latter simple stimuli serve largely to excite the recipient's senses while providing little in the way of a motivation to act. "We see that men eagerly respond to and seek excitation," writes Fromm. "The list of excitation-generating stimuli is endless. The difference between people—and cultures—lies only in the form taken by the main stimuli for excitation. Accidents, murder, a fire, a war, sex are sources of excitation; so are love and creative work; Greek drama was certainly as exciting for the spectators as were the sadistic spectacles in the Roman Colosseum, but exciting in a different way."[23]

The difference between these two kinds of stimuli, and the responses that they induce, has important consequences. Stimuli of the simple kind, when repeated beyond a certain threshold, are no longer registered by the senses and actually lose their capacity to stimulate. This is due to the neurophysiological principle of attenuation, according to which the nervous system eliminates awareness of stimuli that indicate by their repetitiveness that they are unimportant. Continued stimulation thus requires that the stimulus either increase in intensity or change in content; that is, a certain degree of novelty is required if these forms of stimulation are to serve as such. Fromm observes that life in contemporary, industrialized societies operates almost entirely under the influence of simple, sensate-focused stimuli. What is stimulated, he notes, are drives such as sexual desire, greed, sadism, destructiveness, and narcissism. These stimuli find expression in the culture's movies, television, radio, newspapers, magazines, and the commodity markets:

> On the whole, advertising rests upon the stimulation of socially produced desires. The mechanism is always the same: simple stimulation → immediate and passive response. Here lies the reason why the stimuli have to be changed constantly lest

they become ineffective. A car that is exciting today will be boring in a year or two—so it must be changed in the search for excitement. A place one knows well automatically becomes boring, so that excitement can be had only by visiting different places, as many as possible in one trip. In such a framework, sexual partners also need to be changed in order to produce excitation. . . . [T]he more 'passivating' a stimulus is, the more frequently it must be changed in intensity and/or kind; the more activating it is, the longer it retains its stimulating quality and the less necessary is change in intensity and content.[24]

Fromm explores these distinctions at such length because they help to account for human destructiveness and cruelty in interpersonal relationships. They also help to make sense out of the relatively low levels of emotional and psychological maturity that may come to characterize the life of many people:

It is much easier to get excited by anger, rage, cruelty, or the passion to destroy than by love and productive and active interest; that first kind of excitation does not require the individual to make an effort—one does not need to have patience and discipline, to learn, to concentrate, to endure frustration, to practice critical thinking, to overcome one's narcissism and greed. If the person has failed to grow, simple stimuli are always at hand or can be read about in the newspapers, heard about in the radio news reports, or watched on the television or movies. People can also produce them in their own minds by finding reasons to hate, to destroy, and to control others. . . . In fact, many married couples stay together for this reason: the marriage gives them the opportunity to experience hate, quarrels, sadism and submission. They stay together not in *spite* of their fights, but *because* of them.[25]

In the absence of self-transcendent, growth-inducing goals and aspirations the larger project of "character development" goes unaddressed. The result is a proliferation of social pathologies that reflect the character pathologies of those who have come of age within such a milieu. From this perspective, any discussion of the acquisition of traits like emotional intelligence must take into consideration both personal histories and the broader social dimensions of human life.

Research and theory linking social histories, patterns of thought, and cognitive styles to emotions provided the conceptual and methodological underpinnings of the concept of emotional intelligence. Emotional intelligence refers to the capacity to understand and use emotional information. The concept embodies the idea that emotions do not, as had been previously argued, hamper our ability to think; rather, a properly functioning emotional system can serve to enhance a person's ability to relate to both himself and the world. In 1990, Mayer, DiPaolo, and Salovey, pioneers in the development of the concept, defined emotional intelligence as "a type of emotional information processing that includes accurate appraisal of emotions in oneself and others, appropriate expression of emotion, and adaptive regulation of emotion in such a way as to enhance living."[26] They followed in 1999 with an expanded definition. It affirmed that "emotional intelligence refers to an ability to recognize the meanings of emotions and their relationships, and to reason and problem-solve on the basis of them. Emotional intelligence is involved in the capacity to perceive emotions, assimilate emotion-related feelings, understand the information of those emotions, and manage them."[27]

Whatever academic controversies may circle around the idea of emotional intelligence (EI), those most familiar with EI-related research are in agreement that higher EI predicts lower levels of violence and other problem behaviors. Higher EI scores also tend to reflect greater abilities to cope with stress in adaptive, rather than maladaptive, ways; greater capacity to use emotion-related information to get along better with others; and greater capacity to respect and accept one's self. Generally, six basic skills are taught in programs designed to promote emotional intelligence:

- Emotional self-awareness, which consists of the capacity to recognize and label one's own emotions, as well as the ability to understand the psychosocial causes of feelings and the capacity to separate feelings from actions

- The capacity to manage emotions once they are recognized, which consists of increasing one's capacity to tolerate and metabolize frustration

- The ability to express powerful, negative emotions without resort to violence

- The capacity and willingness to be more consciously responsible for one's own actions

- The capacity to experience and express empathy, which consists of increasing one's sensitivity to the emotional needs and feelings of others

- The capacity to solve problems in close relationships with greater understanding and skill[28]

Programs that have been developed and implemented in the United States to promote the development of emotional intelligence have been successful in helping children become more responsible, more helpful to others, more considerate of the feelings of others, better communicators, less impulsive, more "democratic," more competent at solving interpersonal problems without resort to violence or aggression, and better able to work in harmony with others.[29] Although no longitudinal studies have been conducted on the long-term benefits of such training, one might reasonably hypothesize that males (and females) who develop these capacities in youth are far less likely to be violent and abusive as adults.

In discussing the potential role of training in the acquisition of emotional competence, we are animated by far more than the desire to avoid the development of violent and abusive adults. Rather, we turn to such work because we are inspired by the promise it holds for promoting the development of human capital.

8

The Role of Men in Eradicating Gender-Based Violence

Greater inclusion of men in efforts to eradicate gender-based violence, exploitation, and abuse is critical. With respect to gender-based violence, male involvement has traditionally been largely focused on postabuse therapeutic efforts. Such measures include the work of therapists and industries developed to treat sex offenders, the spread of men's support groups for those arrested for battering, and prison-based treatment groups developed to facilitate processing of negative emotions such as anger. While some of the emerging programs show considerable promise, many earlier programs did not tend to contribute significantly to the *prevention* of gender-based violence and may have, in the aggregate, benefited the organizers most.

According to one New York lawyer, for example, sex offender treatment was one of the growth industries of the nineties. The Association for the Treatment of Sexual Abusers in Oregon reports that over the nineties their membership grew from twenty-five to more than a thousand. In addition, the Safer Society, which publishes workbooks, textbooks, and videotapes for sex offender treatment, reports a half-million-dollar-a-year business.[1] Despite decades of work in this area and billions of dollars spent, little progress has been made in the prevention of gender-based violence and exploitation. The failure to achieve meaningful results has led some to begin a search for strategies and perspectives heretofore untried.

For example, in recent years new *prevention-focused* initiatives that engage the active participation of men have begun to emerge. The college-based, all-male sexual assault peer education group 1 in 4, for example, has developed the Men's Program, which focuses on the prevention of rape and other forms of sexual assault among college students. Similar programs have begun to appear across the United States. Another male-centered organization that shows considerable promise is Dads and Daughters (DADs). Its mission is to "create stronger, deeper, more effective relationships between daughters and fathers, and the transformation of cultural messages that value girls more for how they look than for who they are."[2] Since its establishment two years ago, DADs has attracted two thousand members and has convinced several major corporations to change practices that are harmful to women and girls. For example, DADs was able to persuade Campbell's Soup to stop airing a TV commercial that presented their soup to adolescent girls as a diet aid; they convinced Chattem to discontinue a Sun-In ad that encouraged competition among girls based on physical appearance; they persuaded JC Penney to stop carrying misogynist T-shirts; and they rewarded Omni Hotels for their courageous and expensive decision to discontinue in-room pornographic movies.[3]

When one reflects upon the early history of the civil rights movement in North America, the importance of greater male involvement in this campaign is seen in sharper relief.

At its inception the civil rights movement in North America was peopled almost entirely by black Americans. However, as an increasing number of whites began to develop an appreciation of the moral rightness of the movement, they began to lend it their moral, legal, and financial support. Gradually, many whites became highly effective coworkers in the struggle to secure the civil and human rights of African Americans. The National Association for the Advancement of Colored People (NAACP), for example, was founded through partnership between black Americans and white Americans who recognized their responsibility to the moral, social, and legal evolution of American society.

As litigants in the struggle to extend civil rights to black Americans, black and white NAACP lawyers working together became the most effective legal team in the nation's history.[4] Civil rights gains accomplished through the work of the early, highly integrated NAACP resulted in benefits to millions of oppressed peoples within and outside the United States.[5] We believe that efforts to include men more fully in the global campaign to eradicate gender-based violence and to promote the advancement and participation of women is likely to facilitate in a similar way the further development of the movement's potential.

Male involvement in such a campaign may be most effective at the grassroots level. In particular, educational programs that begin in elementary school and that have the strong and visible support of men may inoculate male children against abuse well before they enter into dating and marital relationships. In addition, initiatives that inspire a sense of partnership between men and women on the local level need also to be considered. One initiative that has met with notable success is a three-country project funded by the United Nations Development Fund for Women (UNIFEM) and executed by Global Vision Inc. on behalf of the Bahá'í International Community. This highly participatory project—Traditional Media as Change Agent—endeavored to involve three culturally dissimilar communities in "raising awareness of women's issues, analyzing the consequences of gender stereotypes, and strategizing the pace and direction of change."[6]

Core skills—including qualitative research, management, planning, and evaluation—were taught to indigenous leaders and organizations who used volunteers from throughout the community to study the gender-related problems affecting residents' lives. As a result of the research undertaken by the community itself, a number of problems were identified. Three core concerns, however, were common to all sites: First, women were frustrated by their lack of education and attributed their sense of having no voice within the household to this deficit; second, women felt dominated by men in a variety of contexts; and, third, women voiced concern about men's mismanagement of household finances and expressed a desire to have a greater voice in the allocation and disbursement of the family's resources.

Survey research carried out by the communities themselves also revealed women's frustration at men's alcohol abuse and the physical and/or emotional abuse that tended to accompany their partner's excessive drinking. Focus group discussions revealed, however, that women desired neither to have greater access to money nor to increase their employment. Rather, almost unanimously, their desire was to participate in the redistribution of funds already available and to participate as equal partners in family decision making.[7]

Having identified women's core concerns, the project attempted to bring men into the dialogue and to provide social incentives for them to change their attitudes and behavior. To render men's gender-related attitudes and behaviors more salient, drama, dance, and other traditional media were employed to communicate the concerns of women and the damage done to families and communities when these concerns are not addressed. While all men did not participate, the majority of men in all three sites were clearly moved enough by these depictions to get involved. Factors contributing to men's willingness to participate included the spirit of open and nonjudgmental consultation utilized at every stage of the project; the use of the arts to dramatize the current state of affairs; the willingness of male leaders to participate; and the articulation of a vision of community life in which everyone was able to function at higher levels of unity and effectiveness.

According to the project director, over the three-year period during which the project was carried out, changes in labor patterns between men and women were reported in site after site. Men proved willing to assume a larger share of the household's physical responsibilities; they began to perform tasks formerly considered taboo for them; and the sharing of decision making between husbands and wives was reported by women to have more than surpassed their expectations. In addition, as reported by their wives, men's drinking was substantially reduced, and spousal abuse all but disappeared among participating families.

Insofar as an emphasis on female education resulted in the development of adult literacy programs for women and in almost universal enrollment of girls in primary schools in all three sites, the impact of this intervention is likely to be long term. Furthermore, summary analyses of the project suggest that the economic status of participating families was improved because men began to spend a larger percentage of their own resources on family-related needs, including health and nutrition, education, family farming, and, at one site, family planning. "The significance of this point," notes the project coordinator, "is that these are the sectoral objectives development planners hope to achieve by focusing on women only; in this case, however, they were achieved by focusing on men as well."[8]

With respect to the impact of the project on the lives of women, several positive outcomes were obtained. For example, as a result of their welcomed participation in family and community consultation, women reported improved self-esteem. In addition, because of greater participation of males in household chores, many participating women reported that they had periods of leisure time during which some enrolled in literacy courses and engaged in other forms of self-improvement. In many cases, and most often for the first time, women were elected to leadership positions in social and political organizations. "By all measures," noted a report summarizing the effects of the project, "women's status was raised, family well-being was improved, and community structures were strengthened by participation."[9]

Pertinent to these gains was the deliberate inclusion of men in all aspects of the project, "for while it is true that 'women hold up half the sky,' both halves of the human family are necessary to sustain societies equitably. When partnership models are non-confrontational, and mutually reinforcing, in the long run they greatly expand the bases on which societies remain healthy."[10] Three additional settings in which active male involvement could have important effects include religious communities, educational institutions, and places of employment.

Religious Communities

Notwithstanding the current crisis in the Catholic Church related to the sexual abuse of minors by priests, religious institutions, whose leadership is predominantly male, are among the most influential and stable social institutions in many localities. They thus represent a potentially powerful community resource for assisting in the prevention of violence against women and children. This realization was employed quite effectively by Temple University's Community Child Abuse Prevention Program (C-CAPP), which is part of the university's Center for Social Policy and Community Development (CSPCD). CSPCD works with churches in a poor area of Philadelphia, Pennsylvania, to promote family life in an attempt to reduce the incidence of child abuse. The Spiritual Life Committee was formed by C-CAPP staff in collaboration with religious leaders of the community. This group initiated a variety of activities focusing on public awareness of child abuse, including a training session for the religious community in which pastors, ministers, and laypersons learned about child-welfare issues.

A "sermon search" was also initiated, in which spiritual leaders were encouraged to participate in a friendly competition to preach sermons on the topic of child-abuse prevention. The sermons were collected, published as an anthology, and distributed to the community. In addition, during United Child-Abuse Prevention Day, congregations throughout Philadelphia heard sermons on positive family life. Churches also served as a base for various types of family-life programs, ranging from child-parent play programs, to family conflict resolution programs, to weekly rap sessions on all issues related to the development of more peaceful and happier families. Similar programs might be created and funded by government and nongovernmental agencies that are concerned with the prevention of gender-based violence.

The association between religious fundamentalism and violence against women and girls is another area that deserves careful scrutiny. The conflict between fundamentalist ideas and women's rights of liberty and equality have been brought into sharp relief in recent years. The facts support the charge that many of the world's religions have played active roles in the suppression of women's advancement in three basic ways: first, by insisting upon rigidly defined, differentiated roles for women and men; second, by promoting policies and practices whose intent and/or effect is the subordination and disempowerment of women; and third, by remaining silent in the face of egregious violations of women's basic human rights. Given the interplay in many countries among religious doctrines, cultural practices, and national and civil laws, this area of intervention on the part of males may be among the most important.

A particular doctrine of religious fundamentalism that is having a markedly pernicious effect on women's lives is referred to by Courtney Howland as the "obedience rule." Around the world, and in many religions, the obedience rule requires a woman to submit to the authority of her husband and legitimates the husband's discipline of his wife. The expectation of such subordination renders women vulnerable to physical abuse and often offers no authority to which she can turn for redress and protection. This doctrine, Howland notes, "serves as a clear example of a rule designed to maintain women in a subordinate position, and as such it brings the conflict between rights of religious freedom and women's rights of equality and liberty into sharp relief."[11]

The obedience rule has several implications. It often implies that young girls may be married without their consent; that a husband has a right of sexual access to his wife whenever he desires; and that a husband may forbid his wife to work or may prevent her from continuing her education, if he feels this is best. Another implication already noted is that obedience to the males of the household may be exacted through physical punishment.

Efforts to bring customary and state law into conformity with principles of human rights deserve the urgent attention of male activists around the world.

This is especially urgent since fundamentalist movements tend to be bent on further conforming national law to religious doctrines that further curtail women's development and participation. No clearer example of this can be seen than in the activities of fundamentalist Muslims in Afghanistan. After the Taliban took power in Afghanistan in 1996, women were beaten and stoned in public for not wearing the proper attire, prevented from working or going out in public without a male relative, and were forced from their jobs and confined largely to their homes. Because they were not allowed to work, those without male relatives or husbands were sometimes limited to begging. Few medical facilities existed for women, and as a result of such harsh treatment, suicide and depression appeared to increase rapidly. Prior to 1996, the women of Afghanistan enjoyed relative freedom to work and dress generally as they wanted; they were allowed to drive and to appear in public alone. The resurgence of Islamic fundamentalism deprived women of all of these basic human rights. In other parts of the world, religious fundamentalism poses a similar threat to basic freedoms.[12]

Educational Institutions

Several educational institutions have begun to offer classes focused on teaching nonviolent conflict resolution, parenting skills, consultation, and violence prevention through mediation. Many of these programs have been developed and implemented by men and are beginning to play important roles in male resocialization.[13] Peer groups have also developed among male college students to facilitate education on the impact of pornography on male-female relationships. Since sexual harassment and rape are disproportionately high among subgroups of males in educational settings (for example, athletes and fraternity members),[14] efforts to reduce gender-based violence that focus on these populations are likely to have a significant impact.

From a global perspective, male advocacy and participation in campaigns to improve educational opportunities available to women and girls are likely to be among the most effective means for contributing to women's advancement. Greater access to education would facilitate significant improvement in women's economic and physical health, contribute to improvements in self-esteem and independence, and enable those increasing numbers of families headed by single mothers to care for their children more effectively.

Places of Employment

As women around the world continue to enter the workforce in significant numbers, they must often accept lower wages for work comparable to that performed by their male counterparts; are frequently subjected to subtle and not-so-subtle expressions of inequality that may include paternalistic attitudes, sexual harassment, invisibility, and ostracism; and may not enjoy all of the non-monetary benefits that are owed to them in light of their time at the job and the contributions that they make to their employer's success.

According to Barbara Reskin and Irene Padavic, sex inequality at work is manifested in four distinct forms: sex segregation, sex differences in promotions, sex differences in authority, and sex differences in earnings. With respect to sex segregation, Reskin and Padavic note that "fewer than 10 percent of Americans have a coworker of the other sex who does the same job, for the same employer, in the same location, and on the same shift."[15] When U.S. data on sex segregation are examined more closely, it becomes clear that workplaces are segregated not only by sex but also by race and ethnicity. African American and Mexican women have fewer chances of holding many of the jobs, even in the low-wage sector, that have traditionally been held by European American women. Thus in restaurants, hotels, recreational facilities, airports, and so forth, women of color tend to get assigned to do the most menial work, leaving the higher-status, more-lucrative posts for women of European descent.

Sex differences in promotions are evident when one considers that women tend to be concentrated at low levels of the organizations that employ them, even in predominantly female lines of work. Indeed, as Christine Williams's research shows, the higher the position, the more likely it is that the individual holding the job is a male.[16] Furthermore, when women are placed in positions of power, they tend to supervise fewer subordinates than men, are less likely than men to control financial resources or to make decisions that are vital to the success of their employer, are less likely than men to have health insurance and other benefits, and are more likely to be the targets of various forms of sex stereotypes that often corrode a sense of self-efficacy and effectiveness. Men who are in positions of power are therefore challenged by these data to give consideration both to the sex segregation that may exist in the workplace and to the racial discrimination that renders it a double burden to be both a woman and a person of color. That some men in positions of power are taking up this challenge is evidenced by the fact that Brown University recently became the first Ivy League institution to hire as its president an African American woman. Other bold examples of vision and courage are needed around the world and in all of the professions that have heretofore been dominated by males of European lineage.

9

Why Have Hope?
Some Final Reflections on the Global Campaign to Eradicate Gender-Based Violence

As we embark upon a new century, we can imagine few goals more deserving of the attention of the community of nations and of the peoples of the world than the eradication of gender-based violence. This goal can and should be made an object of concern for both individuals and nations. The goal of eradicating gender-based violence should be proclaimed on billboards, televisions, and radio stations around the world. It should be discussed in classrooms, churches, synagogues, temples, and mosques. Those at the forefront of the campaign should enlist the energy, optimism, and enthusiasm of the world's youth. It should invite the men of the world to play a vital role.

The achievement of such a goal will demand more than publicity. It will require the moral and spiritual vision necessary for the abandonment of old patterns of relating based upon the pursuit of power. It will require the cultivation of an ethic of relational authenticity and will need to encourage all of us to gain greater mastery over our own emotions, impulses, and desires. If it is to enlist the effort of a sizable portion of the world's people, such a campaign will need to demonstrate that the well-being and good fortune of the entire human race depends upon the well-being of the world's women.

Such a campaign will require resources of time, energy, and money. It can be financed not only by governments and nongovernmental organizations around the world but also by private corporations, philanthropists, and common citizens alike. Community-centered institutions, such as the world's colleges and universities, high schools, police departments, commercial industries, artistic communities, and institutions of civil society, have resources at their disposal that could be readily mobilized around such a campaign. While the eradication of interpersonal violence must receive the attention of all the world, we require a special focus on dismantling the root causes of cultural and structural violence by those who are in a position to contribute to the transformation of the corporate, legal, educational, or religious institutions that they have the privilege to serve.

Why Have Hope?

In his important work, *The Topology of Hope,* Calvin Schrag captures a dimension of hope that is made possible by the unique capacities associated with human consciousness:

> We shall first speak of the praxis of hope. Praxis situates hope in the region of social formation and transformation. In this region the phenomenon of hope shows itself as a horizon of social consciousness, bearing implications for the wider cultural life of man. Understood within this modality, hope is the site from which the thought and action of interacting social selves transform the present in response to an envisioned condition of life in the future. The cognition in praxis, which is a form of practical insight and situational decipherment, discloses the present as a time of need, or in its more radical negativity as a time of suffering. Present conditions are seen as threatening personal and social fulfillment. But also the cognition in praxis comports an anticipation of the future as the time for the rectification of the present social ills. The future is envisioned as the coming of the era of emancipation from bondage to an alienated present. Hope is thus postured as a simultaneous awareness of the insufficiency of the present and an anticipation of future fulfillment.[1]

Schrag goes further to distinguish between hope and calculative social planning. In both, he observes, there is dissatisfaction with the present and an orientation toward the future. "However, in the case of social planning, the orientation toward the future is in the mode of a calculation of empirical probabilities that can be manipulated within a simulated plan. In the phenomenon of hoping," by contrast, "the possibilities of the future remain incalculable from an empirico-experimental standpoint. Hope struggles against odds that appear overwhelming from the perspective of calculative thinking and technological control." In this sense, "hope discloses an openness and transcendence of the future which imposes limits on calculation and prediction."[2] It is this transcendent dimension of hope that is a unique characteristic of the human spirit. It is this capacity to see beyond, to transcend, to rise up, and to move forward that is the need of the times.

The transcendent dimensions of hope are captured in the notion of faith. Inasmuch as it embodies theological implications, "faith" is a word much avoided today. Yet, inasmuch as faith involves the intense wish that our goals be realized and our willingness to do everything within our power to make it so and suggests that our effort will require us to call upon resources of heart, mind, and spirit that we are not sure we have, it is best that we are animated by the sprit of faith in such a campaign. Many will denounce faith in our ability to eradicate gender-based violence as unrealistic. Human history is certainly checkered with the juxtaposition of light and dark, good and evil, throughout: Jesus' dramatic teaching of agape love and his followers' subsequent heroic martyrdoms were juxtaposed with the power worship and cruelty of the Roman state; in modern times, scientific advances in the healing of diseases and a dramatic increase in the ease of travel and communications are juxtaposed with the development of weapons of war of unimaginable destructive power. Moreover, history has witnessed the successive rise and fall of civilizations. But, curiously and disturbingly, certain oppressive institutions have been a constant throughout this process. In particular, slavery was the economic basis of every society until the late nineteenth century, and every society has oppressed women, both physically and socially.

Traditionally, the sources of our moral systems have been the great religious and philosophical systems of history: Judaism, Christianity, Buddhism, Confucianism, Platonism, Islam. Yet none of the holy books or the authentic teachings of these great systems contains one single word against either slavery or the oppression of women. One cannot conclude from this that the great teachers condoned slavery and the inferior status of women; rather they were simply silent on the matter, tacitly assuming that these would be a feature of society (e.g., the laws in the Torah governing the use of slaves). Thus, throughout most of human history, not only were slavery and the oppression of women practiced, *they were not regarded as immoral.*

Every one of these systems has regarded murder, say, or adultery as a moral evil. For almost four thousand years (since the Ten Commandments) people generally have considered lying, murder, and adultery as moral evils. Human behavior may or may not conform to this standard, but the standard was there. Nobody, even the perpetrators, claimed that these practices were morally justifiable. But slavery and female oppression were both practiced *and* justified. It is only in the beginning of the nineteenth century that we see the initiation of a discourse that questions these practices, leading up to the current general sentiment that they are indeed immoral. Thus, the way in which the modern world deals with slavery and female oppression (and the two are really two sides of the same coin) is a kind of de facto moral touchstone or index. Here are practices that we ourselves have recognized as immoral. We have not inherited this morality from some mythical past or some tribal norm of behavior. The question before us now is, how will we deal with these immoralities that we ourselves have recognized?

Although it is feasible to eradicate gender-based violence, many doubt that it can be done because of human nature. As has been noted, many regard human nature as incorrigibly selfish and aggressive; thus, they argue that initiatives that depend upon the goodness of human beings for their success are bound to fail. Despite its wide acceptance, this realist perspective on human nature is one that fails to comport either with history or with the most recent developments in human psychology.[3] To the contrary, it would appear that far from expressing humanity's true self, the aggression and conflict that characterize our social worlds represent distortions of the human spirit.

From the psychological literature there is much evidence to suggest that human behavior (including either aggression or altruism) is a function of the relationship between malleable attitudes and prevailing social and/or political conditions. Thus, if we want to explain why a person, a group, or a whole society has acted aggressively, we must know something about the interaction between the actors' world view, beliefs, and values and the social conditions prevailing at the time. Since all human qualities can be strengthened or weakened by training and are subject to immediate and historical social, political, and moral influences, aggression and selfishness are not unalterable features of humanity's behavioral repertoire; rather, they are characteristics that are, in most cases, as remediable as is the inability to read and write.[4]

Furthermore, as we have attempted to argue throughout this book, as it is in the life of the individual, so it is also in the life of humanity. That is, just as the development of the person takes place in stages, so humanity's development is likely to be marked by different levels and stages of progress. Had we not yet witnessed a newborn baby grow into a mature adult, we would not easily believe that a creature that can neither hold its head up nor control its own sputum could someday be able to play the harpsichord, guide an aircraft past the speed of sound, or transplant a kidney from one living person to another. This is the miracle of life and development. Thus when we understand an organism's capacities from a developmental perspective, we are able to nurture it with confidence. We do not, for instance, discard our children because they are helpless, or bothersome, or sometimes even rude, arrogant, and violent; nor do we say that these characteristics are part of the child's immutable nature. We continue to educate children because we have a sense of vision for their potential. The development of the body politic may be understood in much the same way.

A Tale of Two Cities, by Charles Dickens, captures well the sense and spirit of the age in which we live: "It was the best of times, it was the worst of times." The current age does indeed appear to be a powerful mixture of unprecedented hopes and expectations as well as unimaginable contradictions, uncertainties, and setbacks. Some of the positive signs of the age include the end of the Cold War, which dramatically reduced the threat of nuclear war and freed up enormous resources for projects of development; the growing democratization of governments around the world and the establishment of the rule of law in many heretofore authoritarian or despotic regimes; a growing consciousness of the nonmaterial dimensions of development, such that issues of social justice, protection of the environment, and respect for civil and human rights are increasingly a part of the calculus; and finally, advancements in technology that have rendered communications throughout much of the world instantaneous, inexpensive, and reliable. These developments set the stage for further evolution toward peaceful coexistence.

Notwithstanding these hope-inducing processes, growing disparities between rich and poor in access to wealth and technology, the spread of religious fundamentalism with its attendant fanaticism and violence, and the absence of a framework for deciding on moral questions that affect the whole of humanity all contribute to the emergence or entrenchment of problems that challenge human and institutional resources and jeopardize the well-being of women and girls in particular as never before. Many of these challenges are likely to be better met within a new paradigm of international relations that not only arrogates to the nation certain rights and responsibilities but also entrusts to globally elected legislative and judicial bodies responsibilities that protect the interest of the whole, while giving due consideration to the right of nations to self-determination. It is in this respect that we find the expanding vision and programs of the United Nations so vitally important.

Indeed, in light of developments in technology, international communications, and a growing consciousness of human interdependence, it is time for world leaders to give renewed consideration to the establishment of a new international framework based on the idea of collective security. Collective security necessitates the development of peacekeeping institutions with sufficient funding and power to address global concerns, as well as a new attitude toward the concept of the nation and its role in human governance. Unlike the political systems of the present or past that assume the inevitability of conflict between nations and peoples, the system of governance befitting this new millennium must rest upon an emerging consciousness of the oneness and interdependence of humankind. In a letter addressing the implications of this principle at the beginning of the twentieth century, Shoghi Effendi, one of the most astute political observers of our time, writes:

> Let there be no mistake. The principle of the Oneness of Mankind . . . is no mere outburst of ignorant emotionalism or an expression of vague and pious hope. Its appeal is not to be merely identified with a reawakening of the spirit of brotherhood and good-will among men, nor does it aim solely at the fostering of harmonious cooperation among individual peoples and nations. Its implications are deeper. . . . Its message is applicable not only to the individual, but concerns itself primarily with the nature of those essential relationships that must bind all the states and nations as members of one human family. It does not constitute merely the enunciation of an ideal, but stands inseparably associated with an institution adequate to embody its truth, demonstrate its validity, and perpetuate its influence.[5]

It is in this vision of oneness and interdependence, as well as in the establishment of an international framework capable of ensuring collective security, that both realists and idealists may find their highest hopes realized.

We pause here to reflect upon the matter of collective security among nations because it is in times of war that women and girls are subjected to the most horrific forms of violence. As Vesna Nikolic-Ristanovic observes, "War strengthens the already existing dominant marginalization of women. . . . War increases their feelings of helplessness more than it increases their power; attacking their physical and mental health, war makes them dependent on others as it strengthens the social views which tend to maintain or intensify their submissive role."[6] In war, as we have seen, women are frequently subject to sexual violence and harassment; they suffer malnutrition, torture, homelessness, murder, psychological violence, and the loss of their sons, daughters, and husbands. Because of the suffering heaped upon women and girls before, during, and after times of war, the global campaign to eradicate violence against women and girls will need to address the problem of war. In our view, the problem of war can best be avoided within a paradigm of international cooperation and collective security.

If the commonwealth of nations is to have viability, internationally enforceable restrictions on unfettered national sovereignty would seem to be a necessity. At the beginning of the twentieth century, a number of wise observers from a variety of disciplines called for the voluntary imposition of reasonable limits on the sovereignty of nations. Among the most noteworthy of these were Albert Einstein, Bertrand Russell, and Shoghi Effendi. One year after the establishment of the United Nations, Einstein wrote:

> The development of technology and of the implements of war has brought about something akin to a shrinking of our planet. Economic interlinking has made the destinies of nations interdependent to a degree far greater than in previous years. . . . The only hope for protection lies in the securing of peace in a supranational way. A world government must be created which is able to solve conflicts between nations by judicial decision. This government must be based on a clear-cut constitution which is approved by the governments and the nations and which gives it the sole disposition of offensive weapons. A person or a nation can be considered peace loving only if it is ready to cede its military force to the international authorities and to renounce every attempt or even the means, of achieving its interest abroad by the use of force.[7]

Similarly, the British philosopher, Bertrand Russell, notes:

> A much more desirable way of securing world peace would be by a voluntary agreement among nations to pool their armed forces and submit to an agreed International Authority. This may seem, at present, a distant and Utopian prospect, but there are practical politicians who think otherwise. A World Authority, if it is to fulfill its function, must have a legislature and an executive and irresistible military power. All nations would have to agree to reduce national armed forces to

the level necessary for internal police action. No nation should be allowed to retain nuclear weapons or any other means of wholesale destruction. . . . In a world where separate nations were disarmed, the military forces of the World Authority would not need to be very large and would not constitute an onerous burden upon the various constituent nations.[8]

Shoghi Effendi tendered a strikingly similar proposal:

Some form of a world Super-State must needs be evolved, in whose favor all the nations of the world will have willingly ceded every claim to make war, certain rights to impose taxation and all rights to maintain armaments, except for purposes of maintaining internal order within their respective dominions. Such a state will have to include within its orbit an International Executive adequate to enforce supreme and unchallengeable authority on every recalcitrant member of the commonwealth; a World Parliament whose members shall be elected by the people in their respective countries and whose election shall be confirmed by their respective governments; and a Supreme Tribunal whose judgment will have a binding effect even in such cases where the parties concerned did not voluntarily agree to submit their case to its consideration.[9]

To those who suggest that such a framework is either impractical or impossible, we may well reflect upon the federal system that binds the semisovereign states that make up the United States. Because there is interstate cooperation and a greater loyalty to a national constitution and body of laws, it is possible for the states that constitute the union to conduct commerce, protect civil rights, educate the population, share resources, and protect the interests of both individual states and the union more efficiently and cost-effectively. On a global scale, what is both impractical and dangerous is having to carry out those processes necessary for the protection and maintenance of nations as well as the preservation of human rights among citizens within nations without a legal, constitutional, and legislative framework that facilitates and informs the nature of international relations.

Internationally accepted and enforceable laws on human rights; a common global currency; a common universal auxiliary language; a common system of weights and measures; a common commitment to cultivating, safeguarding, and sharing the earth's natural resources; and a well-prepared, universally supported international peace force would be among the most vital elements of such a global framework. Would not the business of preventing war, of protecting human rights, and of sustaining and supporting life on earth be greatly facilitated by such a collective arrangement?

Although mindful of the grievous slaughter and exploitation of America's original inhabitants, in his vision for achieving collective security among nations, Shoghi Effendi also suggests that we might look to the early history of the United States in order to develop greater confidence in the feasibility of a global federal system. In this regard, he writes:

> How confident were the assertions made in the days preceding the unification of
> the states of the North American continent regarding the insuperable barriers
> that stood in the way of their ultimate federation! Was it not widely and emphat-
> ically declared that the conflicting interests, the mutual distrust, the difference of
> government and habit that divided the states were such as no force, whether spir-
> itual or temporal, could ever hope to harmonize or control? And yet, how differ-
> ent were the conditions prevailing a hundred and fifty years ago from those that
> characterize present-day society! It would indeed be no exaggeration to say that
> the absence of those facilities which modern scientific progress has placed at the
> service of humanity in our time made of the problem of welding the American
> states into a single federation, similar though they were in certain traditions, a task
> infinitely more complex than that which confronts a divided humanity in its ef-
> forts to achieve the unification of all mankind.[10]

In addition to addressing the question of war and collective security, universal ratification of the Convention on the Elimination of Discrimination against
Women would do much to advance our confidence in the eventual effectiveness of the global campaign to eradicate gender-based violence. As of May
2001, 168 countries, representing more than two-thirds of the members of the
United Nations, have agreed to be party to the convention. An additional 4
countries have signed the treaty binding themselves to do nothing in contra-
vention of the convention's terms. Inasmuch as the convention permits ratification by countries subject to reservations, provided that the reservations are not
incompatible with the overall objective and purpose of the convention (see appendix A for the full text of the convention), those countries that may have legitimate reservations about its exact wording or implementation need not delay
ratification on those grounds.

Nor can we neglect adoption and implementation of the UN Declaration on
the Elimination of Violence against Women (see appendix B for the full text).
Although not legally binding, the complete and universal adoption of this document, serving as it does as the first set of international standards to address the
problem of gender-based violence, would provide additional fuel for hope in
our ability to translate what has been written into action.

Whatever have been its faults and shortcomings, for more than a half century the United Nations has stood as an important and noble symbol for the collective interests of humankind. In areas of health, education, agriculture, envi-
ronmental protection, the welfare of children, and the advancement of the
rights of women, the UN has demonstrated our capacity for united action
across lines of race, culture, religion, class, and nationality. Such a body deserves the world's support and encouragement.

The United Nations, like the League of Nations before it, can be seen as
representing the earliest steps of humankind toward the realization of a vision

of harmonious cooperation and collective security. While lacking in the material resources necessary to carry out its mandate fully, the UN has, in the judgment of many, been instrumental in averting a number of wars over the course of its short life. To be sure, the UN would be strengthened were it able to rely upon resources that extend beyond voluntary contributions. In addition, the executive and judicial functions of the UN would be carried out to greater effect were it provided the latitude to act even in crises in which the nations involved had not submitted their case for its consideration. Last, as has been suggested throughout this book, in addition to emphasizing the promotion and protection of human rights, the UN would do well to continue to give greater emphasis to the promotion of a consciousness of the psychological, moral, and spiritual dimensions of the global problems it works so hard to remedy.

We derive hope as well from the knowledge that there are, at present, individuals and organizations around the world that are contributing to the amelioration of the harsh consequences of gender-based violence. This work must be able to continue with renewed support. One of the most effective of these organizations, the Tahirih Justice Center, was founded by a young attorney in her first year out of law school. According to its founder, Layli Miller, the Tahirih Justice Center "seeks to bring justice to the lives of women facing international human rights abuses by transforming policies and law, through direct services, outreach and advocacy." The center provides legal advocacy in cases that champion the rights of women and protect them from international human rights abuses. Through litigation, statutory and regulatory development, collaboration with government agencies and like-minded organizations, and public outreach, the center seeks to transform the system so that women are better protected from violence. Recognizing that women facing abuse require a holistic approach to find true justice, the center also coordinates a referral program that assists its clients in accessing medical care and social services. Here are some examples of the advocacy work being carried out at the Tahirih Justice Center.

Female-genital-mutilation related

- A fourteen-year-old Kenyan girl faced forced female genital mutilation (FGM) at the hands of her deceased father's family in Kenya. The center helped her, her mother, and her sixteen-year-old brother gain political asylum in the United States.

- Two U.S. citizens, girls aged five and seven, are facing forced FGM if their father is forced to return with them to Nigeria. The center is representing the girls' father in his withholding-of-removal case, which is currently pending before the Board of Immigration.

- A two-year-old U.S. citizen was threatened with FGM at the hands of her family's elders if she returned to Nigeria with her mother. Her mother had been a victim of FGM herself in Nigeria and had also lost her sister and other female relatives to the practice. The center's legal representation helped her mother gain political asylum in the United States on the grounds that the threat of losing her daughter was persecution and that it was unreasonable to make her choose between leaving her infant daughter in the United States and taking her back to Nigeria to face FGM. The girl's father, who also opposes FGM, will also now be able to emigrate to join his wife and child in the United States.

- A fourteen-year-old Guinean girl of the Fulani/Peuhl tribe was forcibly subjected to FGM at the age of nine by her grandmother, who is now demanding that she return to Guinea to be married to a polygamist man four times her age who has several children her age. The girl is also an active member of the RPG (Rassemblement du peuple du Guinée) youth group, whose parent group is a political movement to which her mother belongs and that speaks out against the current Guinean government. The girl was demonstrating at an RPG rally and was wounded by the repressive measures taken by the Guinean government to suppress the rally. The center has provided the girl with in-depth consultation and guidance regarding her asylum case, as well as a pro bono physician referral.

- The center is currently representing a four-year-old Nigerian girl who will face FGM in Nigeria at the hands of her deceased father's parents if she is forced to return. She is of the Urhobo tribe in Nigeria, and both of her parents are opposed to FGM. However, since her father has died, his parents have taken over control of the family, and they are threatening to circumcise her and also take her away from her mother.

Violence against Women Act–related

- The center represented a five-year-old girl in challenging an order granting full custody to her abusive father in Greece, as opposed to her mother who resides in the United States. The girl's father was charged with abusing and neglecting his daughter and physically and emotionally abusing the girl's mother.

- A one-year-old girl, a U.S. citizen, faced separation from her Ugandan mother and placement in her abusive father's custody. The center helped find her pro bono family law representation to counter the abusive father's claims that the child's mother was "crazy" and "going to be deported." The center also provided free medical services to treat the child's mother's mild depression and anxiety that developed as a result of her abuse. Through a referral by the center, the girl's mother obtained a protection order against the father, who had previously beaten, choked, and threatened her with death.

• The U.S.-citizen father of a six-month-old girl tried to have the girl's mother deported. After an incident in which the father repeatedly punched the mother in the face and then held a gun to her head when she had been breastfeeding the little girl, the mother notified authorities of her husband's attacks. In retaliation for seeking help, the father threatened to have her deported and warned that unless she tried to get the criminal charges against him dropped, he would not attend their green card interview. The center helped the girl's mother obtain legal classification under the Violence against Women Act (VAWA) and thus protected the girl from separation from her mother.

• The Korean wife of a naturalized U.S. citizen was viciously attacked and abused throughout their two-year marriage; she was forbidden to learn English or take driving lessons and was beaten around the head on several occasions. While her husband was at work, she managed to contact the Korean community service center, who in turn referred her to the Tahirih Justice Center. She was able to speak with a Korean-speaking attorney about her abuse and possible protections under VAWA. The center's social services coordinator helped her apply for and enter a local battered women's shelter and put her in touch with a Korean American English tutor. She plans to file for classification as a battered wife of a U.S. citizen.

• The Ukrainian wife of a U.S. citizen suffered mental and physical abuse at the hands of her husband that was so extreme, he was arrested and charged with attempted murder, assault, and battery. While seeking medical attention for her injuries, she told authorities about the abuse she had been suffering. She was eventually granted a protection order and sent to live at a battered women's shelter with her young daughter. Her therapist referred her to the Tahirih Justice Center, which represented her in her effort to obtain immigration relief under VAWA. The Immigration and Naturalization Service (INS) approved her application and gave her a work authorization card; she currently works as an engineer and lives in her own apartment with her child.

Honor Crimes and Gender Apartheid: Afghanistan

• A former schoolteacher came to the United States in 1998 after her family arranged a marriage for her to a U.S. citizen. The Taliban in Afghanistan had forced her to stop teaching in 1996 when they closed the school where she taught. She was being forced to comply with the increasingly restrictive measures being imposed on women by the Taliban. Her father had been imprisoned and her brother-in-law murdered by them, and her family was targeted because of their minority ethnicity. They eventually escaped to Pakistan. She came to the United States after a year and did not marry her arranged husband but developed a relationship with another man, with whom she had two U.S.-citizen children. She could not tell her family about her children, as having children out of wedlock could lead to violence or murder as a means for the family to vindicate its honor. Until very recently the Taliban also inflicted death by stoning on women who have transgressed Muslim laws regarding sexuality. The Tahirih Justice Center represented her before an immigration judge in Arlington, Virginia, and she was granted withholding of removal to both Pakistan and Afghanistan. As a result, she is allowed to live and work in the United States; she lives with her children and their father and intends to continue her teaching career.

Trafficking and Slavery

- A woman who was a member of a persecuted clan in Kenya was brutally raped by police officers on two separate occasions and then was pursued by them. To escape the threat of abuse, she took a job in Saudi Arabia. When she arrived, her "employer" seized her passport and visa and forced her into slavery. She worked long days with no pay, was nearly starved, endured constant physical and emotional abuse, and was threatened with imprisonment and murder if she attempted escape. When her employer moved to the United States, with the help of some acquaintances, the woman was able to escape from her enslavement after two weeks. She is now a client of the Tahirih Justice Center and is seeking political asylum and a special visa that allows victims of human trafficking to remain in the United States while they assist in prosecuting their traffickers.

Domestic Worker Abuse

- A woman from Zimbabwe was legally brought to the United States by a diplomat to be his housekeeper. Upon her arrival in the United States, her employer refused to pay her for her work, forcing her to work strenuously and continuously for very long hours. Afraid to flee her employer for fear of retaliation, she endured this for some time before she finally escaped and brought suit against him for back wages. Although she won the suit, her employer then successfully sued her for slander against him. He also contacted the INS and reported that she had abandoned her employment contract and had therefore violated her immigration status. The Tahirih Justice Center is helping to defend her against deportation by the INS, on the basis that she was forced to violate her status because the employer was not paying her.

Sexual Harassment

- A sixteen-year-old El Salvadoran girl became the victim of constant sexual harassment by an armed gang of men who threatened her with rape. The gang found out where she lived and came to her house on a few occasions with the stated intention of raping her. She was not there at the time, and instead the gang attacked her mother and forced her younger sister to watch the attack. The girl reported the incident to the police, and one gang member was jailed for six months. She was fortunate enough to flee for her life to the United States, but her smugglers subjected her and other women she was with to sexual harassment and abuse as well. The gang member who was imprisoned is now free and has threatened to kill her and has also falsely boasted of raping her, meaning that she will face extreme social ostracism if she returns to El Salvador. In September 2000, the Tahirih Justice Center represented her in her request for political asylum before an immigration judge in Arlington, Virginia, but her case was denied because the law is very unsettled regarding sexual harassment as a basis for political asylum. Her case is currently on appeal before the Board of Immigration Appeals.

Layli's effort, and the work of her able team at the Tahirih Justice Center, is one among a growing number of international programs designed to meet the human rights needs of all women, irrespective of their national, racial, religious, or cultural background. Initiatives such as these nurture our hope and deserve our support and encouragement. We can contribute to this work by contacting the Tahirih Justice Center at www.Tahirih.org.

A Closing Word

There is a children's story that impresses itself upon many of us even in our adulthood. It's Watty Piper's book, *The Little Engine That Could*.[11] As James Maddux recently observed, believing that we can accomplish what we want to accomplish is "one of the most important ingredients—perhaps the most important ingredient—in the recipe for success. Any child who has read 'The Little Engine That Could' knows this is so."[12] In this book, we have made an effort to describe what a very great challenge to all of us this problem of gender-based violence presents. But we have also tried to point out some of the paths that may lead us forward. Now we must say to ourselves that *we can* eradicate gender-based violence, and that *we will*. Such an affirmation, when carried with conviction into action, will no doubt draw down upon us resources that will inspire, encourage, and assist. That is the way that it has been throughout human history.

Appendix A

Declaration on the Elimination of Violence against Women

The General Assembly,

Recognizing the urgent need for the universal application of women of the rights and principles with regard to equality, security, liberty, integrity and dignity of all human beings,

Noting that those rights and principles are enshrined in international instruments, including the Universal Declaration of Human Rights,[1] the International Covenant on Civil and Political Rights,[2] the International Covenant on Economic, Social and Cultural Rights,[3] the Convention on the Elimination of All Forms of Discrimination Against Women[4] and the Convention Against Torture and Other Cruel, Inhuman or Degrading Treatment or Punishment,

Recognizing that effective implementation of the Convention on the Elimination of All Forms of Discrimination Against Women would contribute to the elimination of violence against women and that the Declaration on the Elimination of Violence against Women, set forth in the present resolution, will strengthen and complement that process,

Concerned that violence against women is an obstacle to the achievement of equality, development and peace, as recognized in the Nairobi Forward-Looking Strategies for the Advancement of Women,[5] in which a set of measures to combat violence against women was recommended, and to the full implementation of the Convention on the Elimination of All Forms of Discrimination Against Women,

Affirming that violence against women constitutes a violation of the rights and fundamental freedoms of women and impairs or nullifies their enjoyment of those rights and freedoms, and concerned about the long-standing failure to protect and promote those rights and freedoms in the case of violence against women,

Recognizing that violence against women is a manifestation of historically unequal power relations between men and women, which have led to domination over and discrimination against women by men and to the prevention of the full advancement of women, and that violence against women is one of the crucial social mechanisms by which women are forced into a subordinate position compared with men,

Concerned that some groups of women, such as women belonging to minority groups, indigenous women, refugee women, migrant women, women living in rural or remote communities, destitute women, women in institutions or in detention, female children, women with disabilities, elderly women and women in situations of armed conflict, are especially vulnerable to violence,

Recalling the conclusion in paragraph 23 of the annex to Economic and Social Council resolution 1990/15 of 24 May 1990 that the recognition that violence against women in the family and society was pervasive and cut across lines of income, class and culture had to be matched by urgent and effective steps to eliminate its incidence,

Recalling also Economic and Social Council resolution 1991/18 of 30 May 1991, in which the Council recommended the development of a framework for an international instrument that would address explicitly the issue of violence against women,

Welcoming the role that women's movements are playing in drawing increasing attention to the nature, severity and magnitude of the problem of violence against women,

Alarmed that opportunities for women to achieve legal, social, political and economic equality in society are limited, inter alia, by continuing and endemic violence,

Convinced that in the light of the above there is a need for a clear and comprehensive definition of violence against women, a clear statement of the rights to be applied to ensure the elimination of violence against women in all its forms, a commitment by the States in respect of their responsibilities, and a commitment by the international community at large to the elimination of violence against women,

Solemnly proclaims the following Declaration on the Elimination of Violence Against Women and urges that every effort be made so that it becomes generally known and respected:

Article 1

For the purposes of this Declaration, the term "violence against women" means any act of gender-based violence that results in, or is likely to result in, physical, sexual or psychological harm or suffering to women, including threats of such acts, coercion or arbitrary deprivation of liberty, whether occurring in public or private life.

Article 2

Violence against women shall be understood to encompass, but not be limited to, the following:

a) Physical, sexual and psychological violence occurring in the family, including battering, sexual abuse of female children in the household, dowry-related violence, marital rape, female genital circumcision and other traditional practices harmful to women, non-spousal violence and violence related to exploitation;

b) Physical, sexual and psychological violence occurring within the general community, including rape, sexual abuse, sexual harassment and intimidation at work, in educational institutions and elsewhere, trafficking in women and forced prostitution;

c) Physical, sexual and psychological violence perpetrated or condoned by the State, wherever it occurs.

Article 3
Women are entitled to the equal enjoyment and protection of all human rights and fundamental freedoms in the political, economic, social, cultural, civil or any other field. These rights include, inter alia:

a) The right to life;[6]

b) The right to equality;[7]

c) The right to liberty and security of persons;[8]

d) The right to equal protection under the law;[9]

e) The right to be free from all forms of discrimination;[10]

f) The right to the highest standard attainable of physical and mental health;

g) The right not to be subjected to torture, or other cruel, inhuman or degrading treatment or punishment.[11]

Article 4
States should condemn violence against women and should not invoke any custom, tradition or religious consideration to avoid their obligations with respect to its elimination. States should pursue by all appropriate means and without delay a policy of eliminating violence against women and, to this end, should:

a) Consider, where they have not yet done so, ratifying or acceding to the Convention on the Elimination of All Forms of Discrimination Against Women or withdrawing reservations to that Convention;

b) Refrain from engaging in violence against women;

c) Exercise due diligence to prevent, investigate and, in accordance with national legislation, punish acts of violence against women, whether those acts are perpetrated by the State or by private persons;

d) Develop penal, civil, labor and administrative sanctions in domestic legislation to punish and redress the wrongs caused to women who are subjected to violence; women who are subjected to violence should be provided with access to the mechanisms of justice and, as provided for by national legislation, to just and effective remedies for the harm that they have suffered; States should also inform women of their rights in seeking redress through such mechanisms;

e) Consider the possibility of developing national plans of action to promote the protection of women against any form of violence, or to include provisions for that purpose in plans already existing, taking into account, as appropriate, such cooperation as can be provided by non-governmental organizations, particularly those concerned with the issue of violence against women;

f) Develop, in a comprehensive way, preventive approaches and all those measures of a legal, political, administrative and cultural nature that promote protection of women against any form of violence, and ensure that the re-victimization of women does not occur because of laws insensitive to gender considerations, enforcement practices or other interventions;

g) Work to ensure, to the maximum extent feasible in the light of their available resources and, where needed, within the framework of international cooperation, that women subjected to violence and, where appropriate, their children have specialized assistance, such as rehabilitation, assistance in child care and maintenance, treatment, counseling, and health and social services, facilities and programs, as well as support structures, and should take all other appropriate measures to promote their safety and physical and psychological rehabilitation;

h) Include in government budgets adequate resources for their activities related to the elimination of violence against women;

i) Take measures to ensure that law enforcement officers and public officials responsible for implementing policies to prevent, investigate and punish violence against women receive training to sensitize them to the needs of women;

j) Adopt all appropriate measures, especially in the field of education, to modify the social and cultural patterns of conduct of men and women and to eliminate prejudices, customary practices and all other practices based on the idea of the inferiority or superiority of either of the sexes and on stereotyped roles for men and women;

k) Promote research, collect data and compile statistics, especially concerning domestic violence, relating to the prevalence of different forms of violence against women and encourage research on the causes, nature, seriousness and consequences of violence against women and on the effectiveness of measures implemented to prevent and redress violence against women; those statistics and findings of the research will be made public;

l) Adopt measures directed towards the elimination of violence against women who are especially vulnerable to violence;

m) Encourage the development of appropriate guidelines to assist in the implementation of the principles set forth in the present Declaration;

n) Recognize the important role of the women's movement and non-governmental organizations worldwide in raising awareness and alleviating the problem of violence against women;

o) Facilitate and enhance the work of the women's movement and nongovernmental organizations and cooperate with them at local, national and regional levels;

p) Encourage intergovernmental regional organizations of which they are members to include the elimination of violence against women in their programs, as appropriate.

Article 5

The organs and specialized agencies of the United Nations system should, within their respective fields of competence, contribute to the recognition and realization of the rights and the principles set forth in the present Declaration and, to this end, should, inter alia:

a) Foster international and regional cooperation with a view to defining regional strategies for combating violence, exchanging experiences and financing programs relating to the elimination of violence against women;

b) Promote meetings and seminars with the aim of creating and raising awareness among all persons of the issue of the elimination of violence against women;

c) Foster coordination and exchange within the United Nations system between human rights treaty bodies to address the issue of violence against women effectively;

d) Include in analyses prepared by organizations and bodies of the United Nations system of social trends and problems, such as the periodic reports on the world social situation, examination of trends in violence against women;

e) Encourage coordination between organizations and bodies of the United Nations system to incorporate the issue of violence against women into ongoing programs, especially with reference to groups of women particularly vulnerable to violence;

f) Promote the formulation of guidelines or manuals relating to violence against women, taking into account the measures referred to in the present Declaration;

g) Consider the issue of the elimination of violence against women, as appropriate, in fulfilling their mandates with respect to the implementation of human rights instruments;

h) Cooperate with non-governmental organizations in addressing the issue of violence against women.

Article 6

Nothing in the present Declaration shall affect any provision that is more conducive to the elimination of violence against women that may be contained in the legislation of a State or in any international convention, treaty or other instrument in force in a State.

Notes

1. Resolution 217 A (III).

2. See resolution 2200 A (XXI), annex.

3. Resolution 34/180, annex.

4. Resolution 39/46, annex.

5. Report of the World Conference to Review and Appraise the Achievements of the United Nations Decade for Women: Equality, Development and Peace, Nairobi, 15–26 July 1985 (United Nations publication, Sales No. E. 85. IV. 10), chap. I, sect. A.

6. Universal Declaration of Human Rights, article 3; and International Covenant on Civil and Political Rights, article 6.

7. International Covenant on Civil and Political Rights, article 26.

8. Universal Declaration of Human Rights, article 3; and International Covenant on Civil and Political Rights, article 9.

9. International Covenant on Economic, Social and Cultural Rights, article 12.

10. Universal Declaration of Human Rights, article 23; and International Covenant on Economic, Social and Cultural Rights, articles 6 and 7.

11. Universal Declaration of Human Rights, article 5; International Covenant on Civil and Political Rights, article 7; and Convention against Torture and Other Cruel, Inhuman or Degrading Treatment or Punishment.

Appendix B

Convention on the Elimination of All Forms of Discrimination against Women

The States Parties to the Present Convention,

Noting that the Charter of the United Nations reaffirms faith in fundamental human rights, in the dignity and worth of the human person and in the equal rights of men and women,

Noting that the Universal Declaration of Human Rights affirms the principle of the inadmissibility of discrimination and proclaims that all human beings are born free and equal in dignity and rights and that everyone is entitled to all the rights and freedoms set forth therein, without distinction of any kind, including distinction based on sex,

Noting that the States Parties to the International Covenants on Human Rights have the obligation to ensure the equal right of men and women to enjoy all economic, social, cultural, civil and political rights,

Considering the international conventions concluded under the auspices of the United Nations and the specialized agencies promoting equality of rights of men and women,

Noting also the resolutions, declarations and recommendations adopted by the United Nations and the specialized agencies promoting equality of rights of men and women,

Concerned, however, that despite these various instruments extensive discrimination against women continues to exist,

Recalling that discrimination against women violates the principles of equality of rights and respect for human dignity, is an obstacle to the participation of women, on equal terms with men, in the political, social, economic and cultural life of their countries, hampers the growth of the prosperity of society and the family and makes more difficult the full development of the potentialities of women in the service of their countries and of humanity,

Concerned that in situations of poverty women have the least access to food, health, education, training and opportunities for employment and other needs,

Convinced that the establishment of the new international economic order based on equity and justice will contribute significantly toward the promotion of equality between men and women,

Emphasizing that the eradication of apartheid, of all forms of racism, racial discrimination, colonialism, neo-colonialism, aggression, foreign occupation and domination and interference in the internal affairs of States is essential to the full enjoyment of the rights of men and women,

Affirming that the strengthening of international peace and security, relaxation of international tension, mutual co-operation among all States irrespective of their social and economic systems, general and complete disarmament, and in particular nuclear disarmament under strict and effective international control, the affirmation of the principles of justice, equality and mutual benefit in relations among countries and the realization of the right of peoples under alien and colonial domination and foreign occupation to self-determination and independence, as well as respect for national sovereignty and territorial integrity, will promote social progress and development and as a consequence will contribute to the attainment of full equality between men and women,

Convinced that the full and complete development of a country, the welfare of the world and the cause of peace require the maximum participation of women on equal terms with men in all fields,

Bearing in mind the great contribution of women to the welfare of the family and to the development of society, so far not fully recognized, the social significance of maternity and the role of both parents in the family and in the upbringing of children, and aware that the role of women in procreation should not be a basis for discrimination but that the upbringing of children requires a sharing of responsibility between men and women and society as a whole,

Aware that a change in the traditional role of men as well as the role of women in society and in the family is needed to achieve full equality between men and women,

Determined to implement the principles set forth in the Declaration on Elimination of Discrimination Against Women and, for that purpose, to adopt the measures required for the elimination of such discrimination in all its forms and manifestations,

Have agreed on the following:

Part I

Article 1
For the purposes of the present Convention, the term "discrimination against women" shall mean any distinction, exclusion or restriction made on the basis of sex which has the effect or purpose of impairing or nullifying the recog-

nition, enjoyment or exercise by women, irrespective of their marital status, on a basis of equality of men and women, of human rights and fundamental freedoms in the political, economic, social, cultural, civil or any other field.

Article 2

States Parties condemn discrimination against women in all its forms, agree to pursue by all appropriate means and without delay a policy of eliminating discrimination against women and, to this end, undertake:

a) To embody the principle of equality of men and women in their national constitutions or other appropriate legislation if not yet incorporated therein and to ensure, through law and other appropriate means, the practical realization of this principle;

b) To adopt appropriate legislative and other measures, including sanctions where appropriate, prohibiting all discrimination against women;

c) To establish legal protection of the rights of women on an equal basis with men and to ensure through competent national tribunals and other public institutions the effective protection of women against any act of discrimination;

d) To refrain from engaging in any act or practice of discrimination against women and to ensure that public authorities and institutions shall act in conformity with this obligation;

e) To take all appropriate measures to eliminate discrimination against women by any person, organization or enterprise;

f) To take all appropriate measures, including legislation, to modify or abolish existing laws, regulations, customs and practices which constitute discrimination against women;

g) To repeal all national penal provisions which constitute discrimination against women.

Article 3

States Parties shall take in all fields, in particular in the political, social, economic and cultural fields, all appropriate measures, including legislation, to ensure the full development and advancement of women for the purpose of guaranteeing them the exercise and enjoyment of human rights and fundamental freedoms on a basis of equality with men.

Article 4

1. Adoption by States Parties of temporary special measures aimed at accelerating *de facto* equality between men and women shall not be considered discrimination as defined in the present Convention, but shall in no way entail as a consequence the maintenance of unequal or separate standards; these measures shall be discontinued when the objectives of equality of opportunity and treatment have been achieved.

2. Adoption by the States Parties of special measures, including those measures contained in the present Convention, aimed at protecting maternity shall not be considered discriminatory.

Article 5
States Parties shall take all appropriate measures:

a) To modify the social and cultural patterns of conduct of men and women, with a view to achieving the elimination of prejudices and customary and all other practices which are based on the idea of inferiority or the superiority of either of the sexes or on stereotyped roles for men and women;

b) To ensure that family education includes a proper understanding of maternity as a social function and the recognition of the common responsibility of men and women in the upbringing and development of their children, it being understood that the interest of the children is the primordial consideration in all cases.

Article 6
States Parties shall take all appropriate measures, including legislation, to suppress all forms of traffic in women and exploitation of prostitution of women.

Part II

Article 7
States Parties shall take all appropriate measures to eliminate discrimination against women in the political and public life of the country and, in particular, shall ensure to women, on equal terms with men, the right:

a) To vote in all elections and public referenda and to be eligible for election to all publicly elected bodies;

b) To participate in the formulation of government policy and the implementation thereof and to hold public office and perform all public functions at all levels of government;

c) To participate in non-governmental organizations and associations concerned with the public and political life of the country.

Article 8
States Parties shall take all appropriate measures to ensure to women, on equal terms with men and without any discrimination, the opportunity to represent their Governments at the international level and to participate in the work of international organizations.

Article 9

1. States Parties shall grant women equal rights with men to acquire, change or retain their nationality. They shall ensure in particular that neither marriage to an alien nor change of nationality by the husband during marriage shall automatically change the nationality of the wife, render her stateless or force upon her the nationality of the husband.

2. States Parties shall grant women equal rights with men with respect to the nationality of their children.

Part III

Article 10

States Parties shall take all appropriate measures to eliminate discrimination against women in order to ensure them equal rights with men in the field of education and in particular to ensure, on a basis of equality of men and women:

a) The same conditions for career and vocational guidance, for access to studies and for the achievement of diplomas in educational establishments of all categories in rural as well as in urban areas; this equality shall be ensured in pre-school, general, technical, professional and higher technical education, as well as in all types of vocational training;

b) Access to the same curricula, the same examinations, teaching staff with qualifications of the same standard and school premises and equipment of the same quality;

c) The elimination of any stereotyped concept of the roles of men and women at all levels and in all forms of education by encouraging coeducation and other types of education which will help to achieve this aim and, in particular, by the revision of textbooks and school programs and the adoption of teaching methods;

d) The same opportunities to benefit from scholarships and other study grants;

e) The same opportunities for access to programs of continuing education, including adult and functional literacy programs, particularly those aimed at reducing, at the earliest possible time, any gap in education existing between men and women;

f) The reduction of female student drop-out rates and the organization of programs for girls and women who have left school prematurely;

g) The same opportunities to participate actively in sports and physical education;

h) Access to specific educational information to help to ensure the health and well-being of families, including information and advice on family planning.

Article 11

1. States Parties shall take all appropriate measures to eliminate discrimination against women in the field of employment in order to ensure, on a basis of equality of men and women, the same rights, in particular:

    a) The right to work as an inalienable right of all human beings;

    b) The right to the same employment opportunities, including the application of the same criteria for selection in matters of employment;

    c) The right to free choice of profession and employment, the right to promotion, job security and all benefits and conditions of service and the right to receive vocational training and retraining, including apprenticeships, advanced vocational training and recurrent training;

    d) The right to equal remuneration, including benefits, and to equal treatment in respect of work of equal value, as well as equality of treatment in the evaluation of the quality of work;

    e) The right to social security, particularly in cases of retirement, unemployment, sickness, invalidity and old age and other incapacity to work, as well as the right to paid leave;

    f) The right to protection of health and to safety in working conditions, including the safeguarding of the function of reproduction.

2. In order to prevent discrimination against women on the grounds of marriage or maternity and to ensure their effective right to work, States Parties shall take appropriate measures:

    a) To prohibit, subject to the imposition of sanctions, dismissal on the grounds of pregnancy or of maternity leave and discrimination in dismissals on the basis of marital status;

    b) To introduce maternity leave with pay or with comparable social benefits without loss of former employment, seniority or social allowances;

    c) To encourage the provision of the necessary supporting social services to enable parents to combine family obligations with work responsibilities and participation in public life, in particular through promoting the establishment and development of a network of child-care facilities;

    d) To provide special protection to women during pregnancy in types of work proved to be harmful to them.

3. Protective legislation relating to matters covered in this article shall be reviewed periodically in the light of scientific and technological knowledge and shall be revised, repealed or extended as necessary.

Article 12

1. States shall take all appropriate measures to eliminate discrimination against women in the field of health care in order to ensure, on a basis of equality of men and women, access to health care services, including those related to family planning.

2. Not withstanding the provisions of paragraph 1 of this article, State Parties shall ensure to women appropriate services in connection with pregnancy, confinement and the post-natal period, granting free services where necessary, as well as adequate nutrition during pregnancy and lactation.

Article 13
1. States Parties shall take all appropriate measures to eliminate discrimination against women in other areas of economic and social life in order to ensure, on a basis of equality of men and women, the same rights, in particular:

a) The right to family benefits;

b) The right to bank loans, mortgages and other forms of financial credit;

c) The right to participate in recreational activities, sports and all aspects of cultural life.

Article 14
1. States Parties shall take into account the particular problems faced by rural women and the significant roles which rural women play in the economic survival of their families, including their work in the non-monetarized sectors of the economy, and shall take all appropriate measures to ensure the application of the provisions of this Convention to women in rural areas.

2. States Parties shall take all appropriate measures to eliminate discrimination against women in rural areas in order to ensure, on a basis of equality of men and women, that they participate in and benefit from rural development and, in particular, shall ensure to such women the right:

a) To participate in the elaboration and implementation of development planning at all levels;

b) To have access to adequate health care facilities, including information, counseling and services in family planning;

c) To benefit directly from social security programs;

d) To obtain all types of training and education, formal and not-formal, including that relating to functional literacy, as well as, *inter alia*, the benefit of all community and extension services, in order to increase their technical proficiency;

e) To organize self-help groups and co-operatives in order to obtain equal access to economic opportunities through employment or self-employment;

f) To participate in all community activities;

g) To have access to agricultural credit and loans, marketing facilities, appropriate technology and equal treatment in land and agrarian reform as well as in land resettlement schemes;

h) To enjoy adequate living conditions, particularly in relation to housing, sanitation, electricity and water supply, transport and communications.

Part IV

Article 15

1. States Parties shall accord to women equality with men before the law.

2. States Parties shall accord to women, in civil matters, a legal capacity identical to that of men and the same opportunities to exercise that capacity. In particular, they shall give women equal rights to conclude contracts and to administer property and shall treat them equally in all stages of procedure in courts and tribunals.

3. States Parties agree that all contracts and all other private instruments of any kind with a legal effect which is directed at restricting the legal capacity of women shall be deemed null and void.

4. States Parties shall accord to men and women the same rights with regard to the law relating to the movement of persons and the freedom to choose their residence and domicile.

Article 16

1. States Parties shall take all appropriate measures to eliminate discrimination against women in all matters relating to marriage and family relations and in particular shall ensure, on a basis of equality of men and women:

a) The same right to enter into marriage;

b) The same right freely to choose a spouse and to enter into marriage only with their free and full consent;

c) The same rights and responsibilities during marriage and at its dissolution;

d) The same rights and responsibilities as parents, irrespective of their marital status, in matters relating to their children; in all cases the interests of the children shall be paramount;

e) The same rights to decide freely and responsibly on the number and spacing of their children and to have access to the information, education and means to enable them to exercise these rights;

f) The same rights and responsibilities with regard to guardianship, wardship, trusteeship and adoption of children, or similar institutions where these concepts exist in national legislation; in all cases the interests of the children shall be paramount;

g) The same personal rights as husband and wife, including the right to choose a family name, a profession and an occupation;

h) The same rights for both spouses in respect of the ownership, acquisition, management, administration, enjoyment and disposition of property, whether free of charge or for a valuable consideration.

2. The betrothal and marriage of a child have no legal effect, and all necessary action, including legislation, shall be take to specify a minimum age for marriage and to make the registration of marriages in an official registry compulsory.

Part V

Article 17

1. For the purpose of considering the progress made in the implementation of the present Convention, there shall be established a Committee on the Elimination of Discrimination Against Women (hereinafter referred to as the Committee) consisting, at the time of entry into force of the Convention, of eighteen and, after ratification of the time of entry into force of the Convention, of eighteen and, after ratification of or accession to the Convention by the thirty-fifth State Party, of twenty-three experts of high moral standing and competence in the field covered by the Convention. The experts shall be elected by States Parties from among their nationals and shall serve in their personal capacity, consideration being given to equitable geographical distribution and to the representation of the different forms of civilization as well as the principal legal systems.

2. The members of the Committee shall be elected by secret ballot from a list of persons nominated by States Parties. Each State Party may nominate one person from among its own nationals.

3. The initial election shall be held six months after the date of entry into force of the present Convention. At least three months before the date of each election the Secretary-General of the United Nations shall address a letter to the States Parties inviting them to submit their nominations within two months. The Secretary-General shall prepare a list in alphabetical order of all persons thus nominated, indicating the States Parties which have nominated them, and shall submit it to the States Parties.

4. Elections of the members of the Committee shall be held at a meeting of States Parties convened by the Secretary-General at United Nations Headquarters. At that meeting, for which two-thirds of the States Parties shall constitute a quorum, the persons elected to the Committee shall be those nominees who obtain the largest number of votes and an absolute majority of the votes of the representatives of States Parties present and voting.

5. The members of the Committee shall be elected for a term of four years. However, the terms of nine of the members elected at the first election shall expire at the end of two years; immediately after the first election the names of these nine members shall be chosen by lot by the Chairman of the Committee.

6. The election of the five additional members of the Committee shall be held in accordance with the provisions of paragraphs 2,3, and 4 of this article, following the thirty-fifth ratification or accession. The terms of two of the additional members elected on this occasion shall expire at the end of two years, the names of these two members having been chosen by lot by the Chairman of the Committee.

7. For the filling of casual vacancies, the State Party whose expert has ceased to function as a member of the Committee shall appoint another expert from

among its nationals, subject to the approval of the Committee.

8. The members of the Committee shall, with the approval of the General Assembly, receive emoluments from the United Nations resources on such terms and conditions as the Assembly may decide, having regard to the importance of the Committee's responsibilities.

9. The Secretary-General of the United Nations shall provide the necessary staff and facilities for the effective performance of the functions of the Committee under the present Convention.

Article 18

1. States Parties undertake to submit to the Secretary-General of the United Nations, for consideration by the Committee, a report on the legislative, judicial, administrative or other measures which they have adopted to give effect to the provisions of the present Convention and on the progress made in this respect:

a) Within a year after the entry into force for the State concerned; and

b) Thereafter at least every four years and further whenever the Committee so requests.

2. Reports may indicate factors and difficulties affecting the degree of fulfillment of obligations under the present Convention.

Article 19

1. The Committee shall adopt its own rules of procedure.

2. The Committee shall elect its officers for a term of two years.

Article 20

1. The Committee shall normally meet for a period of not more than two weeks annually in order to consider the reports submitted in accordance with article 18 of the present Convention.

2. The meetings of the Committee shall normally be held at United Nations Headquarters or at any other convenient place as determined by the Committee.

Article 21

1. The Committee shall, through the Economic and Social Council, report annually to the General Assembly of the United Nations on its activities and may make suggestions and general recommendations based on the examination of reports and information received from the States Parties. Such suggestions and general recommendations shall be included in the report of the Committee together with comments, if any, from States Parties.

2. The Secretary-General shall transmit the reports of the Committee to the Commission on the Status of Women for its information.

Article 22

The specialized agencies shall be entitled to be represented at the consideration of the implementation of such provisions of the present Convention as fall within the scope of their activities. The Committee may invite the specialized agencies to submit reports on the implementation of the Convention in areas falling within the scope of their activities.

Part VI

Article 23

Nothing in this Convention shall affect any provisions that are more conducive to the achievement of equality between men and women which may be contained:

a) In the legislation of a State Party; or

b) In any other international convention, treaty or agreement in force for that State.

Article 24

States Parties undertake to adopt all necessary measures at the national level aimed at achieving the full realization of the rights recognized in the present Convention.

Article 25

1. The present Convention shall be open for signature by all States.

2. The Secretary-General of the United Nations is designated as the depository of the present Convention.

3. The present Convention is subject to ratification. Instruments of ratification shall be deposited with the Secretary-General of the United Nations.

4. The present Convention shall be open to accession by all States. Accession shall be effected by the deposit of an instrument of accession with the Secretary-General of the United Nations.

Article 26

1. A request for the revision of the present Convention may be made at any time by any State Party by means of a notification in writing addressed to the Secretary-General of the United Nations.

2. The General Assembly of the United Nations shall decide upon the steps, if any, to be taken in respect of such a request.

Article 27

1. The present Convention shall enter into force on the thirtieth day after

the date of deposit with the Secretary-General of the United Nations of the twentieth instrument of ratification or accession.

2. For each State ratifying the present Convention or acceding to it after the deposit of the twentieth instrument of ratification or accession, the Convention shall enter into force on the thirtieth day after the date of the deposit of its own instrument of ratification or accession.

Article 28

1. The Secretary-General of the United Nations shall receive and circulate to all States the text of reservations made by States at the time of ratification or accession.

2. A reservation incompatible with the object and purpose of the present Convention shall not be permitted.

3. Reservations may be withdrawn at any time by notification to this effect addressed to the Secretary-General of the United Nations, who shall then inform all States thereof. Such notification shall take effect on the date on which it is received.

Article 29

1. Any dispute between two or more States Parties concerning the interpretation or application of the present Convention which is not settled by negotiation shall, at the request of one of them, be submitted to arbitration. If within six months from the date of the request for arbitration the parties are unable to agree on the organization of arbitration, any one of those parties may refer the dispute to the International Court of Justice by request in conformity with the Statute of the Court.

2. Each State Party may at the time of signature or ratification of this Convention or accession thereto declare that it does not consider itself bound by paragraph 1 of this article. The other States Parties shall not be bound by the paragraph with respect to any State Party which has made such a reservation.

3. Any State Party which has made a reservation in accordance with paragraph 2 of this article may at any time withdraw that reservation by notification to the Secretary-General of the United Nations.

Article 30

The present Convention, the Arabic, Chinese, English, French, Russian and Spanish texts of which are equally authentic, shall be deposited with the Secretary-General of the United Nations.

Appendix C

Draft Convention against Sexual Exploitation (January 1994)

The States Parties to the Present Convention,

Considering that, in accordance with the principles proclaimed in the Charter of the United Nations, recognition of the equal and unalienable rights of all members of the human family without distinction as to sex is the foundation of freedom, justice and peace in the world,

Recognizing that those rights derive from the inherent dignity of the human person,

Considering the obligation of States under the Charter, in particular Article 55, to promote universal respect for, and observance of, human rights and fundamental freedoms,

Having regard to Article 3 of the Universal Declaration of Human Rights and Articles 6 and 9 of the International Covenant on Civil and Political Rights, both of which affirm the right of all persons to life, liberty and the security of persons,

Having regard to Article 4 of the Universal Declaration of Human Rights and Article 8 of the International Covenant on Civil and Political Rights, both of which prohibit slavery and the slave trade in all its forms,

Having regard to Article 5 of the Universal Declaration of Human Rights and Article 7 of the International Covenant on Civil and Political Rights, both of which recognize the right of all persons to be free from cruel, inhuman or degrading treatment or punishment,

Noting that the Universal Declaration of Human Rights affirms the principle of the inadmissibility of discrimination and proclaims that all human beings are born free and equal in dignity and rights and that everyone is entitled to all the rights and freedoms set forth therein without discrimination of any kind, including distinction based on sex,

Noting that States Parties to the International Covenant on Civil and Political Rights undertake to secure the equal rights of women and men to enjoy all economic, social, cultural, civil and political rights,

Having regard to the 1949 Convention for the Suppression of Traffic in Persons and the Exploitation of the Prostitution of Others which states that prostitution and the accompanying evil of the traffic in persons for the purpose of prostitution are incompatible with the dignity and worth of the human person and endanger the welfare of the individual, the family, and the community,

Recognizing that the Convention Against Torture prohibits cruel, inhuman and degrading treatment or punishment,

Having regard also to the Convention on the Elimination of all Forms of Discrimination Against Women which obligates States Parties to take all appropriate measures, including legislation, to suppress all forms of traffic in women and exploitation of traffic in women,

Having regard also to the Convention on the Rights of the Child which obligates States Parties to protect the child from all forms of sexual exploitation and sexual abuse and obligates the States Parties to take all appropriate national, bilateral and multilateral measures to prevent (a) the inducement or coercion of a child to engage in any unlawful sexual activity, (b) the exploitative use of children in prostitution or other unlawful sexual practices and (c) the exploitative use of children in pornographic performances and materials,

Noting that the International Convention on the Elimination of All Forms of Racial Discrimination condemns any attempt to justify or promote racial hatred in any form,

Noting that the General Assembly, in the International Convention on the Protection of the Rights of All Migrant Workers and Members of Their Families, reaffirmed the principles and standards set forth in the basic instruments regarding the international protection of human rights,

Concerned that women's rights are seriously threatened by the massive and growing sexual exploitation of women,

Recognizing that sexuality is integral to the human being and that women have the right to sexual integrity and autonomy,

Recognizing further that sexual exploitation, including prostitution, abrogates these rights and subordinates women as a group, and therefore violates human dignity and the right of equality,

Concerned that sexual exploitation inflicts grave harm and often takes the extreme forms of sexual slavery, torture, mutilation and death,

Concerned that sexual violence and prostitution are not inevitable but are forms of sexual exploitation,

Recognizing that the sexual exploitation of any woman is the sexual degradation of all women, deprives women of freedom of movement, and threatens women's safety and security, thus creating the conditions of sexual terrorism,

Concerned that human sexual exploitation, including prostitution, has increasingly become an integral part of national practices which have deprived women of their human rights,

Recognizing the need for a new convention that will affirm and expand the definitions of sexual exploitation which includes violence against women and prostitution as a violation of women's human rights,

Considering that there is no convention presently in existence which addresses sexual exploitation of adults,

Desiring to make more effective the struggle against sexual exploitation,

Have agreed as follows:

Part I: General Provisions

Article 1. Definition of Sexual Exploitation
Sexual exploitation is a practice by which person(s) achieve sexual gratification or financial gain, or advancement, through the abuse of a person's sexuality by abrogating that person's human right to dignity, equality, autonomy, and physical and mental well-being.

Article 2
Sexual exploitation takes the form of, but is not limited to:

a) The denial of life through female infanticide and the murder of women by reason of their gender, including wife and widow murder.

b) Subjection to cruel, inhuman and degrading treatment through the following: battering, pornography, prostitution, genital mutilation, female seclusion, dowry and bride price, forced sterilization and forced child-bearing, sexual harassment, rape, incest, sexual abuse, and trafficking.

c) Subjection to sexual abuse and torture, overt or covert, including sadistic, mutilating practices.

d) Temporary marriage or marriage of convenience for the purpose of sexual exploitation.

e) Sex redetermination.

Article 3
The following shall apply throughout this Convention:

a) Rape is sexual intercourse/sexual assault of any part of the body of a female of any age, by any means.

b) Sexual harassment is the imposition of any unwelcome sexual acts, gestures, speech or materials.

c) Prostitution is the use of a woman's body as a commodity to be bought, sold, exchanged, not always for money, and includes casual prostitution, street prostitution, prostitution sanctioned by socio-cultural practices, brothels, military prostitution, development prostitution, pornography, sex tourism, and mail-order-bride markets.

d) Everything that is herein said about the sexual exploitation of women applies to men and boys in situations of sexual exploitation.

Part II: Sexual Exploitation

Article 4

States Parties condemn sexual exploitation of women and children in all of its forms and agree to formulate policies and practices affecting society to insure freedom from sexual exploitation by protecting control of one's body, sexual integrity, and sexual autonomy.

a) States Parties recognize that some groups of women are rendered particularly vulnerable to sexual exploitation, such as minority and indigenous women, women subjected to racial discrimination, rural women and women in the migrating process, ethnically and socially marginalized women, women workers particularly in free-trade zones, women in the sex entertainment industry, female children, elderly women, women with disabilities that are physical and mental, including learning disabilities and mental retardation, and disabilities caused by substance abuse.

b) States Parties recognize that women are rendered particularly vulnerable to sexual exploitation in the following situations: armed conflict, natural catastrophe, poverty, incarceration, including that of political prisoners and females in immigration and juvenile detention centers, institutional care, certain family contexts, including that of child sexual abuse, domestic violence, forced and child marriages, homelessness, and refugee status.

Article 5

States Parties shall punish perpetrators of sexual exploitation and redress the harm done to victims by developing penal, civil, labor and administrative sanctions. Victims shall be provided with assistance to prosecute their perpetrators. In the formulation and/or application of statutory, common, and customary law:

a) A woman's prior sexual history, including history in prostitution, cannot be used against her in any legal action.

b) Honor shall not be used to justify or defend against any act of sexual exploitation or violence against women.

c) It is an aggravating circumstance and not a defense of sexual exploitation that the perpetrator is the husband, father, other relative, or employer of the victim.

d) A woman's status as an illegal immigrant or stateless person shall not be used against her.

Article 6

States Parties reject any policy or law that legitimates prostitution of any person, female or male, adult or child; that legalizes or regulates prostitution in any way including as a profession, occupation, or as entertainment; and agree to adopt appropriate legislation that recognizes prostitution as an acute form of sexual exploitation, including the following:

a) Punishment of any person who procures, entices, or leads away by any means for the purposes of prostitution, another person, even with the consent of that person; exploits the prostitution of another person, even with the consent of that person; keeps or manages, or knowingly finances or takes part in the financing of a brothel; knowingly rents or lets a building or other place for the purpose of the prostitution of others.

b) Penalization of the customers, recognizing them as perpetrators to be criminalized while rejecting any form of penalization of the prostitute.

c) Where criminal sanctions exist against victims of sexual exploitation, States Parties shall repeal such sanctions.

d) Holding liable the producers, sellers, and distributors of pornography, recognizing that the pornography industry enlarges the demand for, promotes, and is actively engaged in sexual exploitation.

Part III: Global Situations of Sexual Exploitation

Article 7
States Parties agree:

a) To reject State economic development policies and practices which channel women into conditions of sexual exploitation.

b) To insure that State policies and practices provide for the full economic development of women through their integration in dignified paid labor at a decent standard of living from which they have been deprived.

c) To adopt legislative and other measures to prohibit sex tourism and to penalize those who organize tourism for the purpose of sexual exploitation, penalizing the organization of it as a practice of procuring and promoting prostitution. Such measures shall be adopted and implemented in both the countries from which the customers come and the countries to which they go.

d) To provide educational programs to change social and cultural patterns that promote the sexual exploitation of women.

Article 8

a) To adopt measures to prevent and prohibit the trafficking in women for the purpose of sexual exploitation, in particular, prostitution.

b) To enact such regulations as are necessary for the protection of immigrant and emigrant women and children, both at the place of arrival and departure, and while en route.

c) To arrange for appropriate publicity warning the public of the dangers of the traffic in women and children.

d) To insure supervision of railway stations, airports, seaports and en route, and of other public places, in order to prevent international traffic in women and children for the purpose of prostitution.

e) To insure that the appropriate authorities are informed of the arrival of persons who appear, *prima facie,* to be principals and accomplices in or victims of such traffic.

Article 9

States Parties recognize that there are certain types of work in the immigration process, such as domestic labor and entertainment, that are conducive to sexual exploitation and may lead to prostitution and shall take all appropriate measures to provide adequate protection to such victims of sexual exploitation including:

a) Refuge, refugee status and protection, and repatriation of those who desire to be repatriated, whether victims of sexual exploitation have entered a country legally or illegally.

b) Protection to insure that valid written contracts of employment are entered into, monitoring of the provisions of the contract, and protection of the migrant worker from sexual exploitation and abuse in the host country.

c) The right to retain one's own passport and travel documents so that no person can be sold into prostitution or subjected to sexual favors by any other person.

d) The right to shelter, medical care, counseling and other support services.

e) The right of migrant women to be protected under existing labor laws of the recipient countries.

Article 10

States Parties shall insure that:

a) All employers who sexually exploit or abuse migrant workers are held criminally and civilly liable.

b) Persons or enterprises will be prohibited from and punished for promoting, profiting from, or engaging in any business involving the matching of women in marriage to foreign nationals, for example, mail-order-bride selling and pseudo-marriages.

c) Under no circumstances can States construe this article to prevent women from migrating or traveling abroad.

d) Their military, enforcement, and related civilian personnel, whether on or off base in foreign territory or in their own countries, shall be held legally liable and punished for engaging in prostitution of women and children.

e) Their representatives, diplomatic officials, and related personnel shall be held criminally and civilly liable for sexual exploitation.

Article 11

States Parties shall adopt special provisions to prevent the sexual exploitation of women during all wartime conditions, including those of ethnic and communal conflict, civil war, riots, and foreign intervention, and to protect women and children from sexual exploitation in refugee camps and evacuation centers. States Parties recognize the necessity for a special team of observers composed of a majority of women to monitor violations of human rights in the area of sexual exploitation and trafficking.

Part IV: Support Services

Article 12

States Parties agree to take appropriate measures to provide:

a) Restitution to victims of sexual exploitation, and to insure that, notwithstanding the victims' immigration status, their reports of sexual exploitation receive a fair hearing.

b) Women with educational programs and work in order to increase women's economic opportunities and enhance women's worth and status, thereby diminishing the necessity for women to turn to prostitution, notwithstanding the victims' immigration status.

Article 13

States Parties shall create and establish services for victims of sexual exploitation, including prostitution, such as shelters and other social services, and shall fund specialized health services and centers for prostitution alternatives that are voluntary and confidential and would provide the following:

a) Prevention, treatment of, and testing for STDs and HIV.

b) Substance-abuse rehabilitation programs.

c) Training of medical staff to recognize sexual exploitation, including rape and prostitution, to give appropriate treatment, and to make referrals to appropriate services as well as to gather medical evidence for prosecution of crimes of sexual exploitation.

d) Free and elective counseling and education services.

e) Child-care facilities and housing assistance.

f) Income support.

g) Preferential access to credit and loans to begin small-scale business.

h) Non-sexist skills-training programs.

Part V: Procedural Measures

Article 14

States Parties undertake to make the principles and provisions of the Convention widely known by appropriate and active means to adults and children alike.

Article 15

a) For the purpose of examining the progress made by States Parties in achieving the realization of the obligations undertaken in the present Convention, there shall be established a Committee on the Elimination of Sexual Exploitation which shall carry out the functions herein provided. The Committee shall consist of ten persons, consideration being given to equitable distribution of representatives from those countries from which and into which the women are trafficked into sexual exploitation. The members of the Committee shall be elected by States Parties from among their nationals and shall serve in their personal capacity, consideration also being given to equitable geographical distribution, as well as to the principal legal systems.

b) The members of the committee shall be elected by secret ballot from a list of persons nominated by States Parties. Each State Party may nominate one person from among its nationals.

c) Elections of the members of the Committee shall be held at biennial meetings of States Parties convened by the Secretary-General of the United Nations. At those meetings, for which two-thirds of the States Parties shall constitute a quorum, the persons elected to the Committee shall be those who obtain the largest number of votes and an absolute majority of the votes of the representatives of States Parties present and voting.

d) The initial election shall be held no later than six months after the date of the entry into force of this Convention. At least four months before the date of each election, the Secretary-General of the United Nations shall address a letter to the States Parties inviting them to submit their nominations within three months. The Secretary-General shall prepare a list in alphabetical order of all persons thus nominated, indicating the States Parties which have nominated them, and shall submit it to the States Parties.

e) The members of the Committee shall be elected for a term of four years. They shall be eligible for re-election if renominated. However, the term of five of the members elected at the first election shall expire at the end of two years; immediately after the first election the names of these five members shall be chosen by lot by the chairperson of the meeting referred to in paragraph c of this article.

f) If a member of the Committee dies or resigns or for any other cause can no longer perform her Committee duties, the State Party which nominated her shall appoint another expert from among its nationals to serve for the remainder of her term, subject to the approval of the majority of the States Parties. The approval shall be considered given unless half or more of the States Parties respond negatively within six weeks after having been informed by the Secretary-General of the United Nations of the proposed appointment.

g) States Parties shall be responsible for the expenses of the members of the Committee while they are in performance of Committee duties.

Article 16

a) The Committee shall elect its officers for a term of two years. They may be re-elected.

b) The Committee shall establish its own rules of procedure, but these rules shall provide, inter alia, that:

1) Six members shall constitute a quorum;

2) Decisions of the Committee shall be made by a majority vote of the members present.

c) The Secretary-General of the United Nations shall provide the necessary staff and facilities for the effective performance of the functions of the Committee under this Convention.

d) The Secretary-General of the United Nations shall convene the initial meeting of the Committee. After its initial meeting, the Committee shall meet at such times as shall be provided in its rules of procedure.

e) The States Parties shall be responsible for expenses incurred in connection with the holding of meetings of the States Parties and of the Committee, including reimbursement to the United Nations for any expenses, such as the cost of staff and facilities, incurred by the United Nations pursuant to paragraph c of this article.

Article 17

a) The States Parties shall submit to the Committee, through the Secretary-General of the United Nations, reports on the measures they have taken to give effect to their undertakings under this Convention, within one year after the entry into force of the Convention for the State Party concerned. Thereafter the States Parties shall submit supplementary reports every four years on any new measures taken and such other reports as the Committee may request from States Parties, NGOs and other concerned parties.

b) The Secretary-General of the United Nations shall transmit the reports to all States Parties.

c) Each report shall be considered by the Committee which may make such general comments on the report as it may consider appropriate and shall forward these to the State Party concerned and concerned NGOs. That State Party, and concerned NGOs, may respond with any observations to the Committee.

d) The Committee may, at its discretion, include any comments made by it in accordance with paragraph c of this article, together with the observations thereon received from the State Party and any other concerned party, in its annual report made in accordance with this article. If so requested by the State Party concerned, the Committee also may include a copy of the report submitted under paragraph a of this article.

Article 18

a) If the Committee receives reliable information which appears to it to contain well-founded indications that sexual exploitation as defined above is being practiced in the territory of a State Party, the Committee shall invite that State Party to co-operate in the examination of the information and to this end to submit observations with regard to the information concerned.

b) Taking into account any observations which may have been submitted by the State Party concerned, as well as any other relevant information available to it, the Committee may, if it decides that this is warranted, designate one or more of its members to make a confidential inquiry and to report to the Committee urgently.

c) If any inquiry is made in accordance with paragraph b of this article, the Committee shall seek the co-operation of the State Party and any NGOs concerned. In agreement with that State Party, such an inquiry may include a visit to its territory.

d) After examining the findings of its member or members submitted in accordance with paragraph b of this article, the Committee shall transmit these findings to the State Party and any concerned party together with any comments or suggestions which seem appropriate in view of the situation.

e) All the proceedings of the Committee referred to in paragraphs a–d of this article shall be confidential, and at all stages of the proceedings of the co-operation of the State Party shall be sought. After such proceedings have been completed with regard to any inquiry made in accordance with paragraph b, the Committee may, after consultations with the State Party concerned, decide to include a summary account of the results of the proceedings in its annual report made in accordance with article 17. The report of such proceedings should be considered public documents.

Article 19

a) A State Party to this Convention may at any time declare under this article that it recognizes the competence of the Committee to receive and consider communications to the effect that a State Party claims that another State Party is not fulfilling its obligations under this Convention. Such communications may be received and considered according to the procedures laid down in this article only if submitted by a State Party which has made a declaration recognizing in regard to itself the competence of the Committee. No communication shall be dealt with by the Committee under this article if it concerns a State

Party which has not made such a declaration. Communications received under this article shall be dealt with in accordance with the following procedure:

1) If a State Party considers that another State Party is not giving effect to the provisions of this Convention, it may, by written communication, bring the matter to the attention of that State Party. Within three months after the receipt of the communication, the receiving State shall afford the State which sent the communication an explanation or any other statement in writing clarifying the matter, which should include, to the extent possible and pertinent, reference to domestic procedures and remedies taken, pending or available in the matter;

2) If the matter is not adjusted to the satisfaction of both States Parties concerned, within six months after the receipt by the receiving State of the initial communication, either State shall have the right to refer the matter to the Committee, by notice given to the Committee and to the other State;

3) The Committee shall deal with a matter referred to it under this article only after it has ascertained that all domestic remedies have been invoked and exhausted in the matter, in conformity with the generally recognized principles of international law. This shall not be the rule where the application of the remedies is unreasonably prolonged or is unlikely to bring effective relief to the person who is the victim of the violation of this Convention;

4) The Committee shall hold closed meetings when examining communications under this article;

5) Subject to the provisions of subparagraph 3, the Committee shall make available its good offices to the States Parties concerned with a view to an equitable solution of the matter on the basis of respect for the obligations provided for in this Convention. For this purpose, the Committee may, when appropriate, set up an *ad hoc* conciliation commission;

6) In any matter referred to it under this article, the Committee may call upon the States Parties concerned, referred to in subparagraph 2, to supply any relevant information;

7) The States Parties concerned, referred to in subparagraph 2, shall have the right to be represented when the matter is being considered by the Committee and to make submissions orally and/or in writing;

8) The Committee shall, within twelve months after the date of receipt of notice under subparagraph 2, submit a report:

(i) If a solution within the terms of subparagraph 1 is reached, the Committee shall confine its report to a brief statement of the facts and of the solution reached;

(ii) If a solution within the terms of subparagraph 1 is not reached, the Committee shall confine its report to a brief statement of the facts; the written submissions and record of the oral submissions made by the States Parties concerned shall be attached to the report.

In every matter, the report shall be communicated to the States Parties concerned;

b) The provisions of this article shall come into force when five States Parties to this Convention have made declarations under paragraph (a) of this article. Such declarations shall be deposited by the States Parties with the Secretary-General of the United Nations, who shall transmit copies thereof to the other States Parties. A declaration may be withdrawn at any time by notification to the Secretary-General. Such a withdrawal shall not prejudice the consideration of any matter which is the subject of a communication already transmitted under this article; no further communication by any State Party shall be received under this article after the notification of withdrawal of the declaration has been received by the Secretary-General, unless the State Party concerned has made a new declaration.

Article 20

a) A State Party to this Convention may at any time declare under this article that it recognizes the competence of the Committee to receive and consider communications from or on behalf of individuals subject to its jurisdiction who claim to be victims of a violation by a State Party of provisions of the Convention. No communication shall be received by the Committee if it concerns a State Party which has not made such a declaration.

b) The Committee shall consider inadmissible any communication under this article which is anonymous or which it considers to be an abuse of the right of submission of such communications or to be incompatible with the provisions of this Convention.

c) Subject to the provisions of paragraph b, the Committee shall bring any communications submitted to it under this article to the attention of the State Party to this Convention which has made a declaration under paragraph a and is alleged to be violating any provisions of the Convention. Within six months, the receiving State shall submit to the Committee written explanations or statements clarifying the matter and the remedy, if any, that may have been taken by that State.

d) The Committee shall consider communications received under this article in the light of all information made available to it by or on behalf of the individual and by the State Party concerned.

e) The Committee shall not consider any communications from an individual under this article unless it has ascertained that:

1) The same matter has not been, and is not being, examined under another procedure of international investigation or settlement;

2) The individual has exhausted all available domestic remedies; this shall not be the rule where the application of the remedies is unreasonably prolonged or is unlikely to bring effective relief to the person who is the victim of the violation of this Convention.

f) The Committee shall hold closed meetings when examining communications under this article.

g) The Committee shall forward its views to the State Party concerned and to the individual.

h) The provisions of this article shall come into force when five States Parties to this Convention have made declarations under paragraph (a) of this article. Such declarations shall be deposited by the States Parties with the Secretary-General of the United Nations, who shall transmit copies thereof to the other States Parties. A declaration may be withdrawn at any time by notification to the Secretary-General. Such a withdrawal shall not prejudice the consideration of any matter which is the subject of a communication already transmitted under this article; no further communication by or on behalf of an individual shall be received under this article after the notification of withdrawal of the declaration has been received by the Secretary-General, unless the State Party has made a new declaration.

Article 21
The members of the Committee and of the ad hoc conciliation commissions which may be appointed under article 19, paragraph a (5), shall be entitled to the facilities, privileges and immunities of experts on mission for the United Nations as laid down in the relevant sections of the Convention on the Privileges and Immunities of the United Nations.

Article 22
The Committee shall submit an annual report on its activities under this Convention to the States Parties and to the General Assembly of the United Nations.

Article 23
a) This Convention is open for signature by all States.

b) This Convention is subject to ratification. Instruments of ratification shall be deposited with the Secretary-General of the United Nations.

Article 24
This Convention is open to accession by all States. Accession shall be effected by the deposit of an instrument of accession with the Secretary-General of the United Nations.

Article 25
a) This Convention shall enter into force on the thirtieth day after the date of the deposit with the Secretary-General of the United Nations of the twentieth instrument of ratification or accession.

b). For each State ratifying this Convention or acceding to it after the deposit of the twentieth instrument of ratification or accession, the Convention shall enter into force on the thirtieth day after the date of the deposit of its own instrument of ratification or accession.

Article 26

a) Each State may, at the time of signature or ratification of this Convention or accession thereto, declare that it does not recognize the competence of the Committee provided for in Article 15.

b) Any State Party having made a reservation in accordance with paragraph a of this article may, at any time, withdraw this reservation by notification to the Secretary-General of the United Nations.

Article 27

a) Any State Party to this Convention may propose an amendment and file it with the Secretary-General of the United Nations. The Secretary-General shall thereupon communicate the proposed amendment to the States Parties with a request that they notify him or her whether they favor a conference of States Parties for the purpose of considering and voting upon the proposal. In the event that within four months from the date of such communication at least one-third of the States Parties favors such a conference, the Secretary-General shall convene the conference under the auspices of the United Nations. Any amendment adopted by a majority of the States Parties present and voting at the conference shall be submitted by the Secretary-General to all the States Parties for acceptance.

b) An amendment adopted in accordance with paragraph a of this article shall enter into force when two-thirds of the States Parties to this Convention have notified the Secretary-General of the United Nations that they have accepted it in accordance with their respective constitutional processes.

c) When amendments enter into force, they shall be binding on those States Parties which have accepted them, other States Parties still being bound by the provisions of this Convention and any earlier amendments which they have accepted.

Article 28

a) Any dispute between two or more States Parties concerning the interpretation or application of this Convention which cannot be settled through negotiation shall, at the request of one of them, be submitted to arbitration. If within six months from the date of the request for arbitration the Parties are unable to agree on the organization of the arbitration, any one of those Parties may refer the dispute to the International Court of Justice by request in conformity with the Statute of the Court.

b) Each State may, at the time of signature or ratification of this Convention or accession thereto, declare that it does not consider itself bound by paragraph a of this article. The other States Parties shall not be bound by paragraph a of this article with respect to any State Party having made such a reservation.

c) Any State Party having made a reservation in accordance with paragraph b of this article may at any time withdraw this reservation by notification to the Secretary-General of the United Nations.

Article 29

a) A State Party may denounce this Convention by written notification to the Secretary-General of the United Nations. Denunciation becomes effective one year after the date of receipt of the notification by the Secretary-General.

b) Such a denunciation shall not have the effect of releasing the State Party from its obligations under this Convention in regard to any act or omission which occurs prior to the date at which the denunciation becomes effective nor shall denunciation prejudice in any way the continued consideration of any matter which is already under consideration by the Committee prior to the date at which the denunciation becomes effective.

c) Following the date at which the denunciation of a State Party becomes effective, the Committee shall not commence consideration of any new matter regarding that State.

Article 30

The Secretary-General of the United Nations shall inform all States Members of the United Nations and all States which have signed this Convention or acceded to it of the following:

a) Signatures, ratifications, and accessions under Articles 23 and 24.

b) The date of entry into force of this Convention under Article 25 and the date of the entry into force of any amendments under Article 27.

c) Denunciations under Article 29.

Article 31

a) This Convention, of which the Arabic, Chinese, English, French, Russian and Spanish texts are equally authentic, shall be deposited with the Secretary-General of the United Nations.

b) The Secretary-General of the United Nations shall transmit certified copies of this Convention to all States.

Appendix D

Summary of the Global Platform for Action and the Beijing Declaration

The platform for action and the Beijing Declaration, which emerged out of the Fourth World Conference on Women, seeks to uphold the Convention on the Elimination of All Forms of Discrimination against Women while building upon the Nairobi Forward-Looking Strategies. Its overall objective—the empowerment of all women—conforms to the purposes and principles of the Charter of the United Nations; its immediate aim is to establish a basic group of priority actions that should have been carried out in pursuance of women's advancement over the five-year period between 1995 and the turn of the century. The platform for action articulates twelve areas of critical concern that were to receive special attention. These include:

- The persistent and increasing burden of poverty on women

- Inequalities and inadequacies in and unequal access to education and training

- Inequalities and inadequacies in, and unequal access to, health care and related services

- Violence against women

- The effects of armed and other kinds of conflict on women, including those living under foreign occupation

- Inequality in economic structures and policies, in all forms of productive activities, and in access to resources

- Inequality between men and women in the sharing of power and decision making at all levels

- Insufficient mechanisms at all levels to promote the advancement of women

- Lack of respect for, and inadequate promotion and protection of, the human rights of women

- Stereotyping of women and inequality in women's access to, and participation in, all communication systems, especially in the media

- Gender inequalities in the management of natural resources and in the safeguarding of the environment

- Persistent discrimination against and violation of the rights of the girl child[1]

The platform for action is detailed in that it outlines specific actions to be taken by governments to address each of these problem areas. With respect to the elimination of violence against women, governments are called upon to:

1. Condemn violence against women and refrain from invoking any custom, tradition, or religious consideration to avoid their obligations with respect to its elimination as set out in the Declaration on the Elimination of Violence against Women

2. Refrain from engaging in violence against women and exercise due diligence to prevent, investigate, and, in accordance with national legislation, punish acts of violence against women, whether those acts are perpetrated by the state or by private persons

3. Enact and/or reinforce penal, civil, labor, and administrative sanctions in domestic legislation to punish and redress the wrongs done to women and girls who are subjected to any form of violence, whether in the home, the workplace, the community, or society

4. Adopt and/or implement and periodically review and analyze legislation to ensure its effectiveness in eliminating violence against women, emphasizing the prevention of violence and the prosecution of offenders; take measures to ensure the protection of women subjected to violence, access to just and effective remedies, including compensation and indemnification and healing of victims, and rehabilitation of perpetrators

5. Work actively to ratify and/or implement international human rights norms and instruments as they relate to violence against women, including those contained in the Universal Declaration of Human Rights; the International Covenant on Civil and Political Rights; the International Covenant on Economic, Social, and Cultural Rights; and the Convention

against Torture and Other Cruel, Inhuman, or Degrading Treatment or Punishment

6. Implement the Convention on the Elimination of All Forms of Discrimination against Women, taking into account general recommendation 19, adopted by the Committee on the Elimination of Discrimination against Women at its eleventh session

7. Promote an active and visible policy of mainstreaming a gender perspective in all policies and programs related to violence against women; actively encourage, support, and implement measures and programs aimed at increasing the knowledge and understanding of the causes, consequences, and mechanisms of violence against women among those responsible for implementing these policies, such as law enforcement officers, police personnel, and judicial, medical, and social workers, as well as those who deal with minority, migration, and refugee issues; and develop strategies to ensure that the revictimization of women victims of violence does not occur because of gender-insensitive laws or judicial or enforcement practices

8. Provide women who are subjected to violence with access to the mechanisms of justice and, as provided for by national legislation, to just and effective remedies for the harm they have suffered and inform women of their rights in seeking redress through such mechanisms

9. Enact and enforce legislation against the perpetrators of practices and acts of violence against women, such as female genital mutilation, female infanticide, prenatal sex selection, and dowry-related violence, and give vigorous support to the efforts of nongovernmental and community organizations to eliminate such practices

10. Formulate and implement, at all appropriate levels, plans of action to eliminate violence against women

11. Adopt all appropriate measures, especially in the field of education, to modify the social and cultural patterns of conduct of men and women and to eliminate prejudices, customary practices, and all other practices based on the idea of the inferiority or superiority of either of the sexes and on stereotyped roles for men and women

12. Create or strengthen institutional mechanisms so that women and girls can report acts of violence against them in a safe and confidential environment, free from the fear of penalties or retaliation, and file charges

13. Ensure that women with disabilities have access to information and services in the field of violence against women

14. Create, improve, or develop, as appropriate, and fund the training programs for judicial, legal, medical, social, educational, and police and immigrant personnel, in order to avoid the abuse of power leading to violence against women and sensitize such personnel to the nature of gender-based acts and threats of violence so that fair treatment of female victims can be ensured

15. Adopt laws, where necessary, and reinforce existing laws that punish police, security forces, or any other agents of the state who engage in acts of violence against women in the course of the performance of their duties; review existing legislation and take effective measures against the perpetrators of such violence

16. Allocate adequate resources within the government budget and mobilize community resources for activities related to the elimination of violence against women, including resources for the implementation of plans of action at all appropriate levels

17. Include in reports submitted in accordance with the provisions of relevant United Nations human rights instruments information pertaining to violence against women and measures taken to implement the Declaration on the Elimination of Violence against Women

18. Cooperate with and assist the Special Rapporteur of the Commission on Human Rights on Violence against Women in the performance of her mandate and furnish all information requested; cooperate also with other competent mechanisms, such as the Special Rapporteur of the Commission on Human Rights on Torture and the Special Rapporteur of the Commission on Human Rights on Summary, Extrajudiciary, and Arbitrary Executions, in relation to violence against women

19. Recommend that the Commission on Human Rights renew the mandate of the Special Rapporteur on Violence against Women when her term ends in 1997 and, if warranted, to update and strengthen it

Included in the platform are actions prescribed for local governments, community organizations, nongovernmental organizations, educational institutions, the public and private sectors, and the mass media as directed by the state. Among the actions to be undertaken are to:

1. Provide well-funded shelters and relief support for girls and women subjected to violence, as well as medical, psychological, and other counseling services and free or low-cost legal aid, where it is needed, as well as appropriate assistance to enable them to find a means of subsistence

2. Establish linguistically and culturally accessible services for migrant women and girls, including women migrant workers, who are victims of gender-based violence

3. Recognize the vulnerability to violence and other forms of abuse of women migrants, including women migrant workers, whose legal status in the host country depends on employers who may exploit their situation

4. Support initiatives of women's organizations and nongovernmental organizations all over the world to raise awareness on the issue of violence against women and to contribute to its elimination

5. Organize, support, and fund community-based education and training campaigns to raise awareness about violence against women as a violation of women's enjoyment of their human rights and mobilize local communities to use appropriate gender-sensitive traditional and innovative methods of conflict resolution

6. Recognize, support, and promote the fundamental role of intermediate institutions, such as primary health care centers, family-planning centers, existing school health services, mother and baby protection services, centers for migrant families, and so forth in the field of information and education related to abuse

7. Organize and fund information campaigns and educational and training programs to sensitize girls and boys and women and men to the personal and social detrimental effects of violence in the family, community, and society; teach them how to communicate without violence; and promote training for victims and potential victims so that they can protect themselves and others against such violence

8. Disseminate information on the assistance available to women and families who are victims of violence

9. Provide, fund, and encourage counseling and rehabilitation programs for the perpetrators of violence and promote research to further efforts concerning such counseling and rehabilitation so as to prevent the recurrence of such violence

10. Raise awareness of the responsibility of the media in promoting non-stereotyped images of women and men, as well as in eliminating patterns of media presentation that generate violence, and encourage those responsible for media content to establish professional guidelines and codes of conduct; also raise awareness of the important role of the media in informing and educating people about the causes and effects of violence against women and in stimulating public debate on the topic

Actions prescribed for employers, trade unions, community and youth organizations, and/or nongovernmental organizations include:

1. Develop programs and procedures to eliminate sexual harassment and other forms of violence against women in all educational institutions, workplaces, and elsewhere

2. Develop programs and procedures to educate and raise awareness of acts of violence against women that constitute a crime and a violation of the human rights of women

3. Develop counseling, healing, and support programs for girls, adolescents, and young women who have been or are involved in abusive relationships, particularly those who live in homes or institutions where abuse occurs

4. Take special measures to eliminate violence against women, particularly those in vulnerable situations, such as young women, refugee, displaced, and internally displaced women, women with disabilities, and women migrant workers, including enforcing any existing legislation and developing, as appropriate, new legislation for women migrant workers in both sending and receiving countries

The platform for action calls upon the Secretary-General of the United Nations to provide the Special Rapporteur of the Commission on Human Rights on Violence against Women with any assistance that might be required, including the staff and resources needed to perform all functions that have been assigned to the special rapporteur. In addition, governments, international organizations, and nongovernmental organizations are asked to encourage the dissemination and implementation of the UNHCR (United Nations High Commissioner for Refugees) Guidelines on the Protection of Refugee Women and the UNHCR Guidelines on the Prevention of and Response to Sexual Violence against Refugees.

Another set of strategic objectives focuses upon the need for governments and related agencies and institutions to study the causes and consequences of violence against women and the effectiveness of preventive measures. Actions to be taken by governments, regional organizations, the United Nations, other international organizations, research institutions, women's and youth organizations, and nongovernmental organizations include:

1. Promote research, collect data, and compile statistics, especially concerning domestic violence relating to the prevalence of different forms of violence against women, and encourage research into the causes, nature, seriousness, and consequences of violence against women and the

effectiveness of measures implemented to prevent and redress violence against women

2. Disseminate findings of research and studies widely

3. Support and initiate research on the impact of violence, such as rape, on women and girl children, and make the resulting information and statistics available to the public

4. Encourage the media to examine the impact of gender-role stereotypes, including those perpetuated by commercial advertisements that foster gender-based violence and inequalities, and how they are transmitted during the life cycle, and take measures to eliminate these negative images with a view to promoting a violence-free society

To eliminate trafficking in women and to assist victims of violence due to prostitution and trafficking, governments of countries of origin, transit, and destination, as well as regional and international organizations, as appropriate, are encouraged to:

1. Consider the ramification and enforcement of international conventions on trafficking in persons and on slavery

2. Take appropriate measures to address the root factors, including external factors, that encourage trafficking in women and girls for prostitution and other forms of commercialized sex, forced marriages, and forced labor in order to eliminate trafficking in women, including strengthening existing legislation with a view to providing better protection of the rights of women and girls and to punishing the perpetrators through both criminal and civil measures

3. Step up cooperation and concerted action by all relevant law enforcement authorities and institutions with a view to dismantling national, regional, and international networks in trafficking

4. Allocate resources to provide comprehensive programs designed to heal and rehabilitate into society victims of trafficking, including through job training, legal assistance, and confidential health care, and take measures to cooperate with nongovernmental organizations to provide for the social, medical, and psychological care of the victims of trafficking

5. Develop educational and training programs and policies and consider enacting legislation aimed at preventing sex tourism and trafficking, giving special emphasis to the protection of young women and children

Appendix E

Mission Statement
for the Authenticity Project

The Authenticity Project is an international multidisciplinary, collaborative project of research and development focused on the theoretical and practical interpenetration of the science of psychology, on one hand, and the nature of human moral and spiritual development, on the other. The fundamental convictions of the project members are:

- There is a universal, intrinsic human nature that precedes all forms of socialization. From the moment of his/her conception, the human being has inherent spiritual and physical capacities that he/she brings to all interactions with the environment. These capacities, which include the capacity to know, to love and to will, constitute the intrinsic value of the individual human person. We are not Locke's tabula rasa, and, from the beginning of our lives, we participate actively, and with gradually increasing autonomy, in the process of our own becoming.

- For the individual, the fundamental spiritual purpose of life is the proper development of his/her inherent potential through the appropriate deployment of his/her intrinsic capacities. This process of development, made possible by humanity's unique powers of consciousness, is carried forward primarily by the nature and quality of the responses the individual chooses to make to the circumstances of his/her life. These acts of will are primarily value choices in that the objective consequences of a given choice will either be good (tending to an increase in autonomy and well-being) or bad (tending towards morbid dependencies and unpleasant, self-destructive life patterns). There is thus an irreducible ethical or moral dimension to the process of individual growth.

- Although being (essence) precedes becoming (existence), life is nonetheless an experience of continual change. The parameters and laws which

223

govern this process of change (and thus growth) are universal and objective. Proper development thus involves a process of gaining knowledge of these laws and of acquiring the capability (inner resources) to act in a growth-inducing manner with respect to them. Such acts are authentic because they are based on and reflect an accurate understanding of both the inner reality of the self and the outer reality of the self's environment.

- Since change and not stasis is the norm of human life, there is no category of "normal" people who serve as a static reference point for others in relationship to the growth process. Everyone is involved in this process, and the same rules apply to all. The main difference between the growth trajectories of two individuals lies in the degree of functionality (relative to their own potential) with which they first consciously engage the process of self-development. Those who are very dysfunctional in the beginning may need professional help, while more functionally secure individuals may not. However, everyone needs the encouragement and loving support of others in this process. Hence, there is a continuum and harmony between valid psychotherapeutic techniques (e.g., cognitive dynamics) and techniques of spiritual development (e.g., prayer and meditation). Life is a universal process of change in which all are involved, whether willingly or not.

- The primary spiritual purpose of society is to provide the optimum milieu favorable to the growth process of its individual members. All other social considerations, including purely economic ones, are secondary (though important in their own right). The main source of social injustice is the abusive use of power, both individual and collective, and not just the existence of power differentials, some of which are necessary and potentially helpful to all (e.g., parent/child, doctor/patient, teacher/student). In particular, the pursuit of power and dominance, as ends in themselves, is always an abuse of power since such pursuit leads inevitably to asymmetric, adversarial, and conflictual relationships. However, relationships based on the mutual recognition of intrinsic value are authentic, leading as they do to a relational symmetry based on altruistic love (total acceptance of and concern for the other). Thus, ideally society should be structured so as to favor and encourage its individual members to make authentic, autonomous moral choices, instead of blindly following ideology, and to pursue authentic relationships, rather than pursuing power and dominance.

- The process of personal spiritual growth can be taught and learned. The very purpose of the Authenticity Project is to generate a coherent philosophical framework for an understanding of this growth process and to implement this understanding via a pedagogical scheme based on sound and empirically proven principles.

Current members of the Authenticity Project include both women and men who are philosophers, psychologists, educators, corporate trainers, and practicing clinicians from the United States, Canada, and Russia. All members of the Project have vast international experience as well (Africa, China, Europe, Russia).

The work of the Authenticity Project is carried forward by the regular production of both theoretical and pedagogical materials, the holding of seminars and conferences, the training of facilitators, and the active research, both individual and collective, of the Project members.

Incorporated as a nonprofit organization in the United States, the Project is associated with a moral education initiative in Russia. Activities are coordinated by the members of the Project.

Members of the project are:

- Dr. Leslie Asplund, Psychotherapist

- Dr. Sheri Dressler, Psychotherapist and Professor of Counselor Education, University of Central Florida

- Mr. Lonya Osokin, Psychologist and Corporate Trainer

- Dr. Michael Penn, Professor of Psychology at Franklin & Marshall College

- Ms. Mary K. Radpour, Clinical Social Worker

The Authenticity Project can be contacted at:

The Authenticity Project
c/o Mary K. Radpour, Chair
4501 Hixson Pike
Chattanooga, TN 37343
Email: mradpour@usbnc.org

Notes

Preface

1. C. S. Lewis, *The Discarded Image* (Cambridge: Cambridge University Press, 1964), 223–24.

Introduction

1. Nabíl-i-Aʾzam (Muhammad-i-Zarandí), *The Dawn-Breakers* (Wilmette, Ill.: Baháʾí Publishing Trust, 1932), 294–95.

2. Quoted in Shoghi Effendi, *God Passes By*, rev. ed. (Wilmette, Ill: Baháʾí Publishing Trust, 1974), 65.

3. Elizabeth Cady Stanton, *Correspondence, Writings, Speeches*, ed. Ellen Carol DuBois (New York: Schocken, 1981), 28–35, quoted in Bradford Miller, *Returning to Seneca Falls: The First Women's Rights Convention and Its Meaning for Men and Women Today* (Hudson, N.Y.: Lindisfarne, 1995) 19–20.

4. Quoted in UN, *The United Nations and the Advancement of Women* (New York: UN Office of Public Information, 1995), 14.

5. UN, *Advancement of Women*, 16.

6. Quoted in UN, *Advancement of Women*, 20.

7. UN, *Advancement of Women*, 20.

8. Quoted in UN, *Advancement of Women*, 22–23.

9. UN, *Advancement of Women*, 23.

10. UN, *Advancement of Women*, 27.

11. Paraphrased in UN, *Advancement of Women*, 34

12. UN, Convention on the Elimination of All Forms of Discrimination against Women, preamble.

13. UN, *The Nairobi Forward-Looking Strategies for the Advancement of Women*, as adopted by the World Conference to Review and Appraise the Achievements of the United Nations Decade for Women: Equality, Development and Peace, Nairobi, Kenya, 15–26 July 1985, para. 258.

14. United Nations Economic and Social Council, Annex to Resolution 1990/15 of 24 May 1990, recommendation 22.

15. UN, Convention on the Elimination of Discrimination against Women (CEDAW), General Recommendation 19, "Violence Against Women," 1992.

16. UN, *The Vienna Declaration and Programme of Action,* June 1993, pt. 1, para. 18.

17. UN, *Vienna Declaration,* June 1993, pt. 2, para. 38.

18. UN, Declaration on the Elimination of Violence against Women, December 1993, preamble.

19. Radhika Coomaraswamy, *Preliminary Report Submitted by the Special Rapporteur on Violence against Women, Its Causes and Consequences.* UN Doc. E/CN. 4/1995/42 (1994).

20. Marsha A. Freeman, *Human Rights in the Family: Issues and Recommendations for Implementation* (Minneapolis: International Women's Rights Action Watch, April 1993), 10.

21. UN, *Platform for Action and the Beijing Declaration* (New York: UN Department of Public Information, 1996), 76–82.

22. Coomaraswamy, *Preliminary Report.*

23. Cornel West, *Race Matters* (New York: Vintage, 1994), 21.

24. Amede Obiora, "Kindling the Domain of Social Reform through Law," *Third World Legal Studies* 103 (1994–1995): 106.

25. Bahá'u'lláh, *The Kitáb-i-Aqdas: The Most Holy Book,* (Wilmette, Ill.: Bahá'í Publishing Trust, 1993), K14.

26. Harold Berman, *Faith and Order: The Reconciliation of Law and Religion* (Atlanta: Scholars Press, 1993), 7.

27. Roshan Danesh, "Beyond Integration and Separation: The Dynamic Nature of Bahá'í Law," in *Bahá'í World 1999–2000* (Haifa, Israel: World Center Publications, 2001), 223–63.

28. William S. Hatcher in collaboration with the International Moral Education Project, "Ethics of Authenticity," bk. 1, "A Course of Integrated Ethics for Youth and Young Adults" (St. Petersburg, Russia), 4; see also William S. Hatcher, *Love, Power, and Justice* (Wilmette, Ill.: Bahá'í Publishing Trust, 1999).

29. Hatcher, "Ethics of Authenticity," 5–6.

30. Iraj Ayman, ed., *A New Framework for Moral Education* (Darmstadt, Germany: Asr-i-Jadíd, 1993), 15.

31. Irene Taafaki, "A Pedagogy for Moral Education," in *New Framework,* ed. Ayman, 43.

32. Taafaki, "Pedagogy for Moral Education," 41–51.

33. Daniel Goleman, *Emotional Intelligence: Why It Can Matter More than IQ* (New York: Bantam, 1997).

Chapter 1

1. Obiora, "Kindling Social Reform," 114.

2. UN Children's Fund, *Girls and Women: A UNICEF Development Priority* (New York: Programme Publications, 1993).

3. Marianne Frankenhaeuser, Ulf Lundberg, and Margaret Chesney, eds., *Women, Work, and Health: Stress and Opportunities* (New York: Plenum, 1991).

4. Frankenhaeuser, Lundberg, and Chesney, *Women, Work.*

5. Quoted in Neera K. Sohoni, "The Status of Female Children and Adolescents in Development and Corrective Strategies," *Feminist Issues* (Spring 1992): 3–20.

6. UN, *The World's Women, Trends and Statistics 1970–1990* (New York: UN Publications, 1991).

7. R. L. Jarrett, "Living Poor: Family Life among Single-Parent African-American Women," *Social Problems* 41 (1994): 30–49.

8. Coomaraswamy, *Preliminary Report,* 13.

9. Barbara Ehrenreich and Karin Stallard, "The Nouveau Poor," *Ms.*, July/August 1982, 217.

10. Mona Grieser, *Survey Results, "Traditional Media as a Change Agent"* (New York: UNIFEM, 1992).

11. Quoted in Grieser, *Survey Results.*

12. World Bank, *Educating Girls and Women: Investing in Development* (Washington, D.C.: World Bank, 1990).

13. Sohoni, "Status of Female Children," 13.

14. Neera Sohoni, "Child without Childhood," report on the girl child submitted to UNICEF (New York: UNFPA, 1990, mimeographed).

15. Sohoni, "Status of Female Children," 3–20.

16. Hoda Mahmoudi, "Men's Role in Establishing Women's Equality," *World Order* 26 (1995): 27–41.

17. Lori Heise, "Violence against Women: The Missing Agenda," in *The Health of Women: A Global Perspective,* ed. Marge Koblinsky, Judith Timyan, and Jill Gay (Boulder, Colo.: Westview, 1993), 171.

18. Miranda Davis, comp., *Women and Violence* (Atlantic Highlands, N.J.: Zed Books, 1994), 44.

19. K .S. Sunanda, *Girl-Child to Die in the Killing Fields?* (Madras, India: Alternatives for India's Development, 1995), 20.

20. Radhika Coomaraswamy, *Report of Special Rapporteur on Violence against Women, Its Causes and Consequences* (New York: Economic and Social Council of the UN, 1995).

21. Tom Hilditch, "A Holocaust of Little Girls," *South China Morning Post* (Hong Kong), reprinted in *World Press Review,* September 1995, 39.

22. U.S. House of Representatives, Committee on Foreign Affairs, Subcommittee Hearings on International Security, International Organizations, and Human Rights (Sept. 28–29, 1993, and March 22, 1994).

23. See Sohoni, "Child without Childhood"; and Neera K. Sohoni, "The Girl Child: An Investment in the Future" (New York: UNICEF, 1990).

24. Sohoni, "Status of Female Children," 7.

25. Jennifer Horsman, *Something in My Mind besides the Everyday: Women and Literacy* (Ontario: Women's Press, 1990), 27.

26. Coomaraswamy, *Report of Special Rapporteur.*

27. Lee Lee Lou Ludher, "Women in the Informal Sector in Malaysia," in *The Greatness Which Might Be Theirs: Reflections on the Agenda and Platform for Action for the United Nations Fourth World Conference on Women, Equality, Development,*

and Peace (New York: Bahá'í International Community Office for the Advancement of Women, 1995), 31–39.

28. Ludher, "Women in the Informal Sector," 36.

29. W. Mwagiru, "Evaluation Report on the Ghana Project on Enhancing Opportunities for Women in Development (ENOWID), Prepared for the UNDP, United Nations Fund for Women (UNIFEM)," (New York: UNIFEM, 1997).

30. Quoted in Jean G. Zorn, "Women, Custom, and State Law in Papua New Guinea," *Third World Legal Studies* (1994–1995): 169–206.

31. Papua New Guinea Supreme Court, *Annual Report by the Judges 1990,* quoted in Zorn, "Women, Custom, and State Law," 204.

32. From a statement published by the Bahá'í International Community, *The Greatness Which Might Be Theirs.*

33. From an anonymous petition distributed to academics around the world during the 1999–2000 academic year.

34. Mohtarma Benazir Bhutto, "The Fight for the Liberation of Women" (excerpts, remarks, 4 September 1995). Quoted in Shahani Ramos, "Beijing and Beyond: Toward the Twenty-First Century of Women," *Women's Studies Quarterly* 24 (Spring/Summer 1996): 91–97.

35. Coomaraswamy, *Preliminary Report,* 27.

36. Martha Schweitz, "Women's Rights in the Bahá'í Community: The Concept of Organic Equality in Principle, Law, and Experience," in *Women and International Human Rights Law,* ed. Kelly Askin and Dorean Koenig, (Ardsley, N.Y.: Transnational Publications, 2001), 3: 461–509.

37. Carol Gilligan, *In a Different Voice: Psychological Theory and Women's Development* (Cambridge: Harvard University Press, 1993).

38. Jean B. Miller, *Toward a New Psychology of Women* (Boston: Beacon, 1986).

39. Moojan Momen, "In All the Ways That Matter, Women Don't Count," *Bahá'í Studies Review* 4, no. 1 (1994): 1–6.

40. 'Abdu'l-Bahá in *Women: Extracts from the Writings of Bahá'u'lláh, 'Abdu'l-Bahá, Shoghi Effendi, and the Universal Hourse of Justice,* comp. Research Department of the Universal House of Justice (Thornhill, Ont.: Bahá'í Canada Publications, 1986) 13, no. 25.

41. See Schweitz, "Women's Rights," 472.

42. 'Abdu'l-Bahá, quoted in Schweitz, "Women's Rights," 472.

43. Quoted in F. Ferré, *Being and Value: Toward a Constructive Postmodern Metaphysics.* (Albany: SUNY Press, 1996), 294.

44. The antiessentialist movement comprises an eclectic group of theorists who are variously referred to as "postmodern," "neopragmatic," "deconstructionist," "hermeneutical," and so forth. The commitment that unites them is a disdain for *metaphysical realism,* or the idea that there is some determinant way the world "actually" is. Martha Nussbaum, "Apart from the Interpretive Workings of the Cognitive Faculties of Living Beings, Human Capabilities, Female Human Beings," in *Women, Culture, and Development: A Study of Human Capabilities,* ed. Martha Nussbaum and Jonathan Glover (New York: Oxford, 1995), 61–104. Thus, such "entities" as man and woman, justice and truth, causes and effects, are said to be constructed in sociohistorical discourse and have

no objective existence apart from the properties ascribed to them by a community of empowered knowers.

45. William S. Hatcher, "The *Kitáb-i-Aqdas:* The Causality Principle," in *The Law of Love Enshrined,* ed. John S. Hatcher and William S. Hatcher (London: George Ronald, 1996), 117.

46. C. J. Herrick, *Brains of Rats and Man* (Chicago: University of Chicago Press, 1928). Quoted in Erich Fromm, *The Anatomy of Human Destructiveness* (New York: Holt, Rinehart, & Winston, 1973), 239.

Chapter 2

1. National Victim Center and the Crime Victims' Research and Treatment Center, *Rape in America: A Report to the Nation* (Washington, D.C.: Crime Victims' Research and Treatment Center, 1992).

2. I. M. Rosas, *Violencia sexual y política criminal* CLADEM Informativo 6 (Lima, Peru, 1992).

3. P. Handwerker, "Gender Power Differences between Parents and High Risk Sexual Behavior by Their Children: AIDS/STD Risk Factors Extend to a Prior Generation," *Journal of Women's Health* 2 (1993): 301.

4. S. M. Allen, "Adolescent Pregnancy among 11 to 15 Year Old Girls in the Parish of Manchester" (Ph.D. diss., University of West Indies, 1982).

5. See Richard P. Kluft, ed., *Incest-Related Syndromes of Adult Psychopathology* (Washington, D.C.: American Psychiatric Press, 1990).

6. See Michael L. Penn, "Violence against Women and Girls," *World Order* (Spring 1995): 43–54.

7. UNICEF, *Convention on the Rights of the Child: Sexual Exploitation* (New York: UNICEF, 1992), 1.

8. See, e.g., Judith Herman, *Father-Daughter Incest* (Cambridge: Harvard University Press, 1981).

9. Linda Gordon, *Heroes of Their Own Lives: The Politics and History of Family Violence* (London: Virago Press, 1989), 211–12.

10. D. Russell, "The Prevalence and Seriousness of Incestuous Abuse by Stepfathers versus Biological Fathers," *Child Abuse and Neglect* 8 (1984): 15–22.

11. Quoted in Patrick Engle, *Men in Families: Report of a Consultation on the Role of Men and Fathers in Achieving Gender Equality* (New York: UNICEF, June 13–14, 1994).

12. J. Bruce and C. B. Lloyd, *Finding the Ties That Bind: Beyond Headship and Household* (Washington, D.C.: Population Council International Center for Research on Women Series, 1992).

13. In some societies, fathers and other male members of the community are actually prohibited from participating in the early stages of their children's development. The Yandapu Enga of the highlands of New Guinea, for example, have a tradition of postpartum abstinence that lasts for two years, during which time infants are breastfed and looked after solely by their mothers and other female caretakers. In this culture, young babies may not be looked at by men, especially by their fathers, "for fear of the

war magic in which men must participate." The Enga believe that a baby will die if parents cohabit because the father's semen, which is a potent source of his war magic, will mix with the mother's milk and create danger for the suckling child. Although by increasing the gap between subsequent pregnancies this belief functions as a strategy to ensure the survival of infants, it nevertheless prevents Enga men from forming close attachments to their children when it is most critical.

14. In the United States, for example, the Centers for Disease Control report that about 70 percent of American girls now have had sex by their high school graduation. Furthermore, the pregnancy rate for teenagers younger than fifteen has increased from 15.9 per 1,000 girls in 1980 to 18.6 per 1,000 in 1987. Planned Parenthood estimates that 40 percent of girls who are now fourteen years old will become pregnant in their teens. Many of these same studies indicate that a significant number of these children and youths have been impregnated by men in their thirties. Indeed, about a third of all teenage pregnancies in the United States are the result of statutory rape.

15. Andrew Hacker, *Two Nations: Black and White, Separate, Hostile, and Unequal* (New York: Ballantine, 1992).

16. Quoted in Hacker, *Two Nations,* 73.

17. Elijah Anderson, *Streetwise: Race, Class, and Change in an Urban Community* (Chicago: University of Chicago Press, 1990).

18. Cited in Patrice Engle, *Men in Families: Report of a Consultation on the Role of Men and Fathers in Achieving Gender Equality.* New York: UNICEF, 1994.

19. Louise Silverstein, "Fathering Is a Feminist Issue," *Psychology of Women Quarterly* 20 (1996): 4.

20. Patricia Williams, "Spirit-Murdering the Messenger," *University of Miami Law Review* 42 (1987): 127–57.

21. Herman, *Trauma and Recovery* (New York: Basic Books, 1992).

22. K. Lanis and K. Covell, "Images of Women in Advertisements: Effects on Attitudes Related to Sexual Aggression," *Sex Roles* 32 (1995): 639–50.

23. It should be emphasized that the writers do not wish, in any way, to justify this gross violation of children's human rights. To the contrary, every effort must be made both to protect children and to prosecute perpetrators. These insights are offered in the belief that in addition to legal measures, education must play a critical role in prevention efforts. We must also add that while we are mindful of a large body of research that has shown that education of the traditional sort has relatively little impact on people's behavior, we suggest in a number of chapters that follow that when education involves the whole of the human personality over an extended period of time, its effects can be quite profound and lasting. Indeed, were we to believe that education can have no real impact on human behavior, the whole project of "cultivating humanity" would be useless. We are not prepared to submit to the cynicism embodied in such a view.

24. Paul Ehrlich, "Asia's Shocking Secret," *Reader's Digest,* October 1993, 70.

25. J. Jacobson, *Slavery (Yes, Slavery) Returns* (Washington: World Watch, 1992), 5.

26. Lois Chiang, "Trafficking in Women," in *Women and International Human Rights Law,* ed. Kelly Askin and Dorean Koenig (New York: Transnational Publishers, 2000), 2: 332–33.

27. Chiang, "Trafficking in Women," 344.

28. See Andrew Horwitz, "Sexual Psychopath Legislation: Is There Anywhere to Go but Backwards?" *University of Pittsburgh Law Review* 57 (1995): 35–78.

29 Elizabeth Defeis, "Draft Convention against Sexual Exploitation," in *Women and International Human Rights Law,* ed. Kelly Askin and Dorean Koenig (New York: Transnational Publishers, 2000), 2: 323.

30. Defeis, "Draft Convention," 330.

31. As reported in the U.S. House of Representatives, Committee on Foreign Affairs, Subcommittee Hearings on International Security, International Organizations, and Human Rights. September 28–29, 1993; October 20, 1993; and March 22, 1994.

32. Radhika. Coomaraswamy and L. M. Kois, "Violence against Women," in *Women and International Human Rights Law,* ed. Kelly Askin and Dorean Koenig (New York: Transnational Publishers, 2000), 2: 177–217.

33. Rhonda Copelon, "Recognizing the Egregious in the Everyday: Domestic Violence as Torture," *Columbia Human Rights Law Review* 25 (1994): 291–367.

34. Copelon, "Recognizing the Egregious," 201.

35. Patricia Rozée, "Forbidden or Forgiven? Rape in Cross-Cultural Perspective," *Psychology of Women Quarterly* 17 (1993): 504.

36. Rozée, "Forbidden or Forgiven?" 503.

37. Mary P. Koss, Lori Heise, and Nancy F. Russo, "The Global Health Burden of Rape," *Psychology of Women Quarterly* 18 (1994): 514.

38. Diana Banjac. "Rape in Mexico: An American Is the Latest Victim of the Repression," *Progressive,* January 1996, 18–21.

39. Amnesty International, *Rape and Sexual Abuse: Torture and Ill-Treatment of Women in Detention* (New York: Amnesty International, 1992).

40. Rozée, "Forbidden or Forgiven?" 510.

41. Rozée, "Forbidden or Forgiven?" 509.

42. Rozée, "Forbidden or Forgiven?" 507.

43. As reported in Koss, Heise, and Russo, *Global Health Burden,* 514.

44. UN High Commissioner for Refugees (UNHCR), *Sexual Violence against Refugees: Guidelines on Prevention and Response* (New York: UNHCR, 1995).

45. Coomaraswamy, *Preliminary Report,* 21.

46. Koss, Heise, and Russo, "Global Health Burden," 509–37.

47. World Bank, *Violence against Women: The Hidden Health Burden,* discussion paper (Washington, D.C.: World Bank, 1994).

48. Mary P. Koss, "Scope, Impact, Interventions, and Public Policy Responses," *American Psychologist* 48 (October 1993): 1062–69.

49. Koss, "Scope, Impact," 1062–69.

50. Koss, "Scope, Impact," 1065.

51. Koss, Heise, and Russo, *Global Health Burden,* 509–37.

52. Koss, "Scope, Impact," 1063–64.

53. Coomaraswamy, *Report of Special Rapporteur.*

54. Howard French, "The Ritual Slaves of Ghana: Young and Female," *New York Times,* 20 January 1997, A5.

55. Human Rights Watch, *Women and Violence: Shattered Lives—Sexual Violence during the Rwandan Genocide and Its Aftermath* (Washington, D.C.: Human Rights Watch Women's Rights Project, 1996).

56   Judith Matloff, "Rwanda Copes with Babies of Mass Rape," *Christian Science Monitor,* 27 March 1995, 14.

57.   Koss, Heise, and Russo, *Global Health Burden,* 509–37.

58.   A. Richters, *Women, Culture, and Violence: A Development, Health, and Human Rights Issue* (n.p.: Women and Autonomy Center, 1994).

59   Richters, *Women, Culture.*

60.   As reported by Robin Phillips in "Violence in the Workplace: Sexual Harassment," in *Women and International Human Rights Law,* ed. Kelly Askin and Dorean Koenig (New York: Transnational Publishers, 2000), 2: 177–217.

61.   See Louise Fitzgerald, "Sexual Harassment," *American Psychologist* 48 (1993): 1070–76.

62.   Gary Warner, *San Francisco Examiner,* 30 December 1992.

63.   Ron Thorne-Finch, *Ending the Silence: The Origins and Treatment of Male Violence against Women* (Toronto: University of Toronto Press, 1992).

64.   Tim Tate, "The Child Pornography Industry," in *Pornography: Women, Violence, and Civil Liberties: A Radical New View,* ed. C. Itzin (New York: Oxford University Press, 1992), 203–16.

65.   Quoted in Tate, "Child Pornography," 206.

66.   Tate, "Child Pornography," 205.

67.   Liz Kelly, "Pornography and Child Sexual Abuse," in *Pornography: Women, Violence, and Civil Liberties: A Radical New View,* ed. C. Itzin (New York: Oxford University Press, 1992), 113–23.

68.   C. Everett Koop, "Report of the Surgeon General's Workshop on Pornography and Public Health," *American Psychologist* 42 (1987): 945. For a full report, see E. P. Mulvey and J. L. Haugaard, Report of the Surgeon General's Workshop on Pornography and Public Health (Washington, D.C.: U.S. Department of Health and Human Services, Office of the Surgeon General, 1986). For a rebuttal, see also Daniel Linz, Edward Donnerstein, and Steven Penrod, "The Findings and Recommendations of the Attorney General's Commission on Pornography: Do the Psychological 'Facts' Fit the Political Fury?" *American Psychologist* 42 (1987): 946–53.

69.   D. Kaplan, "The Incorrigibles," *Newsweek,* 15 January 1993, 48–49.

70.   Michelle Earl-Hubbard, "The Child Sex Offender Registration Laws: The Punishment, Liberty Deprivation, and Unintended Results Associated with the Scarlet Letter Laws of the 1990s," *Northwestern University Law Review* 90, no. 2 (1996): 788–892.

71.   Statement of Representative James Sensenbrenner, 139 *Congressional Record* (20 November 1993), H10,320.

72.   Earl-Hubbard, "Sex Offender Registration."

73.   Earl-Hubbard, "Sex Offender Registration."

74.   Earl-Hubbard, "Sex Offender Registration," 797.

75.   Horwitz, "Sexual Psychopath Legislation," 36–38.

76.   Quoted in Horwitz, "Sexual Psychopath Legislation," 51.

77.   J. Collins, "Throwing Away the Key," *Time,* 7 July 1997, 29.

78.   M. R. Bawa Muhaiyadeedn, *Islam and World Peace: Explanations of a Sufi* (Philadelphia: Fellowship Press, 1987), 44.

79.   As noted by Charles Guignon in his edited work, *The Good Life: Readings in Philosophy* ([Indianapolis: Hackett, 1999], 19), in the *Odyssey* Polyneices bribes Eriphyles

to persuade her husband, Amphiaraus, to take part in an attack on Thebes. Eriphyle's husband is killed, and she is murdered by her own son in revenge.

80. As quoted in Guignon, *The Good Life*, 18.

81. 'Abdu'l-Bahá, *The Secret of Divine Civilization*, trans. Marzieh Gail and Ali-Kuli Khan (Wilmette, Ill. Bahá'í Publishing Trust, 1990), 59.

82. Constance M. Chen, *The Sex Side of Life: Mary Ware Dennett's Pioneering Battle for Birth Control and Sex Education* (New York: New Press, 1996), 155.

83. Quoted in Senguen Oh, "Beyond the Myth of Love and Sexuality" (M.A. thesis, Landegg International University, 1999), 4.

84. Pitirim Sorokin, *The Crisis of Our Age* (Oxford: One World Publications, 1992).

85. Sorokin, *Crisis of Our Age*, 168.

Chapter 3

1. David Levinson, *Family Violence in Cross-Cultural Perspective* (New York: Sage, 1989).

2. Murray Straus, "Wife Beating: How Common and Why?" *Victimology* 2 (1977): 443–58.

3. Elizabeth S. Cox, "The Battered Women's Movement in Mexico and the United States: An Examination of Strategies and Possibilities for Future Cooperation," *Proceedings of NCIH Conference* (Crystal City, Va.: National Council of International Health, June 1990), 17–20.

4. Joseph Julian and William Kornblum, *Social Problems*, 5th ed. (Upper Saddle River, N.J.: Prentice Hall, 1986).

5. UN, *Trends and Statistics: 1970–1990* (New York: UN, 1991).

6. G. Ashworth, *Of Violence and Violation: Women and Human Rights* (London: Change Thinkbook II, 1986).

7. UN, *Violence against Women in the Family* (Vienna: UN Office at Vienna, Center for Social Development and Humanitarian Affairs, 1989).

8. Charlotte Bunch and Roxana Carrillo, *Gender Violence: A Development and Human Rights Issue* (New Brunswick, N.J.: Center for Women's Global Leadership, Douglass College, 1991).

9. World Health Organization (WHO), *Violence against Women 1993–1994* (Geneva: WHO, 1994), 21.

10. WHO, *Violence against Women*, 21.

11. Lori Heise, Jacqueline Pintanguy, and Adrienne Germain, *Violence against Women: The Hidden Health Burden* (Washington, D.C.: World Bank Discussion Papers, 1994).

12. Heise, Pintanguy, and Germain, *Hidden Health Burden*, 18.

13. Sunanda, "Girl-Child to Die?" 118.

14. WHO, *Violence against Women*.

15. Eva Bu Melhem, "Are Battered Women Hospitalized?" *Al-Raida* 11, no. 65/66 (Spring/Summer 1994): 27.

16. WHO, "Violence against Women."

17. WHO, "Violence against Women," 21.

18. Heise, Pintanguy, and Germain, *Hidden Health Burden.*

19. Heise, Pintanguy, and Germain, *Hidden Health Burden.*

20. Heise, Pintanguy, and Germain, *Hidden Health Burden.*

21. P. Elliott, "Shattering Illusions: Same-Sex Domestic Violence," in *Violence in Gay and Lesbian Domestic Partnerships,* ed. Claire M. Renzetti and Charles H. Miley (Binghamton, N.Y.: Haworth, 1996), 1–8.

22. L. Lockhart et al., "Letting Out the Secret: Violence in Lesbian Relationships," *Journal of International Violence* 9, no. 4 (1994).

23. Gwat-Yong Lie and S. Gentlewarrier, "Intimate Violence in Lesbian Relationships: Discussion of Survey Findings and Practice Implications," *Journal of Social Service Research* 15, nos. 1–2 (1991): 469–92.

24. David Island and Patrick Letellier, *Men Who Beat the Men Who Love Them* (New York: Harrington Park Press, 1991).

25. Coomaraswamy, *Preliminary Report,* 21.

26. Middle East Watch, *Punishing the Victim: Rape and Mistreatment of Asian Maids in Kuwait* (New York: Middle East Watch Women's Rights Project, 1992).

27. Radhika Coomaraswamy and Lisa M. Kois, "Violence against Women," in *Women and International Human Rights Law,* ed. Kelly Askin and Dorean Koenig (Arsdaley, N.Y.: Transnational, 1999), 1: 177–218.

28. Coomaraswamy and Kois, "Violence against Women."

29. Copelon, "Recognizing the Egregious."

30. UN, Convention against Torture and Other Cruel, Inhuman, or Degrading Treatment or Punishment, art. 1 (General Assembly Resolution 39/46, 10 December 1984. Entered into force 26 June 1987).

31. Copelon, "Recognizing the Egregious," 317.

32. Copelon, "Recognizing the Egregious," 329.

33 Copelon, "Recognizing the Egregious," 331.

34. Quoted in Copelon, "Recognizing the Egregious," 343.

35. Copelon, "Recognizing the Egregious," 343.

36. *Planned Parenthood of Southeastern Pennsylvania v. Robert Casey,* 288 U.S. 34 (1992).

37. S. Ford, *Domestic Violence: The Great American Spectator Sport,* Oklahoma Coalition on Domestic Violence and Sexual Assault (July/August, 1991), 3.

38. U.S. Senate Judiciary Committee, "Hearings on Legislation to Reduce the Growing Problem of Violent Crime against Women," Senate Hearing 101-939, part 2 (August 29, December 11, 1990), 142.

39. B. E. Carlson, "Children's Observations of Interpersonal Violence," in *Battered Women and Their Families,* ed. Albert R. Roberts (New York: Springer, 1984), 147–67.

40. R. W. Pynoos and S. Eth, "The Child as Witness to Homicide," *Journal of Social Issues* 40 (1984): 87–108.

41. Laura A. McCloskey, Aurelio J. Figueredo, and Mary P. Koss, "The Effects of Systematic Family Violence on Children's Mental Health," *Child Development* 66 (1995): 1239–61.

42. McCloskey, Figueredo, and Koss, "Systematic Family Violence," 1259.

43. McCloskey, Figueredo, and Koss, "Systematic Family Violence," 1256.

44. Cathy S. Widom, *Victims of Childhood Sexual Abuse,* NCJ 151525 (Washington, D.C.: U.S. Department of Justice, National Institute of Justice, 1995).

45. It should be noted that Widom employed a "matched cohorts" design such that subjects in the comparison group were similar to the abused and neglected subjects in every respect except their abuse and neglect status. This enabled Widom to control for the effects of subjects' socioeconomic and educational backgrounds.

46. Cathy S. Widom, "Childhood Sexual Abuse and Its Criminal Consequences," *Society* (May/June, 1996): 47–53.

47. Erik Erikson, *Identity, Youth, and Crisis* (New York: Norton, 1968).

48. B. Egeland and A. Sroufe, "Developmental Sequelae of Maltreatment in Infancy," in *New Directions in Child Development: Developmental Perspectives on Child Maltreatment,* ed. R. Rizley and D. Cicchetti (San Francisco: Jossey-Bass, 1981).

49. Laurence Steinberg, "The Logic of Adolescence," in *Adolescence and Poverty: Challenge for the 1990s,* ed. P. Edelman and J. Ladner (Washington, D.C.: National Policy Press, 1990, 19–36.

50. Steinberg, "Logic of Adolescence."

51. See Judith Smetana, "Social-Cognitive Development: Domain Distinctions and Coordinations," *Developmental Review* 3 (1983): 131–47; Lawrence Kohlberg, "Stage and Sequence: The Cognitive-Developmental Approach to Socialization," in *Handbook of Socialization: Theory and Research,* ed. D. Goslin (New York: Rand McNally, 1969).

52. L .Camras, G. Grow, and S. Ribordy, "Recognition of Emotional Expression by Abused Children," *Journal of Clinical Child Psychology* 12 (1983): 325–28.

53. Stephen R. Shirk, "The Interpersonal Legacy of Physical Abuse of Children," in *Abuse and Victimization across the Life Span,* ed. M. Straus (Baltimore: Johns Hopkins University Press, 1988).

54. Norma D. Feshback, "The Effects of Violence in Childhood," *Journal of Clinical Psychology* 2 (1973): 284–393.

55. C. George and M. Main, "Social Interactions of Young Abused Children," *Child Development* 50 (1979): 306–18.

56. C. Howes and M. P. Espinosa, "The Consequences of Child Abuse for Peer Interaction," *International Journal of Child Abuse and Neglect* 9 (1985): 397–404.

57. Ann M. Frodi and Michael E. Lamb, "Child Abusers' Responses to Infant Smiles and Cries," *Child Development* 51 (1980): 238–41.

58. Diana Baumrind, "Current Patterns of Parental Authority," *Developmental Psychology,* Monograph 4, no. 1 part 2, 1971.

59. James Garbarino and Ann Crouter, "Defining the Community Context of Parent–Child Relations: The Correlates of Child Maltreatment," *Child Development* 49 (1978): 604–16.

Chapter 4

1. Quoted by Yasmeen Hassan in "Stove Burning, Acid Throwing, and Honor Killings," *Women and International Human Rights Law* 2 (2000): 587.

2. Hassan, "Stove Burning," 590.

3. See K. Olayinka, *The Circumcision of Women: A Strategy for Eradication* (Lon-

don: Zed Books, 1987) for a discussion of the distinctions among these three types of female genital mutilation.

4. U.S. House of Representatives, Committee on Foreign Affairs, Subcommittee Hearings on International Security, International Organizations and Human Rights, Hearings on Human Rights and Abuses against Women, 1st and 2d sess., September 28–29, 1993; October 20, 1993; and March 22, 1994.

5. Celia W. Dugger, "Woman's Plea for Asylum Puts Tribal Ritual on Trial," *New York Times,* 15 April 1996, 1.

6. World Health Organization, *Female Genital Mutilation: The Practice.* (Geneva: WHO, Division of Family Health, 1994).

7. L. Julia and Delia M. Rios, "Conference Targets Mutilation Rite," *Cleveland Plain Dealer,* 5 September 1995; United Press International, "WHO Discusses Female Circumcision," 5 May 1994.

8. Fran P. Hosken, "Genital and Sexual Mutilation of Females," *Women's International News,* Lexington, Mass., January 1994.

9. Halima Embarek Warzazi, *Final Report of the Special Rapporteur on Traditional Practices Affecting the Health of Women and Children* (New York: UN, 1994), (E/CN/.4/Sub.2/1991/6), para. 11.

10. Nahid Toubia, *Female Genital Mutilation: A Call for Action* (New York: Women, Ink, 1995), 29–30.

11. Toubia, *Female Genital Mutilation,* 29.

12. Daphne W. Nitri, "Circumcision and Health among Rural Women of Southern Somalia as Part of a Family Life Survey," *Health Care for Women International* 14 (1993): 227–38. This study, conducted in 1986 in collaboration with the UNESCO (UN Educational, Scientific, and Cultural Organization) and the women's department of the ministry of education in Mogadishu, Somalia, consisted of 859 women in 16 semipastoralist and semiagricultural villages in southern Somalia. The mean age at circumcision was 6.9 years, and in the majority of cases the circumcised girls received no anesthesia.

13. Fran P. Hosken, *Stop Female Genital Mutilation: Women Speak—Facts and Actions* (n.p.: Women's International Network News, 1995).

14. World Health Organization, *Female Genital Mutilation: Report of World Health Organization Technical Working Group* (Geneva: WHO, 1995), 17–19.

15. Barbara L. Calder, Yvonne M. R. Brown, and Donna I. Rae, "Female Circumcision/Genital Mutilation: Culturally Sensitive Care," *Health Care for Women International* 14 (1993): 227.

16. See Hosken, *Stop Female Genital Mutilation.*

17. Hosken, *Stop Female Genital Mutilation.*

18. Toubia, *Female Genital Mutilation,* 17–18.

19. Karungari Kiragu, *Female Genital Mutilation: A Reproductive Health Concern* (Baltimore, Md.: Population Reports Supplement, 1995).

20. Hosken, *Stop Female Genital Mutilation.*

21. WHO, *Female Genital Mutilation,* 17–19.

22. L. L. Wall, "Obstetric Fistulas: Hope for a New Beginning," *International Urogynecology Journal* 6, no. 5 (1995): 292–95.

23. WHO, *Female Genital Mutilation,* 17–19.

24. Toubia, *Female Genital Mutilation,* 19.

25. Toubia, *Female Genital Mutilation*, 43.

26. See Toubia, *Female Genital Mutilation*.

27. Carol P. MacCormack, ed., *Ethnography of Fertility and Birth* (Prospect Heights, Ill. Waveland Press, 1994), 111.

28. It is now clear that there is no primary Islamic, Jewish, or Christian text or tradition that makes female circumcision a religious obligation. The Qur'an, for example, which is the primary source of Islamic law, and the Hadith, a collection of the sayings of the Prophet Muhammad, include no prescription for the practice of female circumcision. Likewise, neither the sacred scriptures of Judaism nor Christianity has mandated the practice of female circumcision. Those Islamic, Christian, and Jewish communities that practice female circumcision thus do so out of cultural requirements rather than religious ones.

29. Quoted in Toubia, *Female Genital Mutilation*, 41.

30. MacCormack, *Ethnography of Fertility and Birth*, 111.

31. Layli Miller-Bashir, "Female Genital Mutilation in the United States: An Examination of Criminal and Asylum Law," *American University Journal of Gender and the Law* 4 (Spring 1996): 415–54.

32. As quoted in Miller-Bashir, "Genital Mutilation in the United States," 431.

33. Toubia, *Female Genital Mutilation*, 45.

34. As quoted in Toubia, *Female Genital Mutilation*, 47.

35. Ellen Gruenbaum, *The Female Circumcision Controversy: An Anthropological Perspective* (Philadelphia: University of Pennsylvania Press, 2001), 220–21.

36. Carol P. MacCormack, "Health and the Social Power of Women," *Social Science and Medicine* 26, no. 7 (1988): 677–83.

37. Molly Moore, "Consumerism Fuels Dowry-Death Wave," *Washington Post,* 17 March 1995, A35.

38. Moore, "Dowry-Death Wave."

39. Moore, "Dowry-Death Wave."

40. Jan K. Black, "Dowry Abuse," *Contemporary Review*, 239.

41. Elizabeth Bumiller, "May You Be the Mother of a Hundred Sons," *New York Times Book Review*, 24 June 1990, 17.

42. Bumiller, "May You Be," 16.

43. Obiora, "Kindling Social Reform," 106.

44. Quoted in Brad Pokorny, "An Unusual Meeting of Bankers and Believers," *One Country* 9, no. 4 (1998): 4.

45. Quoted in Pokorny, "Unusual Meeting," 2.

Chapter 5

1. See appendices A and B for the full text of these documents.

2. Bahá'í International Community, *The Greatness Which Might Be Theirs*, 7.

3. 'Abdu'l-Bahá, *Some Answered Questions*, trans. Laura C. Brown (Wilmette, Ill. Bahá'í Publishing Trust, 1984), 8.

4. UN, *The World's Women 1995: Trends and Statistics* (New York: UN, 1995).

5. UN, *World's Women 1995*, 93.

6. UN, *World's Women 1995*, 94.

7. UNESCO Constitution, November 16, 1945, 275–302.

8. Reported in Margaret E. Galey, "Women and Education," in *Women and International Human Rights Law,* ed. Kelly Askin and Dorean Koenig (New York: Transnational Publishers, 1999), 1: 439.

9. Galey, "Women and Education," 408.

10. Galey, "Women and Education."

11. Hossain B. Danesh, *The Violence-Free Family: Building Block of a Peaceful Civilization* (Ottawa: Bahá'í Studies Publications, 1995), 23.

12. Universidad Núr, *Moral Leadership* (Washington, D.C.: Global Classroom, 1997), 20.

13. Laurie Nagouchi, Holly Hanson, and Paul Lample, *Exploring a Framework for Moral Education*. (Riviera Beach, Fla.: Palabra Publications), 5.

14. Noouchi, Hanson, and Lample, *Framework*, 5.

15. Nogouchi, Hanson, and Lample, *Framework,* 7.

Chapter 6

1. See Martin E. P. Seligman, *Helplessness: On Depression, Development, and Death* (San Francisco: Freeman Press, 1975).

2. Berman, *Faith and Order,* 7.

3. William S. Hatcher, in collaboration with the International Moral Education Project, "Ethics of Authenticity," bk. 1 (Saint Petersburg, Russia, 1997), 4. See also Hatcher, *Love, Power, and Justice.*

4. 'Abdu'l-Bahá, *Selections from the Writings of 'Abdu'l-Bahá,* comp. Research Department of the Universal House of Justice, translated by a committee at the Bahá'í World Centre and Marzieh Gail (Wilmette, Ill.: Bahá'í Publishing Trust, 1997), no. 1381.

5. 'Abdu'l-Bahá, *Selections,* no. 24.

Chapter 7

1. Leonard Berkowitz, *Aggression: Its Causes, Consequences, and Control* (New York: McGraw-Hill, 1993), 3.

2. David Finkelhor et al., *Physical Violence in American Families: Risk Factors and Adaptations to Violence in 8,145 Families* (New Brunswick, N.J.: Transaction, 1990).

2. Murray A. Straus, "Social Stress and Marital Violence in a National Sample of American Families," *Forensic Psychology and Psychiatry: Annals of the New York Academy of Science* 347 (1980): 229–50; and C. Hornung, B. McCullough, and T. Sugimoto, "Status Relationships in Marriage: Risk Factors in Spouse Abuse," *Journal of Marriage and the Family* 43 (1981): 675–92.

4. D. H. Coleman and Murray A. Straus, "Marital Power, Conflict, and Violence in a Nationally Representative Sample of American Couples," *Violence and Victims* 1 (1986): 141–57.

5. R. E. Dobash and R.P. Dobash, "The Nature and Antecedents of Violent Events," *British Journal of Criminology* 24 (1984): 269–88.

6. K. A. Yllo and Murray A. Straus, "The Impact of Structural Inequality and Sexist Family Norms on Rates of Wife-Beating," *Journal of International and Comparative Social Welfare* 1 (1984): 16–29.

7. Finkelhor et al., *Physical Violence.*

8. Berkowitz, *Aggression*, 17.

9. Berkowitz, *Aggression*, 17.

10. Aristotle, *The Nicomachean Ethics*, as quoted by Daniel Goleman in *Emotional Intelligence*, ix.

11. Goleman, *Emotional Intelligence*, 197.

12. Goleman, *Emotional Intelligence*, 198.

13. Seligman, *Helplessness.*

14. Martin E. P. Seligman and Steven F. Maier, "Failure to Escape Traumatic Shock," *Journal of Experimental Psychology* 74 (1967): 1–9; note that in L. B. Alloy et al., "The Hoplessness Theory of Depression: Attributional Aspects," *British Journal of Clinical Psychology* 27 (1988): 5–21, the authors suggest that Seligman's theory is best viewed as a helplessness, rather than a hopelessness, theory of depression, in that "a proximal sufficient cause of depression was the expectation that one cannot control outcomes regardless of hedonic valence or their likelihood of occurrence" (7).

15. Steven F. Maier and Martin E. P. Seligman, "Learned Helplessness: Theory and Evidence," *Journal of Experimental Psychology* 105 (1976): 3–46.

16. D. S. Hiroto and Martin E. P. Seligman, "Generality of Learned Helplessness in Man," *Journal of Personality and Social Psychology* 31 (1975): 311–27.

17. Herman, *Trauma and Recovery*, 112.

18. Hiroto and Seligman, "Learned Helplessness," 311–27; and C. S. Cole and J. C. Coyne, "Situational Specificity of Laboratory Induced Learned Helplessness," *Journal of Abnormal Psychology* 86 (1977): 615–23.

19. See G. H. Brown and T. Harris, *Social Origins of Depression* (New York: Free Press, 1978).

20. Ronnie Janoff-Bulman and L. Lang-Gunn, "Coping with Disease and Accidents: The Role of Self-Blame Attributions," in *Social-Personal Inference in Clinical Psychology*, ed. Lyn Abramson (New York: Guilford, 1989).

21. Roy F. Baumeister, *Escaping the Self: Alcoholism, Spirituality, Masochism, and Other Flights from the Burden of Selfhood* (New York: Basic Books, 1991).

22. Erich Fromm, *The Anatomy of Human Destructiveness* (New York: Henry Holt, 1973), 223–24.

23. Fromm, *Human Destructiveness*, 268–69.

24. Fromm, *Human Destructiveness*, 270.

25. Fromm, *Human Destructiveness*, 271–72.

26. John D. Mayer, M. T. DiPaolo, and P. Salovey, "Perceiving Affective Content in Ambiguous Visual Stimuli: A Component of Emotional Intelligence," *Journal of Personality Assessment* 54 (1990): 772–81.

27. John D. Mayer, D. Caruso, and P. Salovey, "Emotional Intelligence Meets Traditional Standards for an Intelligence," *Intelligence* 27 (1999): 267.

28. Goleman, *Emotional Intelligence.*

29. M. T. Greenberg, C. A. Kusche, and J. P. Quamma, "Promoting Emotional

Competence in School-Aged Children: The Effects of the Path Curriculum," *Development and Psychopathology* 7 (1995): 117–37.

Chapter 8

1. Stephanie Mehta, "Treating Sex Offenders Becomes an Industry, but Does It Work?" *Wall Street Journal*, 24 May 1996, 1.
2. Lane Fisher, "DADs Advocates for Healthy Daughters," *Hope*, no. 26 (Spring 2001): 8.
3. Fisher, "Healthy Daughters."
4. See Richard Thomas, *Racial Unity: An Imperative for Social Progress* (Ottawa: Bahá'í Studies Publications, 1993).
5. In more recent decades, partly owing to public policies, demographic patterns, and growing apathy, white support for civil rights has become less widespread. As black and white communities have become more estranged, the effectiveness born of their co-operative effort has clearly diminished.
6. Mona Y. Grieser, *Women, Poverty, and Income: A Systems Approach*, Reflections on Traditional Media as Change Agent Project (Silver Spring, Md.: Global Vision, 1994).
7. Grieser, *Women, Poverty*.
8. Grieser, *Women, Poverty*, 4.
9. Grieser, *Women, Poverty*, 4.
10. Grieser, *Women, Poverty*, 4.
11. Courtney Howland, "Women and Religious Fundamentalism," in *Women and International Human Rights Law*, ed. Kelly Askin and Dorean Koenig (New York: Transnational Publishers, 2000), 2: 533.
12. See Howland, "Women and Religious Fundamentalism."
13. See Myriam Miedzian, *Boys Will Be Boys: Breaking the Link Between Masculinity and Violence* (New York: AnchorBooks, 1991), for a brief review of such programs.
14. See Peggy R. Sanday, *Fraternity Gang Rape* (New York: New York University Press, 1990).
15. Barbara Reskin and Irene Padavic, *Women and Men at Work* (London: Pine Forge Press, 1994).
16. Christine L. Williams, "The Glass Escalator: Hidden Advantages for Men in the 'Female' Professions," *Social Problems* 39, (1992): 253–57.

Chapter 9

1. Calvin O. Schrag, "The Topology of Hope," *Humanitas* 13 (1977): 271.
2. Schrag, "Topology of Hope," 271.
3. In her synthesis of data from archeology and other disciplines, for example, Riane Eisler (*The Chalice and the Blade: Our History, Our Future* [San Francisco: Harper & Row, 1987]) shows that the bloodiness we associate with human history actu-

ally describes only the last five thousand years or so. This represents less than 1 percent of the time our species has existed. Commenting on Eisler's work, Alfie Kohn noted that "war and other sorts of oppression . . . constitute the historical exception, a detour from the main road of cultural development in which none of the landmarks have to do with destruction" (*The Brighter Side of Human Nature* [New York: Basic Books, 1990], 55). Also, for a review of this literature, see Berkowitz, *Aggression*.

4. For excellent discussions of this issue, see Barry Schwartz, *The Battle for Human Nature: Science, Morality, and Modern Life* (New York: Norton, 1986); and Alfie Kohn, *No Contest: The Case against Competition* (Boston: Houghton Mifflin, 1986).

5. Shoghi Effendi, *The World Order of Bahá'u'lláh: Selected Letters*, rev. ed. (Wilmette, Ill.: Bahá'í Publishing Trust, 1974), 42–43.

6. Vesna Nikolic-Ristanovic, ed., *Women, Violence, and War* (Budapest: Central European Press, 2000), 22.

7. Albert Einstein, quoted in Augusto Lopes-Claros, "Interdependence, Cooperation, and the Emergence of Global Institutions," *World Order* (Summer 1996): 10.

8. Quoted in Lopez-Claros, "Interdependence, Cooperation," 10–11.

9. Shoghi Effendi, *World Order*, 40–41.

10. Shoghi Effendi, *World Order*, 45.

11. Watty Piper, *The Little Engine That Could* (New York: Platt & Munk, 1984).

12. James E. Maddux, *"Self Efficacy: The Power of Believing You Can,"* in *Handbook of Positive Psychology*, ed. C. R. Snyder and S. J. Lopez (New York: Oxford University Press, 2002), 277–87.

Index

About the Authors

RAHEL NARDOS was born in 1974 in Addis Ababa, Ethiopia. She is the only girl in a family of six children, and both of her parents are teachers. She received a scholarship to the International Community School in Addis Ababa where she attended high school, graduating summa cum laude. The International Community School was her first exposure to world diversity. Later, she received a scholarship to attend Franklin and Marshall College in Lancaster, Pennsylvania, where she graduated cum laude with a joint biology and psychology major. After college she worked as a lab technician in the neuroscience departments of Cornell University and Florida State University. Currently she is a fourth-year medical student at Yale School of Medicine and intends to pursue obstetrics and gynecology.

MICHAEL L. PENN is a professor of psychology at Franklin and Marshall College and an affiliate professor of psychology at Landegg International University in Switzerland. He is a core member of the Authenticity Project and a clinical psychologist specializing in the study and treatment of hopelessness-related disorders. His research interests and publications include works in the pathogenesis of hope and hopelessness, adolescent psychopathology, the relationship between culture and psychopathology, psychology and spirituality, and the epidemiology of gender-based violence. He has lectured widely around the world and has been invited to serve as a consultant and speaker at United Nations–related conferences in several countries.